What's Being Said About *No Longer a Child*

Dr. Dixie Yoder is called doctor for a reason. She has captured from her many years of study and experience in discipleship ministry all the "whos, whys and whats":

- Who is God?
- Who am I?
- Why am I stuck in my past and old thought patterns?
- What must I do to break free and discover the abundant life Jesus promised?

As you read *No Longer a Child: Essential Insights for the Growing Christian* you'll discover pieces of the Biblical, common-sense "truth puzzle" that have been missing for years. You'll find truth in understanding what makes you "tick" while facing the difficulties of life. I would subtitle this book *Christianity 101 That Finally Makes Sense.* Dr. Dixie has presented answers to many of the roadblocks to spiritual growth in one book.

No Longer a Child promises one thing: genuine transformation and spiritual maturity from the inside out. I personally wish I could have had this book fifteen years ago! It teaches. It explains. It sets you on the road of incredible freedom to experience your true identity in Christ. Every believer should read this book and share it with others!

—Pam Kanaly, author of *Will the Real Me Please Stand Up*

For years Dr. Dixie has been helping people get to the root of their struggles and complicated life issues by finding their identity in Christ. *No Longer a Child: Essential Insights for the Growing Christian* is an indispensible tool for people who want to live in victory and stay on top of life's circumstances. Everyone who reads this book will find the path to victorious living, and an understanding of what God has for us. This is required reading for all of us!

—Jon Cook, partner and chaplain, Corporate Care, Inc.

NO LONGER A CHILD

NO LONGER A CHILD

ESSENTIAL INSIGHTS FOR THE GROWING CHRISTIAN

Dr. Dixie Yoder

Tate Publishing & *Enterprises*

No Longer a Child

Published by Tate Publishing & Enterprises, LLC
127 E. Trade Center Terrace | Mustang, Oklahoma 73064 USA
1.888.361.9473 | www.tatepublishing.com

Tate Publishing is committed to excellence in the publishing industry. The company reflects the philosophy established by the founders, based on Psalm 68:11,
"The Lord gave the word and great was the company of those who published it."

Cover design by Lance Waldrop
Interior design by Blake Brasor

Published in the United States of America

ISBN: 978-1-61566-457-3
1. Religion, Christian Life, Spiritual Growth
2. Religion, Christian Ministry, Discipleship
10.2.04

Dedication

This book is dedicated to my dad, Richard, who has given me a wonderful foundation for loving God. He has been a constant encouragement to me and has taught me that anything worth having is worth the wait and the effort. He is the most genuinely cheerful and optimistic person I know. I love you, Daddy!

Table of Contents

Introduction

For almost twenty years, I have worked with believers who struggle with life. Sometimes the battles are small, internal, and scarcely visible to others; sometimes the struggles burst out into the open, splintering relationships and lives.

My emphasis has always been on knowing God accurately and intimately as the key to facing our own failures and the failures of others without being destroyed by the disappointment. Twenty years into this work, I am more convinced than ever that knowing God is the only way to live life triumphantly in a world wrecked by sin.

In 2006, I became septic after a routine dental procedure. Nearly three weeks in critical care included a week in a coma, on a ventilator. For several days, I was very near death. During my time in the coma, I spent an incredible interlude in the visible presence of God. Now, although I certainly don't suppose that I even began to know the fullness of His presence, a little bit of my faith has been reinforced by sight, and I teach about the amazing love of God with more passion and confidence than ever before.

God's infinite character cannot be fully described with finite human language. His goodness and perfect justice certainly cannot be judged by the condition of our world or circumstances. The love and tender mercy He *is* toward His beloved humankind is unchangeable and has no beginning or end.

Truly, there is nothing else we can depend on as we walk through each day of life on earth. Certainly, there is no other relationship that will never fail and no other arms that will unfailingly hold us secure.

This knowledge energizes me as I share what I have learned and experienced in my relationship with God, even while I continue to grow up spiritually. With Paul I say,

> For my determined purpose is that I may know Him, that I may progressively become more deeply and intimately acquainted with Him, recognizing and understanding the wonders of His person more strongly and more clearly, and that I may … come to know the power that flows out from His resurrection … and that I may so share His sufferings as to be continually transformed in spirit into His likeness; that I may attain to the … resurrection that lifts me out from among the dead even while in the body. Not that I have already been made perfect, but I press on to make my own that for which Christ Jesus has laid hold of me and made me His own. I have not yet fully captured it and made it my own, but setting aside the failures that lie behind me, I strain forward to the growth that lies ahead. I am pressing on to win and fully enjoy the heavenly prize to which God in Christ Jesus is calling us upward. So let us hold to and build on what we have already attained.
>
> Adapted from Philippians 3:10-16 (Amplified)

Chapter 1
God's Word Is Enough

Enough: Sufficiency is a quantity or quality which satisfies desire; that is adequate to the want or is equal to the power or ability (Dictionary.com).

American Christianity has become, in many ways, a jumbled theology that attempts to be tolerant and all inclusive. This has produced a Church weakened by half truths which sound true, but provide little nourishment for spiritual growth. Satan's lies are always built on some truth. A lie that is entirely untrue would be obvious and so unpleasant that we would quickly reject it. The bit of truth contained in every lie is what makes it feel right and sound right, so that we accept it as right. We believe "if it walks like a duck, quacks like a duck, and looks like a duck, it must be a duck." However, 2 Corinthians 11:14 tells us that Satan looks and acts like an angel of light, but it is a façade that hides the darkest evil. Satan is the originator of all that is false and deceptive (John 8:44), and Paul warns us not to be ignorant of his schemes (2 Corinthians 2:11; 2 Corinthians 11:3).

Aesop and the Bible

"A Wolf found great difficulty in getting at the sheep, owing to the vigilance of the shepherd and his dogs. But one day it found the skin of a sheep that had been flayed and thrown aside, so the Wolf put the fleece on over its own pelt and strolled down among the sheep. The Lamb that belonged to the sheep whose skin the Wolf was wearing, began to follow the Wolf in the Sheep's clothing; so, leading the Lamb a little apart, he soon made a meal of the Lamb, and for some time he succeeded in deceiving the sheep and enjoying hearty meals. Appearances are deceptive" (*Aesop's Fables*, "The Wolf in Sheep's Clothing").

> Beware of false prophets, who come to you dressed as sheep, but inside they are devouring wolves.
>
> Matthew 7:15

> But also in those days there arose false prophets among the people, just as there will be false teachers among yourselves, who will subtly… introduce heretical doctrines… denying and disowning the Master who bought them, bringing upon themselves swift destruction. And many will follow their immoral ways and lascivious doings; because of them the true way will be maligned and defamed. And in their covetousness, lust and greed, they will exploit you with false and cunning arguments.
>
> 2 Peter 2:1-3

> For although they hold a form of piety, they deny and reject . . . the power of it, their conduct belies the genuineness of their profession.
>
> 2 Timothy 3:5

The United States Treasury trains employees to recognize counterfeit bills. Counterfeiters are producing money that is increasingly so much like the real thing that the untrained eye cannot see the difference. But Treasury personnel don't pore over counterfeit bills; they intently study genuine money and become so familiar with every color, characteristic, and watermark that if a counterfeit bill passes through their hands, they identify it immediately as fake.

Believers need to be well acquainted with the genuine Word of God and so carefully informed about its truth that when even the very good counterfeits are presented to us, we quickly recognize and reject them.

"You Were the Closest . . ."

Rick, a recent college graduate with an accounting degree, interviewed for his first salaried job. The company boss asked various questions about him and his education. Finally, he asked, "What is three times seven?" "Twenty-two," Rick replied nervously.

Later, as he drove away, Rick thought over his interview and realized he probably wouldn't get the job since he gave the wrong answer to such an elementary question.

About two weeks later, Rick was surprised when he got a letter in the mail saying he was hired for the job! Although Rick was not the type of person to look a gift horse in the mouth, he was still very curious. As soon as he could, he went in to his boss's office and asked why he got the job, even though he got such a simple question wrong.

"Well," the boss said with a sigh, "you were the closest."

We wouldn't want Rick to do our tax returns, because "closest" isn't good enough. How much more careful and accurate we need to be about eternal things! Our spiritual ignorance can be eternally deadly to those who are asking the hard questions that really do need to be answered from the Word of God. When people ask us questions about God and His Word, it isn't enough to "just be close" in our understanding.

Obviously, we can spend our entire lives studying and learning and still not know all there is to know. But we can know what we *do know* accurately. It would be unrealistic to expect a fourth grader to be able to multiply huge numbers in his head, but it is reasonable to expect him to know that 3x7=21 not 22.

The Word of God Is Not Just a Book of Wise Words

The phrase "the Word of God" is almost exclusively interpreted to mean a book of printed words on thin paper, bound together by a leather cover. And there is truth in that. Our Bible is indeed the written Word of God.

However, if we identify the Word of God exclusively as a leather-bound book, it is easy to think of it as a sort of good-luck charm that we hold up and make demons flee, or if we quote a particular verse often enough, we can make things happen the way we want them to happen, right now. This definition limits the application of the Word of God to a few moments of desperation, a couple of hours in church, or something that only a pastor or priest can enjoy.

If we define the Word of God only as a book that contains wise words, then really any book with wise words will do just as well as Scripture. This restricted view of the Word of God has made it possible for the use of psychology to become pervasive within the church. The truth of God and the words of Freud are considered by many to be equally wise.

We must remember that every book of "wise words" is a written representative of a person whose wisdom is earthly and limited, and who is subject to death. The Christian Bible is the only book ever written whose author lives eternally! The Bible represents the one true and living God, Whose wisdom is eternal and unchangeable. God the Person and His written and spoken Word are inseparable. They are one and the same. As we study the Bible, learn from it, and live by its life-changing principles, we come to know God personally and learn to experience life more and more from His perspective.

God's Word Is…

- God's Word is Jesus: John 1:1-10
- God's Word is the light by which we walk: Psalm 119:105
- God's Word is a sword: Ephesians 6:17; Hebrews 4:12
- God's Word is our armor: Ephesians 6:10-17
- God's Word is our medicine chest: Psalm 107:20
- God's Word is a hammer: Jeremiah 23:29
- God's Word is a fire: Jeremiah 5:14
- God's Word is food: Psalm 119:103
- God's Word is more valuable than gold: Psalm 19:9-10
- God's Word is pure, spiritual milk; absolutely necessary for maturity: 1 Peter 2:2

The parable of the soils (Luke 8:11) says that the Word of God is seed for our lives. When we receive God's Word as unchangeable truth and sow it into the soil of everyday life, we are promised an abundant, beneficial harvest.

> For My thoughts are not your thoughts, neither are your ways My ways, says the Lord. For as the heavens are higher than the earth, so are My ways higher than your ways and My thoughts than your thoughts. For as the rain and snow come down from the heavens, and return not there again, but water the earth and make it bring forth and sprout, that it may give seed to the sower and bread to the eater, so shall My word be that goes forth out of My mouth: it shall not return to Me void or useless, without producing any effect, but it shall accomplish that which I please and purpose, and it shall prosper in the thing for which I sent it.
>
> Isaiah 55:8-11

The Bible gives us many examples of what God's powerful spoken words accomplish:

- God spoke and all creation came into existence. "And God said… " is repeated nine times in the first chapter of Genesis. God's speaking became visible to us as creation.
- God spoke to Noah, and a flood covered the earth. God's

speaking became visible as a flood of tangible, physical water (Genesis 7:11-12).

- God spoke to Abraham, and a ninety-year-old woman and one-hundred-year-old man conceived a child. God's speaking became tangible as a baby was born through impossible circumstances (Genesis 17:19).
- God spoke, and a ram appeared in the thicket to be sacrificed in Isaac's place. God's speaking became visible as an animal (Genesis 22:12-14).
- God spoke through the prophet Isaiah to King Hezekiah, and the sun moved backward ten degrees. God's speaking became visible as the sun moved the "wrong" direction (2 Kings 20:9-11).
- God spoke through Elijah, and no rain fell for three and a half years. God's speaking dried up the rain (1 Kings 17:1).
- God spoke to ravens; they obeyed His voice and brought bread and meat to Elijah in the morning and evening (1 Kings 17:1-6).
- God spoke to Mary, and she became pregnant. When God spoke, His Word put on flesh and walked on earth. God's speaking became audible and visible as a baby born through impossible circumstances (Luke 1:26-38, John 1:14-18).

When God Speaks

We are made new through the Word of God:

> You have been regenerated, not from a mortal origin or seed, but from one that is immortal—you have been regenerated by the ever living and lasting Word of God.
>
> 1 Peter 1:23

We receive salvation through the eternal Good News:

> For all flesh (humankind) is like grass, and all its … honor like grass. The grass withers and the flower drops off, but the Word of the Lord, His divine instruction … endures forever. And this Word is the good news which was preached to you.
>
> 1 Peter 1:24-25

The good news of the Gospel is not just words about a person. The Gospel *is* a Person who was spoken into His incarnation by the Father. The Word put on flesh and walked into our world to accomplish what the Father's words intended to bring to pass:

> In the last of these days He has spoken to us in the person of a Son, Whom He appointed Heir and lawful Owner of all things; also through Whom He created the worlds ... and space and the ages of time ... Jesus is the sole expression of the glory of God ... and He is the perfect imprint and very image of God's nature, upholding and maintaining and guiding and propelling the universe by His mighty Word of power. When He had by offering Himself accomplished our cleansing of sins and riddance of guilt, He sat down at the right hand of the divine Majesty on high ...
>
> Hebrews 1:2-3

> For the Word that God speaks is alive and full of power ... making it active, energizing, and effective; it is sharper than any two-edged sword, penetrating to the dividing line of the ... soul and the immortal spirit, and of joints and marrow—of the deepest parts of our nature—exposing and sifting and analyzing and judging the very thoughts and purposes of the heart.
>
> Hebrews 4:12

Words Are More Than Sounds

Our American understanding of words is limited. We treat words as sounds that fall out of the mouth and cease to exist as soon as the word is no longer audible to our ears. But the Bible indicates that a word is a *lasting power* that continues to accomplish what was spoken, long after we no longer hear the sound.

> Death and life are in the power of the tongue, and they who indulge in it shall eat the fruit of it, for death or life.
>
> Proverbs 18:21

To illustrate how words become tangible, read *aloud* this obituary written for a woman by her daughter:

> Deborah left us on August 7. She will be met in the after-life by her husband, her son and her daughter. She is survived by numerous grandchildren and great-grandchildren.
>
> Deborah had no hobbies and made no contribution to society and rarely shared a kind word or deed in her life. I speak for the majority of her family when I say her presence will not be missed by many; very few tears will be shed and there will be no lamenting over her passing.
>
> Her family will remember her among ourselves in our own way. Our life with her was mostly troubling throughout the years. We may have some fond memories of her, and perhaps we will think of those times too. But I truly believe at the end of the day all of us will really only miss what we never had—a good and kind mother, grandmother and great-grandmother. I hope she is finally at peace with herself.
>
> There will be no service, no prayers and no closure for the family she spent a lifetime tearing apart. We cannot come together in the end to see to it that her grandchildren and great-grandchildren can say their goodbyes. So I say here for all of us, "Good-bye, Mom."

What a sad assessment of a life! Those words on the page, read aloud, produce a heaviness; a sorrow for a family so deprived of love.

Now read *aloud* these true statements made by children:

- Three-year-old Reese prayed, "Our Father, Who does art in heaven, Harold is His name. Amen."
- A mother had been teaching her three-year old daughter the Lord's Prayer. For several evenings at bedtime, she repeated the lines from the prayer. Finally, she decided to go solo. Mom listened with pride as she carefully enunciated each word right up to the end of the prayer: "Lead us not into temptation," she prayed, "but deliver us some e-mail. Amen."
- A mom was preparing pancakes for her sons, Kevin, five, and Ryan, three. The boys began to argue over who would

> get the first pancake. Their mother saw the opportunity for a moral lesson. "If Jesus were sitting here, He would say, 'Let my brother have the first pancake. I can wait.'" Kevin turned to his younger brother and said, "Ryan, you be Jesus!"

These two accounts show how *actually real* words are. First there were the sad words that produced heaviness and a tangible sorrow. The next words produced laughter as we enjoyed the innocence of these children.

Words are an audible representation of who we are. We might say of someone:

- "He is so critical and judgmental." And how do we know that? By the words he speaks.
- "She is so kind. She makes everyone feel so good about themselves!" How do we know that? By the words she speaks.

Words are not just sounds that fall out of our mouths and disappear. Jesus said:

> But I tell you that every careless word that people speak, they shall give an accounting for it in the day of judgment. For by your words you will be justified, and by your words you will be condemned.
>
> Matthew 12:36-37 (NASU)

We are finite, but our words are forever existent after we speak them and they carry the power to represent us and affect our world. How much more the Word that God speaks! His Word is not just ink marks on a page. God's Word is a representation of Himself that becomes visible and audible through the results of His speaking.
Write out these Scriptures:

Proverbs 18:21

____

____

____

Proverbs 26:28

____

____

____

Isaiah 40:8

____

____

____

The "Insufficiency" of God

From the beginning, in the Garden of Eden, Satan has been described as subtle and crafty. The word *crafty* means to be skillful in the art of deception and fraud; to be cunning, sly, deceitful, and shrewd (Dictionary.com). In his attack on the credibility of God's Word, Satan's most common tactic is to cast doubt on the usefulness of God's instruction to us and then offer ungodly counsel instead. He is always careful to make sure that the false words of instruction he offers sound logical and reasonable and appeal to our flesh.

The importance of God's Word is so frequently minimized or ignored that we have become indifferent to the rejection of its sufficiency. The result is statements like these:

- "The Bible? Oh yes, I think it's a good book. Not very relevant though."
- "The Bible is an incredible piece of literature—I think everyone should read it, along with other great works like Plato and Aristotle."
- "Well, I try to read my Bible every day, but it doesn't make

much sense to me. It's too hard to understand, and I just don't have time to study it the way I probably should."

- "Well, I think the Bible is fine, as far as it goes. But there are a lot of life's problems that it really doesn't address."
- "I'd like to believe the Bible. There's a lot of good stuff in it, but I've heard other Christians say that there are contradictions and some of the stories are myths. I don't know what part I can believe."

Because the written representative of God, the Bible, cannot be separated from the Person of God, when we say that the Bible is not enough, we are also saying that God is not enough. When we believe that God is not enough, we have accepted *The Lie* of Satan, as surely as the first man and woman did, and we will continually turn to other people and other things to try to find solutions for the difficulties and longings we face.

"Expert" Authority

Our culture routinely grants authority to people based on a particular level of education or training and insists that only "experts" or "professionals" really have the answers. We've heard this so often and for so long we've accepted it as true. Consequently:

We accept the authority of a physician who tells us that we are in need of a particular treatment because of the diplomas we see on the walls in the exam room. He is the medical "expert." As a result, people are taking less initiative in their own health issues, expecting the "experts" to care as much about their bodies as they do themselves.

We defer to the teacher who tells us that our child needs special instruction or medication at school because she is the education "expert." Today's parents seldom question the pronouncement the teacher makes over their child. They allow their children to take dangerous drugs and wear psychological labels that are often more damaging than the original "problem," because we have been taught to believe the "expert system" always has the best interest of each child as their highest priority.

We listen to the mental health professional assign one or more of the thousands of psychological labels available to the "experts." The patient often accepts without question that the rest of life must be lived under the burden of the label or dependent upon the prescribed medication and therapy. This mind-set seriously hinders the power and work of God.

In Church history, before this dependence on the "experts" began to be promoted, it was accepted that hurting people could go to pastors and mature Christians when it came to matters of the spirit and the soul. It was readily acknowledged by the saved and the lost that when someone was afraid or sad or there were problems in the home, the pastor was the one to call. Now however, few consider calling their pastor when trouble strikes, and most believers neglect to read their Bibles because they're convinced that only the seminary "experts" can really know what the Bible means.

Consider the following story that illustrates how pervasive the belief in "experts' has become:

The Parable of the Uncertain Pastor

Pastor James Curtis walked into the studio with his usual confidence and enthusiasm. His voice was cheerful as he greeted his staff. James was thirty-eight years old and had pastored the same church for the past seven years. He was just completing his first full year of television ministry, an outreach that was rapidly expanding his congregation. There was a growing rapport between him and the people as they continued to mature spiritually, fed weekly by his simple and clear presentation of the Scripture.

Pastor James faced the cameras and his studio audience, confident that he was well prepared with his current teaching about the sufficiency of the Scriptures.

"Let us pray," James invited. And as people bowed their heads, James prayed with heartfelt compassion for the hurting people listening to the truth from God's Word and reminded himself and others that the Word of God is truth that sets people free from the bondage that holds them. He closed the prayer by asking the Holy Spirit to remind each one that the Word of God reveals everything that is needed to live life with confidence and enthusiasm and to empower believers to be salt and light in the way God has designed.

"Let's turn to 2 Timothy 3:16-17." James read the passage confidently. "Every Scripture is God-breathed, given by His inspiration, and is profitable for instruction, reproof and … for correction of error … and for training in righteousness … so that the man of God may be complete and proficient, well fitted, and thoroughly equipped for every good work."

Pastor James continued, "Now let's turn to 2 Peter 1:3-4." The rustle of Bible pages made James feel good. *They are really with me this morning!* he rejoiced silently. He resumed reading.

"For His divine power has bestowed upon us all things that are requisite and suited to life and Godliness, through the full, personal knowledge of Him who called us … by His own glory and excellence … by means of these He has bestowed on us His precious and exceedingly great promises, so that through them you may escape … from the moral decay … that is in the world, because of covetousness, lust, and greed, and become partakers of the divine nature."

James placed his Bible on the pulpit and let his eyes roam over the studio. He noticed a shy looking man in his midthirties sitting near the back and, knowing that he had not seen him before, made a mental note to meet him when the taping was finished.

"I want to show you this morning that no matter what your situation is; no matter what difficulty you face, God has the solution. Notice that Peter does not say that 'God has given us *almost* everything we need' or that 'His divine power has bestowed upon us all but a few of the things that are needed for a life of godliness!' We are not instructed to find the answers from the latest "guru" on afternoon television. Science and philosophy do not have the answers to humankind's deepest needs. God has those answers, and He pleads with us to come to *Him* for the solution."

James saw the young man duck his head and rub his eyes and imagined that he heard a sigh as he closed with a prayer of blessing. By the time James got to the back of the studio, the man was gone.

The next day, as James looked through his scheduled appointments for the week, his phone buzzed. "Pastor James, you have a call on line one," his secretary's pleasant voice informed him.

"Pastor James speaking,'" he answered cheerfully.

A husky voice responded, "Pastor Curtis, my name is Justin Thomas, and I visited your service yesterday."

"Yes," James said, "I remember seeing you. What can I do for you?"

"Well, I was so intrigued by your sermon. You answered some questions for me that I have had for a long time, and I was wondering if I could make an appointment with you for counseling sometime this week?"

James moved uneasily in his chair. "Well, you see, Mr. Thomas, I don't usually take counseling appointments, but I know several very competent psychologists, and I could give you a referral."

"Well, no, that wouldn't be helpful," Justin replied. "I've already tried that route—I've been to psychiatrists and several Christian psychologists. They all immediately recommended medication for the anxiety I was feeling. I tried it, but it just made me feel like a zombie. After listening to your sermon yesterday, I thought you would have the real answers that I need."

James had a sinking sense of inadequacy, remembering how he had emphasized that God's Word is enough for all of life. "I think I have some time about three o'clock tomorrow afternoon," he offered hurriedly.

He heard relief in Justin's voice. "Great! I look forward to talking to you."

Three o'clock arrived more quickly than James wanted it to. He hadn't slept well the night before, wondering just how to convince the young man to see the psychologist he usually referred people to. He couldn't help but think that if he had already been to several he must be very troubled.

He cleared his throat. "Now, Mr. Thomas, how can I be of help to you?"

"Well," he said with a slight smile, "I have an anger problem. I do a lot of yelling—I've hit the wall a couple of times, and my wife is afraid that it is going to escalate to physical abuse. She is threatening to leave me if I don't deal with the issues that are causing the problem."

"And what are those issues?" James asked. His palms felt

sweaty, and he couldn't help but hope that the eager young man would change his mind about wanting to talk to him.

"Well, my stepfather abused me sexually from the time I was six until I was fourteen. I told my mom about it, but she just screamed at me to shut up and said I was lying and that I was never to mention it again. When I was fourteen, my stepdad choked me and left a bruise on my neck that my school counselor noticed. When she started asking questions, I told her about the situation, and I ended up in foster care until I was eighteen. During that time, I was molested by two of the men in the foster homes. I don't trust men at all, even though I really want friends, and because my mom rejected me, it's hard for me to make myself be close to my wife. I don't trust her either." He smiled wistfully. "No one seems to know quite what to do with me. You seemed different though—like you really have confidence in the Bible, so I thought I would take the chance. I really want help."

Pastor James swallowed hard. He had heard about cases like this—even listened to talk shows dealing with issues of homosexual incest and abuse but had never personally dealt with something this painful. He adopted his kindest tone. "I am so sorry that all of this happened to you. I'm sure that it grieves the heart of God and He deeply desires that you be healed from this trauma. But honestly, I just think this is beyond my experience—it's clear to me that you need professional help to move past this."

"What do you mean?" The hopelessness that had been so evident in Justin's posture the previous day became visible again as his shoulders sagged.

"I just think that your problems are so deep—you really need to consult with a professional."

Justin bit his lip. "But you said that knowing what the Bible says would give me peace in my heart. I'm desperate—I've got to get rid of this anxiety and resentment that I feel. It's killing me, and it's destroying my marriage!"

James cleared his throat. "Listen, Justin. What I learned in seminary is how to deal with *spiritual* issues. For abuse and disorders that are as complicated as yours, you need professional help from someone who has had psychological training. You may very well need medication. I mentioned earlier that I would be glad to give you a referral to a competent psychologist."

Justin shook his head in bewilderment. "But I don't understand. I thought you said yesterday that everything we need to live life can be found in the Bible."

"Well, yes—of course, we can find many of the answers to our problems, but we also need scientific research to give us understanding. Professional counselors have specialized training that helps them uncover the subconscious causes of the presenting problems. Then they are able to apply special therapies for specific dysfunctions and disorders."

"Have you ever gone through psychotherapy?" Justin asked. Pastor James shook his head.

"Well, I have, and I'm telling you there are no answers there. They use the latest psychological model and ask a few questions. They rephrase and repeat back to you what you've just said to be sure that they have "understood" you. Then when that and some of the other "old faithful" models don't make you feel better immediately, they prescribe the latest medication so that you don't feel the pain. And when you say, "The pain is less," they cheer this latest miracle drug that "takes away" the problem."

"Well yes, I understand that is standard therapy, but I'm talking about *Christian* psychologists." James hurried to defend his position. "You surely realize that there is a difference?"

"No, I told you, I've been down that *Christian* therapy road." James heard the bitter note in Justin's voice as he emphasized the word *Christian*. "Not one of those men ever prayed with me, and at best, a couple of them quoted some Scripture before they handed me a prescription. I really thought you could help."

James felt sick. "Well," he said lamely, "I hope you will continue to study with us. We're on the air weekly, and I know that the study of the Word will help you." Justin looked at him without expression. "Thank you," he said, and walked out the door.

The practical reality is that pastors do not usually have the in-depth training or the time it takes to be full-time counselors. But the reluctance of both pastors and non-ordained Christians to apply Scripture to life's painful problems has been strongly influenced by the current cultural mind-set that "spiritual issues" and "psychological issues" are not connected, or that only "mental health experts" are qualified to help. This has left the church with limited confidence in the extraordinarily effective tool that we have been given—God's Word. Knowing God and His Word is the only real way to face the difficulties of life with hope.

Hybrids and Sterility

Hybrid describes the composite produced by the interaction or cross-breeding of heterogeneous elements such as animals, cultures or philosophies. Many hybrids are sterile.

Our focus on psychology in this study is *not* because it is the *only* system in our culture that opposes the Word of God but because *it is the system that has replaced the Word of God in the church* for spiritual and emotional health.

- Psychology is defined as the science that studies the mind, the mental states, and processes, human nature, and behavior. Psychology is the study of humankind by humankind. It is people and problem centered. We call this *humanism.*
- The Word of God is the study of humankind from the perspective of our Designer-Creator. Biblical guidance is focused on God and is centered on the solutions He presents.

There are two words often used in the ongoing attempt to blend Christianity with psychology:

- *Integration* is defined as "the knitting together" (not fusing) of psychology and theology. Integration is the process by which both disciplines retain their own identity while benefiting from each other's perspective and communicating the same truth."[1]
- *Syncretism* is defined as "the attempted reconciliation or union of different or opposing principles or practices, as in philosophy or religion."[2]

Because the Bible and psychology are opposing philosophies, it is impossible to "knit them together." Therefore this attempt to blend is *syncretism* rather than *integration*. Since the two systems are diametrically opposed, the same "truth" cannot be communicated by both, and theology never benefits in any way from the attempted inclusion of psychology.

As the attempt to blend these opposing philosophies continues, psychology is not becoming more Biblical. Instead, the American understanding of Biblical truth is being significantly infiltrated by the humanistic philosophy of psychology, which emphasizes feeling good and being happy. Personal responsibility for failure tends to be minimized, and when human answers fall short, blame for the problem is shifted to others. Instead of doing the hard work of personal change, we plunge into shopping, entertainment, sex, food, or drugs—both illegal and prescribed—in an attempt to bury the failure.

Trying to blend two incongruent systems has produced a sterile hybrid called *Christian psychology* that lacks power to produce spiritual and emotional wholeness. To expect human beings to have the answers to human problems is like asking a broken lawn mower to figure out its own mechanical failure, choose what parts to order, and decide which mechanic it wants to install the new parts.

Because God is the Designer, Creator, and Sustainer of the human race, it is reasonable to expect that His solutions will be far more insightful and effective than those devised by people. God is as interested in the process as the result, and He is not in a hurry. His goal is not that we be happy but that we become holy. A focus on holiness produces joy; a focus on happiness ends in emptiness.

Who is Teaching the Kids?

The number of young men and women raised in Christian homes who graduate from both secular and parochial schools with a degree in psychology, compared to those who are being taught to receive and give counsel from the Word of God, is shockingly unbalanced. This is happening because Christians believe the myth that psychological counseling, with all its theories and techniques, is a science. It has even been given a name: psychotherapy.

Science is defined as a branch of study dealing with a body of facts which are systematically arranged. True science shows the operation of the general laws of the physical or material world gained through observation and experimentation. Present-day psychology does not fit into that definition.

In 1983, in an attempt to advance the acceptance of psychology as a science, the American Psychological Association appointed Sigmund Koch to plan and direct a study which was subsidized by the National Science Foundation. This study included eighty scholars skilled in assessing the facts, theories, and methods of psychology. The results were published in a seven-volume series entitled *Psychology: A Study of Science.* Koch describes their findings:

> The *hope* of a psychological science became indistinguishable from the *fact* of psychological science. The entire subsequent history of psychology can be seen as a *ritualistic endeavor to emulate the forms of science in order to sustain the delusion that it already is a science.*[3]

Psychology as a study can offer observations about human development and behavior. The problem is that psychology has moved from *observation* into the field of *explanation*. That indicates a move from objective, observational science to subjective opinion. An unsubstantiated opinion presented as science is described as *pseudoscience*: a system of theories, assumptions, and methods erroneously regarded as scientific.[4] Pseudoscience uses scientific labels to protect and promote opinions that cannot be scientifically proven or disproven.

Psychotherapy has mushroomed into a mass of conflicting explanations of human behavior. Gary Collins has this to say:

> Newcomers to the study of psychology, psychiatry, and counseling view it as a rather unified discipline. However, because psychology is the study of humankind from a human perspective, there is no solid, unchanging standard upon which to build. The result is literally hundreds of contradictory therapeutic models with thousands of conflicting techniques and approaches, all claiming to cure the human psyche! All psychological models give sin a *disease* label. *The solution offered is usually some method of cultivating self-esteem along with the newest medication to alleviate discomfort.*[5] (emphasis added)

Psychologist Roger Mills, in his 1980 article, "Psychology Goes Insane; Botches Role as Science," says:

> The field of psychology today is literally a mess. There are as many techniques, methods, and theories around as there are researchers and therapists. I have personally seen therapists convince their clients that all of their problems come from their mothers, the stars, their bio-chemical make-up, their diet, their lifestyle and even the "karma" from their past lives.

With over 250 separate systems of psychotherapy, each claiming superiority over the others, it is hard to view such diverse opinions as scientific or even factual.

Carl Jung, one of the founders of psychology, viewed all religions, including Christianity, as collective mythologies, but he clearly understood that the "whys" of behavior and the "hows" of changing that behavior must be viewed as religious in nature. He wrote, "Religions are systems of healing for psychic illness... that is why patients force the psychotherapist into the role of a priest, and expect and demand of him that he shall free them from their distress. That is why we psychotherapists must occupy ourselves with problems which, strictly speaking, belong to the theologian."

In contrast, Sigmund Freud reduced all religious beliefs to the status of an evil illusion, calling it "the obsessional neurosis of humanity." He considered religion to be delusionary and the source of mental problems. Both views are anti-Christian. One denies Christianity and the other mythologizes it.

Repudiating the God of the Bible, both Freud and Jung led their followers in the quest for alternative understandings of humankind and alternative solutions to life's problems. They turned inward to their own limited imaginations and evaluated their patients from their own anti-Christian subjectivity. Because of its humanistic roots, psychology cannot explain the meaning and purpose of human beings as God created us, especially those of us who are redeemed and are in Christ.

Psychology: Food for the Flesh

Psychology is a valuable support system for our selfish flesh! Instead of being denied, self is now esteemed and promoted. We hear much the same message from the pulpit and through Christian media that we hear from secular radio, television, books, and magazines; that the greatest human need is to develop self-love, self-esteem, self-worth, and positive self-image. Step-by-step, we are being led to substitute the truth of Scripture with good feelings and a positive self-image.

It is often difficult to distinguish what is offered as "Christian therapy" from secular therapy. This includes unbiblical forms of meditation, inner healing, positive confession, visualization, and exorcism. Each of these is based on a Biblical truth, but just a slight twist changes the focus from God to self and takes it into the realm of humanism.

It is paradoxical that at a time when secular psychological researchers are demonstrating less confidence in psychological counseling, more professing Christians are pursuing it. "Christian" counseling centers are springing up all over the nation, offering what many believe is the perfect combination: Christianity plus psychology. In an attempt to be relevant, many preachers, teachers, counselors, and writers promote a psychological perspective of life rather than a Biblical one, and multitudes of professing Christians view psychology with respect and awe.

This humanistic theory that has become so popular in the church has not produced even what the world hoped for. *Newsweek's* cover of February 17, 1992 announced its feature article in large letters: "The Curse of Self-Esteem: What's Wrong with the Feel-Good Movement."

Portland's *Oregonian* included an article in the November 23, 1995 issue entitled, "Note to California: Drop self-esteem; Self-control is most important." Based upon years of research, the author declares: "If we could cross out *self-esteem* and put in *self-control*, kids would be better off and society in general would be much better off." This is precisely what the Bible has always said about this essential fruit of the Spirit. Yet the theory of self-esteem continues to invade Christian counseling in the church.

A Critical Choice

To whom should Christians go for counsel and insight when there is the need for the changing of core beliefs and attitudes? Our only two choices are:

- humanistic philosophies and theories that constantly change
- the inspired Word of God that never changes

Imagine that you are a gifted pianist and you own an expensive Steinway baby grand piano. One day as you are playing, you hear a "thunk" and a "twang." A bit of investigation reveals that one of the strings is broken. You have two choices for repair: one is an unemployed neighbor down the street who has taken some classes at vo-tech in piano tuning so he has some rudimentary knowledge about the insides of pianos. He could probably come over in a few minutes and hook that old string back up somehow.

Your other choice is to call the Steinway dealer in the large city a hundred miles away, knowing that it will take much longer and be considerably more expensive. But which one would you rather have working on your Steinway baby grand?

When we hear "thunk" and "twang" in our lives, and we know that some major repair work needs to be done, well-meaning people immediately offer "solutions" in the form of psychiatrists, medications, new things, and different relationships, instead of taking us to our Maker, the One who really understands our inner workings.

All the Counsel of God

In Acts 20:20-27, Paul says emphatically that in his spiritual guidance of the new church, he "kept back nothing that was profitable... for I have not shunned to declare unto you all the counsel of God."

Paul is not talking about things that made his listeners feel better about themselves or that gave them a roadmap to greater wealth. He was referring to all that is necessary for a joyful, fruitful, triumphant Christian life, no matter when, where, or under what circumstances that life was lived. Those early Christians were encouraged and inspired by the knowledge that all the counsel of God was available to them at any time. What could be more thrilling than having God Himself as our personal Counselor and to be assured that the Bible is the counsel and wisdom of God!

Paul wrote to Timothy at a time when life was looking really tough for a rather timid young man in ministry who had a Jewish-Christian mother and a Gentile father. He was evidently being criticized for being so young, and he carried tremendous responsibility. No doubt he was anxious and stressed, but there is no suggestion from Paul that Timothy should work on his "self-image." Paul's counsel to Timothy:

> O Timothy, guard and keep the deposit entrusted to you! Turn away from the irreverent babble and godless chatter, with the vain and empty and worldly phrases, and the subtleties and the contradictions in what is falsely called knowledge and spiritual illumination.
>
> 1 Timothy 6:20

> Study and be eager and do your utmost to present yourself to God approved, tested by trial; a workman who has no cause to be ashamed, correctly analyzing and accurately dividing, rightly handling, and skillfully teaching the Word of Truth. But avoid all empty, vain, useless, idle talk, for it will lead people into more and more ungodliness. And their teaching will devour; it will eat its way like cancer or spread like gangrene.
>
> 2 Timothy 2:15-17

> For the time is coming when people will not tolerate or endure sound and wholesome instruction, but, having ears itching for something pleasing and gratifying, they will gather to themselves, one teacher after another... chosen to satisfy their own liking and to foster the errors they hold, and will turn aside from hearing the truth and wander off into myths and man-made fictions.
>
> 2 Timothy 4:3-4

> For the Word that God speaks is alive and full of power, making it active, operative, energizing, and effective; it is sharper than any two-edged sword, penetrating to the dividing line of the breath of life, the soul and the immortal spirit, and of joints

> and marrow, the deepest parts of our nature, exposing, sifting, analyzing, and judging the very thoughts and purposes of the heart.
>
> Hebrews 4:12

Paul instructed Timothy:

- to guard and keep the deposit of truth entrusted to him.
- to avoid empty chatter.
- to study eagerly.
- to avoid useless, idle talk.
- to continue to hold to the things he had learned from God's sacred writings.
- to lay these instructions before his brothers and sisters.
- to refuse impure fictions and old wives tales.
- to train himself toward godliness.
- to express his disapproval of silly myths.

All of Paul's instruction is pointed toward encouraging Timothy to grow up in his understanding and application of God's Word so that he would not be drawn into the vain talk and empty solutions that were so prevalent in the world around him.

Is psychology empty, idle talk? Read this excerpt from a review entitled, "What is Christian Psychology?"

> The first thing we must do is to admit we are not perfect. Intellectually, this sounds easy, but it is the emotions that have a difficult time with self-limiting statements. Jesus taught in the Beatitudes that it is advisable to feel another's pain. He taught that being empathic to others would take one away from themselves and the selfish instinct of humanness... Psychologists are required to follow a carefully thought out set of ethical standards. *These high standards of practice do not promote a particular standard but use positive societal norms in which to guide behavior.* The Christian psychologist also follows these standards of conduct but *in addition he or she uses the standards set forth by God.* These combined resources must be considered an improved position. [6]

Admit that we're not perfect? Actually, the Bible says that there is nothing about us that is in any way acceptable to God, apart from the blood of Jesus. And when did Jesus ever make a *self-limiting* statement? His entire life, death, and resurrection were directed toward the *death* of self, not its limitation.

And what about the "high standards" that do not promote a particular standard (including Biblical truth) but use "a positive societal norm" to guide behavior? What if a "positive societal norm" says it is all right to kill babies, the handicapped, or the elderly who don't contribute? What if the "positive societal norm" sees same-sex relationships as a good thing or rewards grand larceny through the manipulation of the banking system or stock market? Is this really an improved position?

If the Christian psychologist follows these so-called "high standards" and then adds as a kind of afterthought, "we also use standards set forth by God," the result will be exactly the same solutions that the world offers. When the Word of God is recommended *in addition to* anything else, what is offered is a sterile hybrid; its power is nullified.

Consulting the Owner's Manual

The Bible has been called our manufacturer's handbook. God is our Maker (Proverbs 22:2), and He wrote our handbook, intending that His people would regularly consult it. The manufacturer of any machine, appliance, or toy includes instruction for every situation or repair. How much more complete our infinite Designer has made His operating manual for us (2 Peter 1:3-4; Romans 8:32)! Surely God has not overlooked any possible problem or malfunction which might happen, nor has He failed to provide complete instructions and the appropriate remedy.

So what if we become angry, frustrated, fearful, anxious, insecure, and lonely or perhaps we feel misused and abused or useless? We can turn to our Designer for counsel and help because He knows everything about us. In His Word we are given clear instruction that will take us through the process of growth and maturity. Jesus is named the Wonderful Counselor (Isaiah 9:6).

Men and women who have been powerful in the kingdom of God depended on God for their physical, spiritual, and emotional needs and triumphed by faith. For example Joseph was alternately spoiled and criticized by his father. His brothers hated him and wanted to kill him. He was sold into Egypt as a slave. While trusting God and living with integrity, he was falsely accused of rape and imprisoned. How did he survive with no medication or inner healing? He was gloriously triumphant over insurmountable difficulties because he trusted the unfailing goodness of God.

Write out the following verses:

Proverbs 22:2

____

____

____

2 Peter 1:3-4

____

____

____

Romans 8:32

____

____

____

Psalm 56:3

____

____

____

Isaiah 9:6

____

____

____

What Would Jesus Prescribe?

From *The Church Snatchers: The Ultimate Identity Theft*
by Dr. Dixie Yoder

Let's just pretend for a moment that the Biblical writers and their contemporaries had access to the same psychological "solutions" that are so accessible to us, and that Jesus embraced the same mind-set. If Scripture writers who suffered from fear, disappointment, depression, guilt, and grief like we do had turned to psychology and medication in the same way that modern believers do, what would our Bible say?

Isaiah, writing the prophecy of the coming Messiah, might have exclaimed, "The Spirit of the Lord God is upon me, because the Lord has anointed me to bring the good news of the latest antidepressant to the afflicted; He has sent me to bind up those who feel brokenhearted because of low serotonin levels; to proclaim liberty and the freedom of Zoloft to prisoners of anxiety ... to bring the comfort of Paxil to all who mourn, to grant those who mourn a new miracle drug, giving them a prescription to take away their sorrow, Prozac instead of mourning, the mantle of Ritalin instead of a spirit of fainting" (Isaiah 61:1-3).

What about the time that Jesus's disciples tried to stop parents from bringing the children to Him? If Jesus and Luke had known about Ritalin, perhaps Jesus would have said, "These children are making absolutely too much noise! They are disrupting everyone, and I certainly can't preach with them fidgeting around like this. Luke, when they have taken their Ritalin and can sit still, then bring them to Me" (Mark 10:13-16).

When Jesus confronted the issue of "overload," which often results in anxiety, He would have said, "Come to the neighborhood pharmacy, all you who have jetlag because of your heavy work and travel schedule. When you are heavy laden with anxiety, depression, and the pressures of "life in the fast lane," the newest anti-anxiety drug will cause you to rest. It will ease and relieve and refresh your souls. Take two each day, and you will find rest, relief, and ease for your souls, with no effort on your part" (Matthew 11:28-30).

Jesus, on His way to the Garden of Gethsemane with His disciples, crying out His distress to His Father, would have said, "Now My soul has become troubled and distressed; and what shall I say, 'Father, I can't stand this emotional pain! I know I must have a chemical imbalance, and that's why I feel so anxious'" (John 12:27).

Paul, praying for the struggles he had to face might have said, "Because of the surpassing greatness of the revelations I have received, I have every reason to feel good about myself. It simply is not fair that there was given me a thorn in the flesh, a messenger of Satan to torment me! So concerning this, I have implored the Lord three times that it might leave me. And He has said to me, 'Since My grace isn't a tangible thing and doesn't feel sufficient for you, there is a new medication on the market that will help you to feel better about yourself and your situation.' Most gladly, therefore, I will take the medication and continue to boast about my accomplishments, so that my self-esteem will remain high. I don't have to be content with weaknesses, with insults, with distresses, with persecutions, with difficulties. After all, God wants me to be happy and to feel good" (2 Corinthians 12:7-10).

"Yes, but…"

If there is any "disorder" that has reached epidemic proportions in the church, it is the "yes, but…" disorder.

- We hear that the Bible is God's sufficient, inerrant Word, and we reply, *"Yes, but I've tried it and it doesn't work."*
- Don't we have the indwelling Holy Spirit to guide and empower us? *"Yes, but how do I know it's really Him speaking?"*
- Hasn't the Word of God and the comfort and guidance of the Holy Spirit been enough for suffering, persecuted, and misunderstood Christians for the first nineteen hundred years? *"Yes, but the world is so much more complex today and we need additional help."*
- Jesus said that we are to come to Him when we are weary and overburdened. *"Yes, but He lived in such a different time. He couldn't possibly understand the pressure of the twenty-first century."*

- The men and women of faith mentioned by the writer of Hebrews were victorious in fierce persecution without psychology. *"Yes, I know that, but you just don't understand my situation. You just don't know my children... my husband... my wife... my boss... the abuse I suffered as a child."*

The issue is not complicated. God said through Peter that the wisdom and instruction written down for us is sufficient; it is everything necessary to live a Godly life (2 Peter 1:3-4). That statement is either true, or God lied and has failed us. If the Word of God requires twenty-first-century psychology and medication to be truly effective, then God unjustly left His church to struggle for 1900 years without the additional tools they needed.

The Twenty-First-Century Eden

Things really haven't changed much since the Garden of Eden. Like the first man and woman, humankind still runs away from the voice of God, and even those of us who have a face-to-face relationship with Him through salvation still try on the self-help "fig leaves" of the newest theories. They are just as fragile, dry, and uncomfortable as those first fig leaves. We still try to hide behind the "trees" of unbelief and rebellion, and God still continually calls us to step out and talk to Him about our lives.

How God must grieve as He watches His children seeking "earthly, natural, and demonic wisdom" in place of the unfailing wisdom found in His Word (James 3:15)! When we do that, we accuse our Creator of not understanding the men and women He so tenderly fashioned or of not caring enough to provide everything that He promised.

It is essential that God's sons and daughters grow up in knowledge of the whole Bible—not just the parts that make us "feel good." We need to cultivate a deep desire to know and apply all of the counsel of God. It will not happen automatically.

God plans for eternity, and He builds to last forever, but it takes time and patience. If we fulfill our own desires, we will be like the Samaritan woman at the well; we will soon thirst again. But if we allow

God to provide for our thirst, He fills us with living water, and we are filled in ways we could never have known on our own.

Asking and Answering the Five W Questions

A good journalist obtains information by asking five questions about the person or situation that is being investigated:

1. Who?
2. What?
3. Why?
4. When?
5. Where?

These five words will show us why we can be confident that God's Word is adequate and fully able to correct and train His children in every area of life, even those that are not spelled out in great detail.

1. *Who* is involved in this situation? First and foremost, God is! As we will see in the study "A Toaster Can't Fry Waffles," God is the Designer, Creator, and Engineer of humankind. Just as the inventor of a complex machine is involved in every aspect of carefully designing each part, large or small, so our Designer is intimately familiar with every physical cell of our bodies, the deepest thoughts and motives of our soul, and the eternal condition of our spirit.

   Write Acts 17:28

   ____

   ____

   ____

2. *What* is involved in this situation? The written Word of God: God is the author of His Word even though it came to us through the agency of human beings. God, has presented us with a carefully written guide that includes the doctrines, principles, and instruction we need for living life with the Holy

Spirit. Other written material may give us interesting and sometimes useful information, but only God's Word has the power to protect, change, comfort, and energize us. Because God is our Creator, we go to Him and His Word when we have questions about our design and function.

Write Psalm 119:99

____

____

____

Write Romans 15:4

____

____

____

Write 2 Peter 1:19-21

____

____

____

3. *Why* do we need God's Word? We live in a world that is being ripped apart by the effects of sin, and even after we have received the gift of salvation, our bodies and our souls (mind, will, and emotions) are subject to the effects of our sinful world. In order to withstand the pressure and repair the damage so that we live in victory, it is essential that we be familiar with our "owner's manual."

   Write Psalm 119:105

   ____

   ____

   ____

Write Psalm 119:50

____

____

____

Write Psalm 119:9,11

____

____

____

4. *When* does the Word of God apply? It is applicable for all time and throughout eternity.

Write Psalm 119:160

____

____

____

Write Isaiah 40:8

____

____

____

Write 1 Peter 1:24-25

____

____

____

5. *Where* is the Word of God? It stands both in heaven and on earth. Jesus is the Living Word of God. In Scripture we have

been given a written description of the Living Word and how to be in relationship with Him.

Write Psalm 119:89

____

____

____

Write Psalm 147:15

____

____

____

Write Psalm 89:2, 5

____

____

____

God's Word Is Enough!

Sometimes we hear the argument that Scripture is not complete or sufficient for what we need because it doesn't tell us how to drive a car or build a house. However, we can find information in abundance about the attitudes needed to drive a car without giving in to "road rage" or to build a home with diligence and excellence. The Bible does not outline in legal detail how to establish a corporation, but it does tell us that we are to be honest in our business dealings and pay employees a fair wage. Although Scripture is not exhaustive in detail, its principles and wisdom cover every area of life.

The written Word of God, and the insight we receive from the Holy Spirit as we read it provides humankind with everything necessary to enjoy abundant living. Along with this revelation from God, He also gives us the ability to gain insights from the world around us. However, we are born with a fallen nature and corrupted soul (mind, will, and emotions). Without the Presence and prompting of the Holy Spirit, we will depend on the interesting, sometimes wonderful—but always temporary—knowledge gained from our world, without receiving eternal insight into how to live life.

When we fail to carefully evaluate the information available to us, many marginal ideas and principles, which may sound good but fundamentally reject the authority of Scripture, will be mixed with Scriptural truth. This mixture will always result in confusion.

> As His divine power has given to us all things that pertain to life and godliness, through the knowledge of Him who called us by glory and virtue.
>
> 2 Peter 1:3 (NKJV)

> For the Word that God speaks is alive and full of power, making it active, operative, energizing, and effective; it is sharper than any two-edged sword, penetrating to the dividing line of the breath of life (soul), and the immortal spirit, and of joints and marrow—of the deepest parts of our nature, exposing and sifting and analyzing and judging the very thoughts and purposes of the heart.
>
> Hebrews 4:12

> The entrance and unfolding of Your words give light; their unfolding gives understanding, discernment, and comprehension to the simple.
>
> Psalm 119:130

To be adequate or sufficient means to "be equal to." It conveys the idea of that which satisfies the requirement exactly; it is neither too much nor too little for what is needed. To say that Scripture is "adequate" or "enough" is to say that it is exactly what is needed for human beings to live life.

Bible Study

Read Psalm 119. List ten verses that mention God's Word, His testimony, His law, His statutes, etc. Write out the benefit the psalmist observed when he obeyed.

1. Reference and descriptive phrase (word, testimony, law, etc.)

 ____

 Benefit:

 ____

 ____

2. Reference and descriptive phrase (word, testimony, law, etc.)

 ____

 Benefit:

 ____

 ____

3. Reference and descriptive phrase (word, testimony, law, etc.)

 ____

 Benefit:

 ____

 ____

4. Reference and descriptive phrase (word, testimony, law, etc.)

 ____

 Benefit:

 ____

 ____

5. Reference and descriptive phrase (word, testimony, law, etc.)

 ____

 Benefit:

 ____

 ____

6. Reference and descriptive phrase (word, testimony, law, etc.)

 ____

 Benefit:

 ____

 ____

7. Reference and descriptive phrase (word, testimony, law, etc.)

 ____

 Benefit:

 ____

 ____

8. Reference and descriptive phrase (word, testimony, law, etc.)

 ____

 Benefit:

 ____

 ____

9. Reference and descriptive phrase (word, testimony, law, etc.)

 ____

 Benefit:

 ____

 ____

10. Reference and descriptive phrase (word, testimony, law, etc.)

____

Benefit:

____

____

Questions for Personal Reflection

1. Do you believe that the application of Scripture is necessary in every area of life? (This would include work, leisure, relationships, emotions, and thinking) If yes, how? If no, explain why not.

____

____

____

____

2. As you go through your day and you hear and see the ideas being promoted through movies, TV, books, music, magazines, the educational system, and churches, do you stop to filter what you are receiving through a Biblical perspective? Give examples:

____

____

____

____

3. Are you intentionally placing your private thoughts and your personal life—when no one else is around—under the guidance of God and His Word? In what ways?

____

____

4. How do your thoughts, attitudes, and behavior with your family reflect the instruction you receive from Scripture?

5. Does the way you do your work and the way you interact with fellow employees or employers show a determination to be like Jesus in the workplace? Give examples:

6. Would others evaluate your life as one of Godliness or selfishness? In what area do you see the need for change?

7. Do your friendships and use of leisure time show a love for the Word of God and its instruction for these areas? Why or why not?

8. Does your interaction with people show a love for Jesus rather than a legalistic determination to make them do what you believe they are "supposed" to do? In what way?

9. When you feel angry, depressed, lonely, or anxious, do you seek understanding from the Word of God first, or do you turn to people and "expert" information for a solution? How?

10. When someone asks you for help or advice, is your first impulse to take them to the Word of God, or do you give them information designed to make them feel better? How? (For example, do you share how a particular scripture has been helpful to you or made a change in your life?)

11. Briefly describe one specific issue you are currently struggling with in your own life.

____

____

____

____

12. What have you done about this problem?

____

____

____

____

13. In the past, as you have tried to deal with the problem, did your attempts to solve it depend more upon your friends, books, yourself or God and His Word? In what way?

____

____

____

____

14. Did this method work? Why or why not?

____

____

____

____

15. What does the Bible tell you that God thinks about your situation? Write out the verse(s) and reference.

____

16. What promises in the Word of God are applicable to your situation? Write them out.

17. Write out a prayer thanking God for His work in your life and His solution to your situation.

Chapter 2
Our God Image:
Who Do You Think He Is?

What I Believe About God

1. What is God's attitude toward you?

   ____

2. What is God's opinion of you?

   ____

3. What are God's intentions toward you?

   ____

4. What does God need from you?

   ____

5. What does God expect of you?

   ____

6. How does God feel toward you when you fail?

   ____

7. Does your private behavior shame or embarrass God?

   ____

8. Can you disappoint God?

   ____

9. How would God describe you?

   ____

10. Describe God's personality.

    ____

11. Without using the words *conditional* and *unconditional*, describe the difference between God's love and human love.

____

12. The thought of being alone with God makes me feel…

____

13. When it seems that my life is out of control, and I have to trust God, I feel…

____

14. I get frustrated when God insists that I…

____

15. I enjoy God when…

____

16. God would like me better if I could just change this one thing about myself:

____

17. Reading the Bible and all of God's commandments makes me feel…

____

18. I wish God would…

____

19. I can depend on God when…

____

20. I am always sure that God will…

____

21. The thing that frightens me the most about God is…

____

22. God surprises me when…

____

Love! It's a word that is constantly tossed around. We say that we "love" our pets; we "love" ice cream; we "love" our families; and as believers in Jesus, we "love" God. More or less, we also believe that God "loves" us.

If we have grown up in a church atmosphere, we might even be able to quote 1 John 4:8, which tells us that "God is love," but in the midst of all this talk about God and love, we live as though God isn't very real. Since God is love, if God does not seem real to us, then genuine love will not seem real to us either, and we'll spend our lives trying to find a substitute in what surrounds us.

Unfortunately, we have learned to describe God according to how our circumstances look. We equate good circumstances with a good, benevolent God and difficult circumstances with a harsh, angry, punishing God. The result is a terribly wrong conclusion about God: that He is moody, capricious, and undependable.

The historic church taught that the "chief end of humankind is to glorify God and enjoy Him forever." Modern American Christianity has a strong humanistic perspective, too often teaching that the *chief end of God is to gratify people.* Humankind is assumed to be the center of God's plan from creation to the complete restoration of all things. Consequently, the predominating theme in most Christian writing and teaching today is:

- How we sinned
- What our needs are
- How God is going to provide for our needs

When we perceive God as existing only to benefit and care for humankind, we place ourselves in the center. From this humanistic perspective, we may think of God as the "Man Upstairs," or the "Great Vending Machine" out there somewhere. Perhaps we approach Him as the "Infinite Magician in the Sky" who will perform signs and wonders while we sit watching passively from our front row seat, telling Him what He needs to be doing and how, when and where "it" should be done.

The Reality of God

A college professor wanted to impress on his students how important it is to observe a situation from more than one perspective in order to have a more complete understanding. As he stood before the class, he made three dots on the large whiteboard and drew lines between the dots, constructing a triangle. Then he asked, "What do you see?" The students sat quietly for a few moments, thinking that what was there was pretty obvious, but to humor the professor, the students described their perspective of the dots and lines on the whiteboard. Finally the professor asked, "Do any of you see the whiteboard?" The students sat silently, embarrassed that they had missed the most obvious object and the one that had been there long before the dots and lines had been drawn!

Our ability to see God, who exists eternally as a Father, often gets diverted by what we see "drawn" around us—our daily circumstances, other people and our own perspective of life. We fix our attention on what is temporary, rather than on the One who creates; giving life and meaning to everything that exists.

The human concept or understanding of God was fractured when Adam and Eve chose to disobey God and declared their independence from Him. Ever since that catastrophic event, each human being has tried to determine what is right or wrong, true or false, good or evil, according to our circumstances, emotions, and our faulty, limited human reasoning.

All our concepts of God are inadequate, simply because any concept of His infinite deity that is within the grasp of our finite minds will inevitably limit and, therefore, distort the reality that lies behind the name "God." So we might ask the question, if all concepts are distorted, does it really matter which one we have? The answer is an unqualified,

"Yes, it does matter!" Even when our understanding fails to encompass God, an increasingly accurate concept of Him will draw us into greater intimacy with Him.

Oxytocin (Ox-ee-toe'-sin): God's "Superglue" for Human Bonding

A baby and its parents "imprint" themselves into the very cells of each other's brains and bodies by making direct eye contact while talking and touching. In a natural childbirth setting, when the mother is holding her baby for the first time, endorphins and oxytocin are released in the mother's brain, promoting joy and contentment. Oxytocin is thought to be released during hugging, touching, and orgasm in both sexes. Oxytocin is involved in social recognition and bonding, and may be involved in the formation of trust[7] and generosity[8] between people. It is God's "superglue" for human relationships.

Physical closeness of the baby to his parents immediately following delivery is extremely important for the development of the infant's senses as they are stimulated by the sounds, scents, and touch of his parents. Babies learn their mother's scent while nursing and as the mother, father, and baby look into each other's eyes, the infant's developing sense of sight is stimulated. This also familiarizes the baby with the parents' facial features and expressions, which is crucial for developing the ability to mimic these expressions. Parents talk and sing to their new baby, identifying their voices to the infant and stimulating his developing sense of hearing. Human infants and parents are physically "wired" for bonding to occur.[9]

Infants who have minimal human contact develop attachments to inanimate objects, such as blankets and teddy bears. The fact that even healthy, well-adjusted toddlers have a favorite cuddly toy confirms the research that human beings are designed to need touch, closeness, and intimacy.

Love: God's "Superglue" for Spiritual Bonding

A baby that is born physically alive and with no physical defect is, nonetheless, spiritually separated from the life of God. In that sense, we are spiritual "orphans" from the moment we are conceived by our mother and father. Bonding or "imprinting" with our Father God cannot take place until we are reborn through a love relationship with Jesus. Until that rebirth, we are "imprinted" with the fallen family traits of First Adam, and changing the imprint is often painful, as those family ties are relinquished. We have all watched a child's hands being pried away from a blanket, a bottle, or some other object that needed to be given up. The same is true of the spiritual "security blankets," such as harmful relationships and habits, that God knows we need to put aside.

Because imprinting with our Father God is a process, even after we are born into His family, we can know *about* Him but not have a personal and intimate relationship with Him. Closeness of the spiritual baby to the heavenly Father immediately following "delivery" (salvation) is extremely important for the development of the spiritual infant's senses as they are stimulated by the sounds, scents, and touch of the "new" Dad.

Tattooed on His Hands

Using the parallel of human bonding and growth, God gives us a visual illustration of what the bonding and growth in Him is to be like. In Isaiah, God compares Himself to a human mother but says emphatically that even though she may reject or forget her child, He never will. He has tattooed, or "imprinted," a picture of us in the palms of His hands, and His "wall" of protection is always around us. In the Hebrew culture, to be without a wall meant to be without protection. God promises to be our unfailing Protector (Isaiah 49:14-16).

In Hosea 11, God likens Himself to a tender father who taught His son (Israel) to walk and continues to love His people even when they persistently turned to idols and refused to acknowledge that it was God who gently fed, clothed, and healed them. In verse four, He says that He intertwines Himself with them. He goes on to describe the suffering they will experience as God separates them from their wrong "security blankets"—the idols of other nations. In verses eight and nine, we hear the anguish in the Father heart of God as He cries out, "Oh, Ephraim, how can I give you up?" He describes the pain He feels as He watches them struggle through the consequences of wrong choices.

And then comes the reassurance, "But I am God, not a man; therefore, I will not come to you in wrath" (Hosea 11:1-9).

God also gives us a visual picture of our spiritual conception, birth, and growth through our own human families.

Spiritual conception: Peter explains how we were spiritually conceived and born: "You have been regenerated (born again), not from a mortal origin (seed, sperm), but from one that is immortal by the ever-living and lasting Word of God" (1 Peter 1:23).

Newborn spiritual babies: After we are born again, Peter compares us to "newborn babies" who should crave or "earnestly desire the pure, untainted spiritual milk" of the Word of God, so that we will grow up into healthy maturity in our spirit-person (1 Peter 2:2).

Spiritual little children: Jesus admonishes us to become like little children—not child*ish*, but child*like* when it comes to trusting, loving, and forgiving (Matthew 18:3-4).

Spiritual childishness: In 1 Corinthians 3:1-2, Paul scolds believers in Corinth because he could not talk to them as spiritual adults but as he would talk to babies in the new life in Christ. He said, "I fed you with milk, not solid food, for you were not yet strong enough; but even now you are not … ready for it." Paul's dismay over their childish, selfish immaturity tells us that it is not normal to still be drinking spiritual "milk" years after our birth into God's family.

The writer of Hebrews dealt with the same problem:

> For even though by this time you ought to be teaching others, you actually still need someone to teach you over again the very first principles of God's Word. You have come to need milk, not solid food. For everyone who continues to feed on milk is obviously inexperienced and unskilled in the doctrine of righteousness … for he is a mere infant, not able to talk yet! But solid food is for full-grown men, for those whose senses and mental faculties are trained by practice to … distinguish between what is morally good … and what is evil and contrary either to divine or human law.
>
> Hebrews 5:12-14

Spiritual adulthood: 1 John 4:6-8 describes how we resemble our Father in attitude and behavior, as we receive the imprint of our Father God:

> "We are children of God . . . progressively learning to know God . . . let us love one another, for love springs from God; and he who loves his fellowmen is born of God and is coming . . . to a better and clearer knowledge of Him. He who does not love has not become acquainted with God and does not know Him, for God is love."

Love for other people is the visible imprint of God in His children.

Spiritual Maturity

We bond with our heavenly Father in much the same way that we bond with our physical parents: when we make eye contact, when we are held close and become familiar with scent and voice. There are many references in Scripture to God's eye, ear, voice, and touch. This is generally referred to as an *anthropomorphism* or giving human characteristics to God. Sometimes when we think of God in terms of being a person, we end up with a mental picture of:

- A Stern Very Big Man who is watching from a distance with a critical eye to see what is going on down here on earth.
- A Grandfatherly Very Big Man who listens tolerantly with no intent to become involved.
- An Imaginary Very Big Man who helps us to pretend that He is touching us.

We think of God as a person, because He does such person-like things toward us—such as loving, forgiving, persuading, and teaching. He tells us about His tender gaze, eye-to-eye; His face is always turned toward us as He speaks and listens attentively, holding us in His strong arms. Thinking of God as a person is not wrong; it is reducing God to fallen humanness that becomes problematic. The Bible describes His personhood and interaction with us:

Eye contact:

Behold, the Lord's eye is upon those who fear Him and worship Him with awe, who wait for Him, and hope in His mercy and loving-kindness to deliver them from death, and keep them alive in famine. Our inner selves wait (earnestly) for the Lord; He is our help and our shield (Psalm 33:18-20).

For the eyes of the Lord are upon the righteous (those who are upright and in right standing with God), and His ears are attentive to their prayer (1 Peter 3:12).

Sense of smell:

I will accept you graciously, as a pleasant odor when I lead you out from the peoples and gather you out of the countries in which you have been scattered, and I will manifest My holiness among you, in the sight of the nations who will seek Me because of My power displayed in you (Ezekiel 20:41).

And walk in love (esteeming and delighting in one another), as Christ loved us and gave Himself up for us, a slain offering and sacrifice to God (for you, so that it became) a sweet fragrance (Ephesians 5:2).

Sound of voice:

And after the fire (a sound of gentle stillness and) a still, small voice. When Elijah heard the voice, he wrapped his face in his mantle and went out and stood in the entrance of the cave. And behold, there came a voice to him and said, "What are you doing here, Elijah? (1 Kings 19:12-13).

And when the trumpeters and singers were joined in unison, making one sound to be heard in praising and thanking the Lord, and when they lifted up their voice with the trumpets and cymbals and other instruments for song and praised the Lord, saying, "for He is good, for His mercy and loving-kindness endure forever," then the house of the Lord was filled with a cloud, so that the priests could not stand to minister because of the cloud, for the glory of the Lord filled the house of God (2 Chronicles 5:13-14).

Listen to my words, O Lord, give heed to my sighing and groaning. Hear the sound of my cry, my King and my God, for to You do I pray. In the morning, You hear my voice, O Lord; in the morning I prepare a prayer, a sacrifice for You and watch and wait for You to speak to my heart (Psalm 5:1-3).

The sheep that are My own, hear and are listening to My voice; and I know them, and they follow Me (John 10:27).

Touch:

If I take the wings of the morning or dwell in the uttermost parts of the sea, even there shall Your hand lead me, and Your right hand shall hold me (Psalm 139:9-10).

Fear not for I am with you; do not look around you in terror and be dismayed, for I am your God. I will strengthen and harden you to difficulties, yes, I will help you; yes, I will hold you up and retain you with My (victorious) right hand of rightness and justice (Isaiah 41:10).

Nevertheless I (David) am continually with You; You do hold my right hand. You will guide me with Your counsel (Psalm 73:23-24).

Hold me up, that I may be safe and have regard for Your statutes continually (Psalm 119:117)!

For, as we all know, He (Christ) did not take hold of angels (the fallen angels, to give them a helping and delivering hand), but He did take hold of (the fallen) descendants of Abraham, to reach out to them a helping and delivering hand (Hebrews 2:16).

Taste:

O taste and see that the Lord [our God] is good! Blessed and to be envied is the man who trusts and takes refuge in Him (Psalm 34:8).

How sweet are Your words to my taste, sweeter than honey to my mouth (Psalm 119:103)!

Our God Image

Even though our relationship position with God changes eternally in the instant we are born into His family, the experience of being separated from God has affected our perspective of Him as our Father. Our beliefs about God are inaccurate because they were developed while we were "fatherless," often in a system that doesn't know God intimately.

- We form our perspective of God by looking at people. When we see someone loving others generously or kindly, we say "that is what God's love is like." But, in reality, even when a person loves really well, we are still seeing conditional, fallible love, with a little glimpse of God's love mixed in. What God's love is really like only becomes evident as we see the Father's love for us, expressed through the death and resurrection of Jesus.

- We form our perspective of God by how we love our own children. We say that we love our children "unconditionally," yet we place conditions on them in many different ways. So we misunderstand what it means when God tells us that He loves us truly unconditionally. Human beings are needy; it is, therefore, impossible for us to love without preconditions. Only God, who needs nothing from us, can love without condition or expectation.
- We form our perspective of God by observing the church body around us. The result is a confusing mix: we believe God is demanding, unforgiving, sometimes loving, sometimes close, often very distant or completely absent.
- We form our perspective of God by looking at weather disasters and reading our insurance policies. The sin-provoked destruction of earthquakes, storms and drought are almost invariably referred to as "acts of God," and we learn to believe that He is capricious and unreliable.
- We form our perspective of God by looking at the world around us. We insist that God is "in control" of the brokenness in creation trashed and torn by sin. It follows then, in our sin-twisted logic, if "it" (rape, divorce, murder, cancer) happened, "it" must be His will, and we learn to believe that God is cruel and unsympathetic.

When believers lay the blame for everything that happens at God's door, they are as mistaken as an atheist who blames everything on blind chance. Things happen, both good and bad, because God bestowed incredible freedom on humanity. The freedom from which evil comes is also an essential aspect of all goodness. The guaranteed absence of evil would equally guarantee the absence of good, because a puppet without the freedom to choose wrong also cannot choose to do that which is good.

Unless we recognize what is happening and deliberately sort

through the lies and deceptions of the enemy, our view of God will grow increasingly twisted and inaccurate.

The Parental "Filter"

Our view of God is powerfully influenced by our earthly parents. As we grow up in our family structure, we build a "grid" through which we view God, ourselves, and all of life. When we grow up in a healthy, balanced family in which love is expressed and modeled, it becomes possible to accept God's love as real and true. When the family system is dysfunctional—not operating according to God's design for the family—our view of God grows twisted and inaccurate. There are several general categories of dysfunctional earthly fathers into which we might unknowingly place God:

- The dictatorial father: This type of father is more interested in having control over his children than he is in having a relationship with them. He doesn't want them to express a differing opinion, and if they do, he accuses them of disrespect and rebellion. He demands that they want what he wants, and when they don't, he uses intimidation and manipulation to force compliance. Because of their earthly experience, these children are likely to be rebellious toward God as adults, sometimes completely denying His existence (atheism).
- The abusive father: This father hurts his children intentionally, inflicting pain through emotional, physical, or sexual abuse. Children who grow up in this family system have no sense of their own worth. They find it extremely difficult to trust anyone. Because they believe they have no value, they choose relationships in which the abuse continues and they are used as objects to gratify the lust or rage of someone else. A very high percentage of prostitutes come from an abusive family system.
- The indifferent father: This father expresses little or no affection. He may be a hard worker and a good financial provider, but he does not interact with his family, especially

emotionally or spiritually. He rarely says "I love you" and does not take part in the triumphs, failures, joys, and sorrows of his children. Often his parents didn't know how to support him emotionally, and he never learned how. Sometimes a dad withdraws emotionally from the children because there is trouble between him and their mother, even though a divorce has not occurred. These children learn to believe that God is not interested in the "unimportant" everyday things of their lives.

- The distant or absent father: This father may be absent from his children because of divorce or workaholism, perhaps because of death. Or, like the indifferent father, he may be present physically and absent emotionally. He may have learned in his growing-up years to believe that the home is the mother's domain. He lives there but provides no tangible emotional support or input. He withdraws to other activities that make him feel more successful such as work, sports, or church work. His children grow up feeling neglected and abandoned, believing that God abandons and neglects them as well.
- The critical father: This father is negative and judgmental. His children cannot do anything that will bring a complement or encouraging statement from him. Their best effort is never enough. His intent is to motivate his children to try harder to do better, but the result is that they become discouraged and give up. These children grow up believing they can never measure up to God's impossible standards and no matter how hard they try, He will never be pleased or satisfied with them.

God compares Himself to a "nursing mother" in Isaiah 49:14-16. Our mothers also have an important impact on our understanding of God. There are several general categories of dysfunctional earthly mothers into which we might unknowingly place God:

- The controlling mother: This mother is determined to bring up her children in the way *she* thinks they should go.

She will justify her rigid control by insisting that a mother always knows what is best for her children. She wants to be her child's "best friend" and often tries to experience life vicariously through her children. Because they've learned that "God is in control," they resent God as much as they do the constant infringement from their mother into their adult lives.

- The abusive mother: This mother takes her frustration out on her children with constant yelling, harsh language, and facial expressions intended to intimidate and force compliance with her demands. Her children learn to resent all correction and will not easily accept spiritual instruction.
- The passive mother: This mother is often married to the abusive father. Her fear of being rejected by him and her belief that "no one else would have her" causes her to ignore the abuse directed at their children. They feel abandoned and believe God doesn't care about them either.
- The busy mother: This mother always has a "greater mission" than her children. She serves on committees, works full time, and is the bustling homeroom mother that all the other kids love. The busy mother is often a single mom. She has projects going on at home in her "spare time." Her children often fend for themselves, going to bed by themselves at night. Her children grow up believing that God is always occupied with "important" things, not them.
- The critical mother: This mother is negative and judgmental. Her children cannot do anything that brings a complement or encouraging statement from her. Their best effort is never enough. Her intent is to motivate her children to try harder to do better, but the result is that they become discouraged and give up. These children grow up believing they can never measure up to God's impossible standards and no matter how hard they try, He will never be pleased or satisfied with them.

The Impact on Children

The effects on the children are extensive. A distorted view of God built within a damaged family system produces adults who are unequipped to build good human relationships. Girls and boys who grow up in poorly functioning families respond differently. A girl's response will fall somewhere in the following categories:

- She may reject her appearance and her femininity. After all, if her parents, especially her dad, did not find her appealing and pleasing and did not want to spend time with her, then she believes no one will ever find her attractive. She feels ugly and undesirable, no matter how attractive she may be. She may try to imitate the airbrushed, glossy pictures in magazines. Her excessive focus on appearance often produces an eating disorder.
- She may obsessively crave attention and affection from men. Because she longs to be held, she may become promiscuous, because there are plenty of young men who will gladly exchange a few moments of "holding" for sex.
- At the other extreme, she may resent all men so deeply that she desires no attention from them whatsoever and longs instead for the companionship from women that she didn't receive from her mother. This makes her vulnerable to homosexual behavior because she still needs attention and affection and she still needs to be held.
- She becomes a living, walking model of rejection. The smallest slight or disagreement from friends and family reinforces the lie she believes — that no one could ever love her. She will withdraw and accept any form of abuse that comes her way, believing she doesn't deserve any better treatment.
- Her need for assurance and approval will be insatiable; she will likely become extremely dependent and "clingy" in every relationship, including with her children.
- She will find it difficult or impossible to trust God because she has no visible pattern on which to build a trust relationship.

A boy's response will fall somewhere in the following categories:

- He may reject his own appearance and imitate a man he admires. Good spiritual role models are rare, so boys often emulate the lifestyle of actors or musicians, trying to achieve the same kind of body, copying tattoos, hairstyles, and piercings.
- He may obsessively crave attention and affection from men and may resent women deeply. This makes him vulnerable to homosexual relationships. He will find it difficult to form relationships with men in a nonsexual context.
- He may resent men so deeply that he becomes promiscuous with women. If he had a controlling, critical mother, he will need women to tell him what to do, but resents them for "nagging." He will likely become an abuser. He will find it almost impossible to build a life-long marriage relationship, because one woman will not be able to meet the needs that even he doesn't understand.
- He becomes a living, walking model of rejection. The smallest slight or disagreement from friends and family reinforces the lie he believes—that no one could ever love him. He will likely become cocky, loud, and belligerent, very possibly abusive to his wife, children, or coworkers.
- His need for assurance and approval will be insatiable. He will tend to become jealous, suspicious of every conversation his wife has and any "extra" miles driven in the car. He will check on her by calling or texting any time of the day or night.
- He will find it impossible to trust God because he has no visible pattern on which to build a trust relationship.

Omnipotence Is Not Control

When children who grew up under the control of harsh, dictatorial parents hear of God's omnipotence and are told that *God is in control*, they immediately assume that God is responsible for everything bad that happens. Later on, when they also begin to learn that God holds people accountable for sin, they reject Him as being mean and unfair. "*After all*," they think, "*He makes it happen and then blames us!*" Because they experienced parental abuse, the deplorable misuse of human power that hurt them so terribly in their growing-up years, they cannot trust a God who seems like the controlling parent.

Norman Pittinger describes God's power this way: "God's power is the kind of power exercised by a wise and effective parent—the power to persuade. He is the living, dynamic personal Love who is ever at work to establish more love and goodness in the world; hence more justice and righteousness. It is profoundly unbiblical to think of Him as a despotic ruler. A much better model would be the man whose character is sheer goodness, who is always faithful to his purpose and loyal to his friends, who 'lets them be' but is affected by what they think and do, and who yet has enough resources of love to adapt himself to new circumstances and situations, and to make the best that can conceivably be made of them."

To be able to trust God, we must set aside the perspective of God as a powerful authority figure who constantly opposes humankind and replace it with the Biblical picture of One who loves and gives Himself to humanity. He is perfect love; He does not enslave us, nor will He hamper our development. Instead, His unconditional love draws us to our highest and fullest potential. God is the very embodiment of the quality of love that leads to freedom without selfishness and service without enslavement.

The Parable of the Prodigious Father

(Luke 15:11-32: paraphrased by Dr. Dixie Yoder)

We have been given a beautiful picture of God's kind of love in a parable that Jesus told about two rebellious sons and a loving dad. This account is usually referred to as the "prodigal son," but it is really more accurate to see the father in the story as the one that is extravagant—almost recklessly wasteful—in the love that he pours out on two sons, both with bad attitudes. *Prodigious* means to be remarkably or impressively great in extent, size, or degree.

> A man had two sons. The younger son showed incredible disrespect by saying to his father, "In a sense I wish you were dead. I want what is coming to me now! And if it creates a hardship for you, that's your problem. You'll just have to deal with it."
>
> The father graciously divided his estate between his sons, one-third to the younger and two-thirds to the elder. A few days later, the younger son turned his property into cash, left the community, and spent everything he had with no restraint.
>
> About the time his money ran out, the economy in that city became very unstable. He couldn't find work or pay his bills, and he was terribly hungry. He found a farmer and made a nuisance of himself asking for work until the farmer finally sent him into the field to feed his pigs. He was so hungry he tried eating the carob pods the pigs were eating, but they didn't satisfy his hunger.
>
> One day, he took an honest look at himself. "What am I thinking?" he asked himself. "Here I am in the worst place a Jewish man can possibly be—in the middle of a pigpen—yet my dad has plenty of food. Even his servants aren't hungry, but I'm his son, and I'm literally starving to death! I know what I'll do. I'll go home and tell my dad that I realize what I did was wrong. And I'll tell him I realize that he probably won't accept me as his son after what I did, but that I am willing to be a hired man. At least I'll have enough to eat."
>
> He started home. He wasn't even close when his dad, who had come out several times every single day to watch the road for his son, ran to meet him. He grabbed his son and whirled around with excitement, kissing him and shouting with joy the whole time. The son kept trying to interrupt his dad with the speech he had prepared. "Dad, I know that you won't want me to be your son any longer. I don't deserve that, and I don't expect it."
>
> But the father didn't seem to hear him at all. He said to the servants who were with him, "Hurry, bring the best suit out of

my closet. Bring those new shoes I just bought this week and that gold ring on my dresser. Bring them quickly. I want him to walk in the house looking like who he is—my son! And start to prepare a barbeque! Call all the neighbors! My son is home again! I thought he might be dead, but he's here! He's home for good!"

As the sun was setting, the elder son was coming in from a hard day of work in the fields. He was irritated because he had been thinking all afternoon about how much more work he had to do since that worthless brother of his left home. "Stupid kid! And I know just what he's been doing," he muttered angrily to himself. "Does he think we're deaf to the rumors?"

Just then he heard the sound of laughter coming from the house and saw people dancing on the patio. He called one of the hired men over and asked him what was going on.

"You'll never believe it!" he answered with a broad grin. "Your brother has come home, and your dad has killed that wheat-fattened calf that he was saving for a special occasion. Come on! It's a great party!"

"Of all the nerve," the older brother spat out indignantly. "I wouldn't eat a bite of that calf if I was starving." He stomped angrily into the machine shed and slammed the door.

A few minutes later, the door opened quietly. He looked up and saw his father standing there. "Son, come on in and join us. I've waited a long time for this day."

The elder son's rage spilled out in hot angry words. "I've spent my entire life slaving for you on this stupid farm, and you've never given me a party. This other son of yours robs us blind, throws it all in the sewer, and the minute he shows his face, you act like nothing ever happened. You don't even care that he has trashed our family name. People have done nothing but talk about us since he left home."

"Son," the father said gently. "Everything that I have here is yours now. I gave it to you. And even though you are filled with bitterness, resentment and anger, you are always here with me, and in my heart. But your brother, who we thought might be dead, is home again. How could I not be excited and throw a celebration!"

This story is a picture of the tender, forgiving heart of Father God, the Dad Who is always with His children through immaturity, rebellion, and wrong attitudes. His design from the beginning was for us to grow up in a family in which He is the center, loved by a female mother and male father. When we watch Mom and Dad love God, each other, and other people, we have a model of life that makes it much easier to accept the love of God. Our enemy, the devil, knows that. He is bent on the total destruction of the family so that our concept of God will hinder us from receiving His love.

Our Covenant Father

We view life from the inside out through our "grid" of beliefs; we also filter everything that comes into our minds via our five senses through that grid. That's why it is so incredibly important that our "grid" be Biblically accurate, especially in how we know God.

The Bible tells us that God is Spirit. He does not have a spirit: He is spirit in His essence. The Bible lists many character traits that make God who He is. Galatians 5:22-23 names nine of these traits. List them:

God is…

____

____

____

God does not *have* these characteristics; He *is* each one, fully and perfectly. He has promised through covenant to share Himself with us as completely as we will receive Him.

> As surely as God is trustworthy and faithful and means what He says, our speech and message to you have not been Yes (that might mean) No. For the Son of God, Christ Jesus (the Messiah)…was not Yes and No; but in Him it is (always the divine) Yes. For as many as are the promises of God, they all find their Yes (answer) in Him (Christ). For this reason we also utter

> the Amen (so be it) to God through Him (in His person and by His agency) to the glory of God.
>
> 2 Corinthians 1:18-20

A covenant is a promise made by speaking words that last forever. Words don't cease to exist when the sound of them fades away; the power contained in words that are thought and spoken continues to operate. A covenant is a solemn verbal agreement that binds the participants together for life and, after death, through their descendents.

In Biblical culture, making a covenant with another person or nation was a deeply serious matter. The participants understood that the agreement between them would not only affect them but all of the generations who would be born from their families. They understood that a covenant did not cease to exist simply because someone failed within the agreement. Because of their insight into the workings of covenant, they chose their covenant friends and partners very carefully. Elements of covenant included:

- Exchange of weapons: This declared, "Your enemies are now my enemies, and mine are yours. If anyone attacks you, they are attacking me. I am your protection."
- Exchange of clothing: This declared, "In wearing your clothing, I am 'wearing' you and you are 'wearing' me. All that I have is yours; all that you have is mine. I die to independent living and to any independent rights I have claimed before this covenant. I am your provision."
- Exchange of the girdle or belt that held their clothing: This declared, "When you are weak, my strength will be yours. I am your strength."
- A walk into death: The participants walked around the pieces of the sacrificial animals in a figure eight, the symbol of eternity. As they walked through the blood from the animals that splashed on their feet, they pointed first to heaven and then to the dead animals, saying, "May what happened to these animals happen to me if I ever break this covenant."
- Mingling their blood: Each one entering into the covenant

made a cut on his wrist or palm, and as they clasped hands, their blood was mingled and they declared, "It is agreed. We are now one."
- Tattooed: The covenant participants would rub ashes into the cut on the wrist to make a tattoo mark that would never wash away. Each declared, "No matter where I go; no matter what I do; when I see this tattoo on my wrist, I will remember that I am no longer independent in what I do and say. I have a covenant partner."
- Exchange of names: This declared, "I will answer to your name as though it is mine. Because we are in covenant, I am now known by who you are, and you are known by who I am."
- Covenant meal: This was a meal in which they placed a piece of bread in the covenant partner's mouth. It was a symbol of becoming so much a part of each other that they were as one, never again to be independent, *even in succeeding generations*.
- Covenant memorial: At the end of the meal, a visible memorial was set up where the cutting of the covenant took place. Sometimes it was the planting of a tree, perhaps a pile of stones, perhaps a written and signed memorial.

We still see some scattered remnants of covenant in our culture, even though we have very little understanding of it:

- Handshakes
- Written contracts
- Wedding rings (symbol of eternity)
- Bride and groom feeding each other wedding cake
- Wedding vows
- Cultic or occultic jewelry
- Mantras
- Tattoos—these can represent a covenant with the culture that encourages them. In the context of forbidding idolatry, God says, "Do not put tattoo marks on yourself" (Leviticus 19:28).

In Genesis 15:1-17 we read the account of God coming to Abram to cut a covenant with him.

> Verse 1: God tells Abram that He is his shield, representing the exchange of weapons. God says He is Abram's abundant compensation, a declaration that "all I have is yours."
> Verses 4-5: God promises to provide Abram with an heir from his own body and that his descendents will be too numerous to count. The covenant included all future generations.
> Verses 6-8: Abram believes God and asks Him for confirmation of the promise.
> Verses 9-11: God tells Abram which animals to bring. Abram prepares them for the covenant ceremony.
> Verses 12-16: God puts Abram to sleep, and he has a frightening vision of what God explains is the enslavement of his descendents in Egypt.
> Verse 17: As darkness becomes deep, a "flaming torch" passes in a figure eight around the pieces of the dead animals.
> Verse 18: "And on that day, the Lord made a covenant pledge with Abram."

There is significance in Abram's deep sleep. Abram could not enter into covenant with perfect God, saying, "May this death happen to me if I break this covenant." It is obvious that an imperfect man cannot make and keep a covenant with perfect God. God put Abram to sleep, and Jesus, the Light of the world, appeared as the flaming torch, passing between the pieces and taking into Himself both His and Abram's role of the covenant making. The rest of the story in Scripture tells us that in actual fact, Jesus's body was torn and broken because of the failure of humankind. His crucifixion was the death that He pledged Himself to as He passed between the torn pieces of the sacrificial animals.

David and Jonathan: Covenant Friends

In western cultures, if we think about covenant at all, we think of it as a contract, which is only as good as the shrewdest attorney. A contract is really not very binding or permanent, and we certainly don't think about it in terms of future generations.

There is a beautiful story in the Old Testament that helps us gain a deeper understanding of how a covenant was always made by someone who represented a family or a people group. For example, in the Biblical account of the battle between David and Goliath, David represented Israel, so he *became* the nation of Israel. As the Philistine representative, Goliath *became* the Philistine nation. Whatever happened to the representative happened to the entire nation, which is why the Philistines fled when Goliath fell even though they had the military advantage. When Goliath died, the Philistine nation was defeated. When David won the battle, the nation of Israel was victorious.

A few years after his victory over Goliath, when David was about twenty years old, he was forced to run for his life because of King Saul's jealousy. Before David fled to hide in desert caves, Saul's oldest son, Jonathan, who was David's closest friend, entered into a blood covenant with him. The entire account is recorded in 1 Samuel 18—2 Samuel 9.

- 1 Samuel 18:1: Cutting the covenant: "The souls of David and Jonathan were knit together." They cut a covenant and made a mark on the wrist or palm.
- 1 Samuel 18:3-4: Exchange of weapons and clothing: "Then Jonathan renewed the covenant with David, because he loved him as his own life. And Jonathan stripped himself of the robe that was on him and gave it to David, and his armor, even his sword, his bow, and his girdle."
- 1 Samuel 20:15-17: Jonathan reminds David of his obligation to Jonathan's offspring because of their covenant: "But also you shall not cut off your kindness from my house forever—no, not even when the Lord has cut off every enemy of David from the face of the earth."
- 1 Samuel 20:42: Reminder of the covenant: "And Jonathan told David, Go in peace, forasmuch as we have sworn to each other in the name of the Lord, saying, 'The Lord shall be between me and you, and between my descendants and yours forever.' And Jonathan arose and departed into the city."
- 1 Samuel 23:16-18: Jonathan, Saul's eldest son, is heir-apparent to the throne of Israel. However, he realizes that because he loves David and wants to be obedient to God, he will have to give up his right to inherit the throne. "And Jonathan,

> Saul's son, rose and went into the wood to David . . . he said to him, 'Fear not . . . you shall be king over Israel, and I shall be next to you. Saul my father knows that too.'"

David lived in caves in the wilderness for about ten years, avoiding Saul and his death threats. Then the day came that Saul, Jonathan, and both of Jonathan's brothers were all killed in the same battle (1 Samuel 31:2). There was panic in the household of Saul because they knew David would be coming to claim the throne. In that culture, the incoming king often destroyed any remaining members of the outgoing king's family. So the entire household ran for safety.

Mephibosheth: A King in Exile

At the time of his death, Jonathan had a five-year-old son named Mephibosheth. As his terrified nanny ran with him from the palace in Jerusalem, she fell. Both of Mephibosheth's legs were injured, and he was permanently crippled. He was taken with the rest of the household to Lo-Debar, an area north of the Yarmuk River in Transjordan at the tip of the Golan; a region that was allied with Saul. It seems to be in the same area as the cities of refuge. Joshua 21:27 gives this information: "and to the Gershonites of the families of the Levites they gave . . . the city of Golan in Bashan, as the city of refuge for the slayer."

These cities were located so that they were easily accessible to those who needed protection. The roads leading to them were to be kept in good repair and clearly marked. There were signs at all the crossroads pointing the way to the nearest city of refuge so that a person who unintentionally killed someone could run there and present his case to the elders of the city. By going to one of these cities, the one who was being pursued was safe until the facts of the case could be examined and a verdict declared. If found innocent, the manslayer was allowed to live safely in the city of refuge until the death of the high priest serving at the time. Even though he was innocent, he still paid a price for accidentally killing another human being, because if he left the city of refuge, the elders could no longer protect him.

As far as Mephibosheth and those who took him to safety and lived with him were concerned, Mephibosheth was a king in exile. It does not appear that he was aware of the covenant between David and Jonathan; after all, he was only five when Jonathan died.

So Mephibosheth lived in the desert city from the age of five, fearful of leaving his refuge. Over and over again, he must have heard the accusations: "David stole your throne. You are the rightful heir to the throne. Your grandfather was king. Jonathan, your dad, would have been king if he had not died. You should be on that throne. David took it away from you, and he would kill you if he could get to you. You're a threat to him. He's probably looking for you right now. David is an imposter—an illegitimate king."

Because Mephibosheth was the sole survivor of the deposed king's family, it isn't hard to imagine that he lived in an atmosphere of bitterness and resentment. Perhaps he lived as a terrorist, lord of a tribe of dessert raiders, picking away at the edges of David's kingdom at every opportunity. He married and had a son named Micah (1 Chronicles 8:34).

David was thirty years old when he began his forty-year reign (2 Samuel 5:4). Sometime after he ascended to the throne, David remembered again his covenant with Jonathan, in which he had sworn that he would treat Jonathan's descendents as though each one was Jonathan himself. He began to look for Mephibosheth.

Mephibosheth had reason to be afraid when he heard that King David was looking for him. He was fully aware of the custom of eliminating anyone who might challenge the new king's right to the throne. However, when David's men found Mephibosheth, he had no choice but to go with them to the palace to face King David.

Mephibosheth's fear was evident as he bowed before the king. His obeisance was not offered out of respect and honor for David as king, but because he assumed he was going to die (2 Samuel 9:6). Perhaps there was a snarl on his face, hidden against the floor as he thought, *"He took away my throne, and now he is going to take my life."* However, to Mephibosheth's astonishment, David received him with respect, acknowledging him as the rightful heir to Saul's estates. King David's generosity included the command to *eat continually at his table* in a position of honor.

Mephibosheth's father, Jonathan, had accepted that David would be king. In order for Mephibosheth to enjoy the benefits of David and Jonathon's covenant, he not only had to surrender his own right to the throne, he also had to accept that his son, Micah, would never ascend to that place of power. He had to give up even the title of "king in exile." He knew that he was exchanging the limited freedom and protection of the city of refuge for the much greater freedom and protection of the king. So the crippled man bowed again, this time in gratitude, and accepted the gifts offered by King David.

The statement "he ate at the King's table" is repeated often. Every meal was a reminder of the covenant between David and Jonathan that now provided benefit to Jonathan's son, Mephibosheth, and his grandson, Micah.

> So Mephibosheth dwelt in Jerusalem, for he ate continually at the king's table, even though he was lame in both feet.
>
> 2 Samuel 9:13

It seems significant that Mephibosheth's crippled legs are mentioned several times, but we might ask why it is mentioned in the context of eating at the king's table? After all, he doesn't eat with his feet!

Mephibosheth must have needed help to get to the table since he couldn't walk. And because he was crippled, he couldn't carry out any of the duties that David's soldiers, guests, and residents of the palace performed every day. It must have seemed that he didn't deserve all that the king gave him—he couldn't contribute much to the household. But when David looked at Mephibosheth, he did not see a crippled, bitter terrorist. He didn't even see a reformed terrorist. He saw Jonathan.

King David *imposed* a pardon upon Mephibosheth. He *imposed* gifts upon him. He *imposed* upon him the privilege of sitting at his covenant table. He gave all this to Mephibosheth, not because Mephibosheth asked him for it, or even because he wanted it. David gave it because of the covenant with Jonathan. It was not because Mephibosheth had done anything to deserve what David was doing; in fact he had done everything not to deserve it! Mephibosheth was rewarded for Jonathan's faithfulness to David. David did not say, "Now Mephibosheth, if you will do this and that, and if you will refrain from doing this and that, then I will bring you into my house." Rather he acknowledged that Mephibosheth was exiled by rebellion and then announced that he was imposing the covenant of his father upon him. All Mephibosheth had to do to enjoy it was to say *no* to his desert refuge and *yes* to David's table.

It must have been hard for both Mephibosheth and those already living in the court of David to adjust to his presence. Think of it! In the morning, he was a terrorist, hating David and all that he stood for; by evening of the same day, he had become a part of the king's family.

Knowing how people think and react, it is not hard to imagine that as Mephibosheth sat at the table waiting to be served, someone probably said something like, "You have no right to be here in the king's palace. We know that your grandpa hated King David! We know your history, and we know how you've lived your life. You don't deserve to be here."

Mephibosheth didn't even have to defend himself. In fact, he could not because the accusations were true. It was only necessary for him to say, "Go ask King David about the mark on his wrist. He'll tell you why I'm here."

We Are Mephibosheth

The Lie that Satan planted in the Garden of Eden was that if human beings just know enough, we can be exactly like God out of natural knowledge and wisdom, without having to depend on God.

First Adam rebelled against God and chose to believe *The Lie* that Satan told. He placed his attention on *The Lie* and determined to live life from it. When he did, the entire human race became infected with the sin of rebellion against the King. As the first man and woman were sent out of the Garden, they began life in a "desert" of frustration and sabotaged effort.

Satan has kept up a constant, slanderous attack against God, the King of the universe. We hear his message in so many ways: "God is withholding from you. You really deserve to be just like God. He has taken your rights away. He would probably kill you if He could—in fact, that's probably what He's trying to do right now. Why else would He let you suffer like this? Why else would He allow such hard things to happen?"

Adam and Eve and every descendent since creation have lived in the angry, bitter "desert" atmosphere of a fallen world, often living as terrorists, controlling, manipulating, and picking away at the edges of God's kingdom by lying and stealing at every opportunity. We were born in the spiritual "Lo-Debar" of a world wrecked by sin. In this barren desert, we are constantly surrounded by *The Lie* that slanders the character of God. Because we've heard it so often, we came to believe it as truth.

We have every reason to be afraid when we first hear that God is looking for us, because we know that anyone who challenges the throne of God has to be eliminated. Our fear shows as we bow before the King, and often we bow more out of resentment than from respect and honor. We make the correct assumption that self will die, and often snarl in frustration before we truly know the love of God. "He took away my throne, and now He is going to take my life."

The Covenant between God the Father and God the Son

God loves His human beings with an immeasurable love. In order for us to be reconciled to Him, He has imposed a covenant upon the human race, not because we wanted it, but because He wants us! He did not say, "If you will do this and that, then I will enter into covenant with you." Rather, He acknowledged that we were exiled because of rebellion, and He declared His intent to impose His covenant of love upon humankind. All we have to do to enjoy it is receive the truth that we are accepted in His Son. We have to say *no* to the desert of the sinful world and *yes* to the King's table.

> For I will take you from among the nations and gather you out of all countries and bring you into your own land. Then will I sprinkle clean water upon you, and you shall be clean from all your uncleanness; and from all your idols will I cleanse you. A new heart will I give you and a new spirit will I put within you, and I will take away the stony heart out of your flesh and give you a heart of flesh. And I will put My Spirit within you and cause you to walk in My statutes, and you shall heed My ordinances and do them.
>
> Ezekiel 36:24-27

In order to make this covenant valid, there had to be a representative from the human side; someone who could walk forward and connect with God. But no human being has ever lived who could be worthy or adequate. Since there were no qualified human prospects, God, out of His unrelenting love, became human, taking on our very nature.

Jesus entered the world through the Incarnation. He became a human baby and lived life fully human, choosing to do nothing on earth as God (Philippians 2:5-7). He is the representative of the human race, and if He ever did anything as God while on earth as a man, He would not have accurately represented the human race. He was fully tempted in every way that we are and experienced all that we encounter in our humanity. His life on earth was so utterly, ordinarily human that there are only a couple of events recorded about the first thirty years of His life. As a human being:

- He got up each morning and washed His face.
- He ate breakfast.
- He went to work.
- He gave estimates for His carpentry work.
- He collected money for the work He did.
- He probably supported His family after Joseph's death.
- He came home at night tired and ready to go to bed.

Jesus, Son of Man, perfect humanity, went to the cross and cut a covenant with God the Father as the representative of the entire human race. What happened to Him happened to us. We died with Him, and when we acknowledge Him as King, we receive His life and step into the covenant with God that is only available through Jesus. His victory becomes ours.

When we enter into the blood covenant through Jesus, all that we are becomes His:

- Our debt
- Our poverty
- Our deadness
- All the rottenness and corruption associated with death

All that He is becomes ours. We don't just inherit God's "things," we inherit *Him*:

> And if we are (His) children, then we are (His) heirs also: heirs of God and fellow heirs with Christ (sharing His inheritance with Him) only we must share His suffering if we are to share His glory.
>
> Romans 8:17

When God the Father looks at His children, He does not see crippled, bitter terrorists. He doesn't even see reformed terrorists. He sees Jesus.

God, through His Son, *imposed* pardon upon us. He *imposed* gifts upon us. He *imposed* upon us the privilege of sitting at His covenant table. He did this, not because we sought Him out and asked Him; not even because we understood and wanted what He was offering! Romans 5:8 tells us "God shows and clearly proves His own love for us by the fact that while we were still sinners, Christ the Messiah, the Anointed One died for us."

This covenant relationship is ours, not because we have done anything to deserve what God has given us—in fact we have done everything not to deserve it! We have been rewarded for the faithfulness of Jesus, as He represents us in the covenant He made with God the Father. But in order to sit at the King's table, we have to abdicate our right to the throne of our lives and acknowledge that Jesus is the rightful King.

Rags to Riches

When we first come into the King's house and sit at His table, it is often very hard for us and for those who have lived with the King for a while to adjust to our being there. Just think—in the morning we hated God and all that He is, and by evening of that same day we are a part of the King's family! It takes a lifetime to fully work this out.

When we are sitting at the King's table and someone, either human or demonic, begins to whisper, "What do you think you're doing here? We know your history, you're no good. You don't deserve to be here. We know how you thought and acted last week."

We do not have to defend ourselves. In fact, we cannot, because the accusations are true. It is only necessary for us to say, "Go ask King Jesus about the mark on His wrist. He'll tell you why I'm here."

> The people in captivity said, "The Lord has forsaken me, and my Lord has forgotten me." And the Lord answered, "Can a woman forget her nursing child, that she should not have compassion on the son of her womb? Yes, they may forget, yet I will not forget you. *Look! I have indelibly tattooed a picture of you on the palm of each of My hands.*"
>
> Isaiah 49:14-15

Bowing before the King and sitting down at His covenant table started the process of knowing the goodness and love of God instead of regarding Him with suspicion; learning to trust Him for our daily provision instead of believing we have to fix and provide everything ourselves. As we know Him better, we relax in His faithfulness instead of "wondering when the other shoe is going to drop."

We no longer live in Lo-Debar. Let's stop acting like it! Instead, let's grow in our enjoyment of the privilege of sitting at the King's table.

Questions for Personal Reflection

Describe your dad:

____

____

____

Describe your mother:

____

____

____

Describe your favorite teacher:

____

____

Describe your favorite pastor when you were growing up:

What was your parents' attitude toward God, church, and religion?

What assumptions have you made about God as a result of your observations of your parents and other authority figures while growing up?

Chapter 3
A Toaster Can't Fry Waffles

God's Design for People

Most of us have a small appliance in our kitchen designed to toast sliced bread, English muffins, and other pre-baked bread products. Imagine what would happen if you decide one morning that you're tired of toast and you want fresh waffles instead. You stir up a batch of waffle batter, pour a serving into the toaster slot, and push the button down. Very soon, as the wires heat and turn red, black smoke pours out of the toaster, the kitchen begins to smell like burnt waffles and the toaster shorts out and stops working. The mess is the result of using the toaster in a way that it was not designed to be used.

Human beings are designed to be fulfilled primarily in our spirit person through a relationship with God. If we don't have a good understanding of how we're designed and the purpose we were created to fulfill, we go through life trying to get our spiritual, emotional and physical needs met entirely through our five senses, other people and our physical surroundings. A primary dependence on things, people, and circumstances produces the "black smoke" of disappointment and broken relationships. When this happens, our life experience "smells bad" and people "short out" and give up as the cycle of failure continues. This happens because we are trying to live life in a way that disregards our God-designed blueprint.

The Bible says "if any man is in Christ, he is a new creation" (2 Corinthians 5:17). But if we are going to understand what it means that we are "new creatures in Christ," especially when our behavior doesn't seem so new, it is important to be aware of:

- How and why humankind was originally created.
- The impact sin had on our wonderful human design.
- How we have been restored through a relationship with Jesus Christ.

Before God created the *'aadam*, or *humankind*, He submitted a proposal. God said, "Let us (Father, Son, and Holy Spirit) make humankind in Our image, after Our likeness, and let them have complete authority over the fish of the sea, the birds of the air, the (tame) beasts, and over all of the earth, and over everything that creeps upon the earth" (Genesis 1:26). This kind of planning session between God the Father, God the Son and God the Holy Spirit is not recorded during any other part of the creative process and seems to indicate that God was designing something special and different.

The word image is defined as: *one like another or one who complements the other*. It also includes the meaning of a visual impression, such as the likeness we see reflected when we look into a mirror. The way we reflect our God image to others became fractured when sin entered in, but that reflection in our spirit-person has been restored through a relationship with Jesus.

A reflection cannot be present without the existence of the one who produces the reflection. The existence of humankind is simple proof of the existence of God, just as the visible physical realm is proof of the existence of the invisible spirit realm. All that is visible has its origin in the invisible.

> We look at this Son and see the God who cannot be seen. We look at this Son and see God's original purpose in everything created. For everything, absolutely everything, above and below, visible and invisible ... everything got started in Him and finds its purpose in Him. He was there before any of it came into existence and holds it all together right up to this moment ... He was supreme in the beginning and — leading the resurrection parade — He is supreme in the end. From beginning to end He's there, towering far above everything, everyone. So spacious is He, so roomy, that everything of God finds its proper place in Him without crowding. Not only that, but all the broken and dislocated pieces of the universe — people and things, animals and atoms — get properly fixed and fit together in vibrant harmonies, all because of His death, His blood that poured down from the Cross. (Colossians 1:15-20 from *The Message: The Bible in Contemporary Language*)

God created human beings to live in a love relationship with Him. The purpose for the existence of humankind is simply to receive the love of God, invite Him to live as a "roommate" in the body we have been given, and from the intimacy of that relationship, reveal the love, mercy, and tenderness of God to others through human relationships and behavior.

A light bulb cannot be explained apart from electricity. There is no part of a light bulb that has any meaning apart from the flow of electrical power, and a bulb cannot be used for anything else. Every component of a bulb is designed for one purpose—to receive electricity—and, as the invisible current flows into the filament, to reveal that electricity as visible light. Apart from electricity, the bulb has no purpose.

In the same way, every aspect of humankind was designed with one purpose in mind: to receive God Who is invisible to our physical eyes, into ourselves. When we have received Him, He is revealed and becomes visible to others through the activity of our lives. Any person who is living life apart from that one purpose is broken and inoperative—dysfunctional in the sense that the "components" that form a human being are being used for the wrong purpose.

Saved to Serve?

We often hear that we are "saved to serve" or that we were created to be "used by God." But God did not create us for good works. In fact, Ephesians 2:10 says that He created the good works for us! God did not design human beings to be a race of slaves He could use to get His work done. Rather, God created us so that He could love us and, as we receive His love, walk through every day of our lives in partnership with Him, bringing His will and His kingdom into operation right here on earth.

God does not use us. He doesn't even want to! What would you think about someone who says, "I'm your friend," and then you find that they have used you to benefit themselves? That's not a positive situation, and that relationship will likely end in resentment and humiliation. If we dislike this kind of treatment from our fellow human beings, why would we attribute such selfish behavior to a perfectly loving God? God does not use us. Rather, He invites us into relationship, friendship, and partnership with Himself.

Satan is the one who uses; he manipulates, humiliates, and takes advantage of us anytime we believe his deceptions. The truth that we are created so incredibly like God that we can walk and talk with Him is mixed with *The Lie* that we can do exactly what He does apart from Him, in our own strength, or by drawing on whatever is around us. This emphasis on the physical, natural world is the pagan religion of Naturalism.

Our Three-Part Design: Spirit, Soul, and Body

Part One: The Human Spirit

Each person is a spirit being whose dwelling place is a body marvelously created by God. Our spirit or nature is the very essence of who we are, and it is in that fundamental nature that we are *God aware* and respond to Him as He draws us into a relationship with Himself. John 4:24 says, "God is Spirit, and those who worship Him must worship Him in spirit and in truth." Our human spirit is the part of us that gives life to our body. "For . . . the human body apart from the spirit is lifeless" (James 2:26).

Part Two: The Human Soul

Another part of God's amazing design for human beings is the soul. The soul is made up of three parts:

- The mind (thinker)
- The will (chooser)
- The emotions (feeler)

The soul is the personality. It is the part of us that is *self-aware* and makes it possible for us to know ourselves and express ourselves to others. We cannot see the soul, but it becomes observable to others as our thoughts find visible and audible expression through our choices and emotional responses.

Each person is given a unique combination of these "thinker, feeler, chooser" qualities. For example, some people are more task or "chooser" oriented and less sensitive emotionally. Some are deep thinkers who have great ideas but have difficulty carrying the thoughts to a goal. "Feelers" have great empathy for other people and may laugh or cry easily but often don't think deeply about issues at hand. There is not a right or wrong combination. Personalities are simply different, and these differences are part of what makes interaction with other people uncomfortable, exciting, and frustrating, sometimes all at once.

Part Three: The Human Body

Of all of God's wonderful creation, human beings are unique in being equally at home both in the physical realm and the spirit realm. Because we are spirit in nature, but also have a physical body, we go through life with "one foot in each realm."

Interaction with other people and the world around us requires a body. This is the element in our God-given design that is *world aware*. Through the body we are able to communicate with others, receive from them, and give to them.

When God created *'aadaam* (humankind), this new creation came to life fully mature and completely equipped to live in relationship with the Creator. The Hebrew word *'aadaam* (pronounced aw-dawm´) simply means ruddy; human species or humankind. As He breathed life into His humankind, God declared that He had given this new creature His own capacity to exercise benevolent stewardship over the rest of creation, an assignment which clearly signifies intelligence, language, creativity, and the ability to reason and choose.

Name the three parts of a human being:

____

____

____

Name the three part of the human soul:

____

____

____

Write Romans 8:10. What part of a person is mentioned here?

____

____

____

Write Deuteronomy 6:5. What part of the soul is mentioned here?

Write Job 6:7. What part of the soul is mentioned here?

Write Lamentations 3:20-21. What part of the soul is mentioned here?

Write Proverbs 14:30. What part of a person is mentioned here?

The following chart lists verses that mention the three parts of humankind: spirit, soul, and body.

Spirit	Soul	Body
Numbers 16:22	Genesis 2:7	Psalm 31:9
Psalm 51:10	Deuteronomy 6:5	Psalm 38:4-8
Ecclesiastes 12:7	Deuteronomy 30:2	Proverbs 14:30
Zechariah 12:1	Job 6:7	Romans 6:12-13
Acts 7:59	Psalm 19:7	1 Corinthians 6:13-15a
Matthew 26:41	Psalm 63:1	1 Corinthians 9:26-27
Luke 1:46-47	Psalm 119:28	Philippians 3:20-21
Luke 8:54-55	Song of Solomon 1:7	James 2:26
Romans 8:10	1 Thessalonians 5:23	James 3:5-6
1 Corinthians 6:17	Hebrews 4:12	
	1 Peter 2:11	

First There Is One—Then There Are Two

The *'aadaam* was a single human being whose nature contained all of the possibilities of both male and female; not yet separated into two persons, and this new creation was placed in authority over all of the handiworks of God.

Genesis 2:8 from the Hebrew text says that God placed the humankind in the Garden of Eden, and to this single human was given the task of naming all the animals that had been previously created. God brought the animals to *'aadaam* for naming to give His new creation the opportunity to develop his intellectual capacity and to carry out the assignment of ruling over God's perfect handiwork. This capacity, unique to humankind, is a clear reflection of our Creator.

Naming indicates dominion and authority. The *'aadaam's* acceptance and completion of the task of naming the animals declared his lordship and superiority over them. As each pair of animals passed before him, the *'aadaam's* sense of aloneness increased. He became intensely aware that there was no one like himself to share this wonderful world over which he now ruled. Surprisingly to us, he was lonely even in the presence of God!

God knew exactly what He was doing. He did not just suddenly notice that the *'aadaam* was alone in his humanness. The separation of His creation into two bodies was not a modification of the original plan. Rather, it seems that God gave the humankind the opportunity to experience loneliness, and realize the deep need for human companionship. Our appreciation of other people will be in proportion to our understanding of how deeply alone and incomplete we are without others.

In Genesis 2:18b, God announces His solution to the humankind's aloneness. A more expansive translation expresses in English what the Hebrew conveys:

> To end the loneliness of the single human, I will make another power,[10] another being like it, corresponding to it, of the same species, facing it, standing opposite in an equal relationship; another human, its equal.[11]

In Genesis 2:21-23 the gender separation occurs as God fashions a woman from the rib or side of the *'aadaam*. At that time, the words *'iysh* (eesh) and *'ishshah* (eesh-shaw') are introduced. In contrast to *'aadaam*, a general term referring to the human race, these new words mean more specifically *a male human being* and *a female human being;* terms that could also be understood as *lord* and *lady*. The words emphasize that they are now separated into two distinct bodies, each one equally reflecting the image and likeness of God.

In describing people, we sometimes say, "she has such a funny side" or "he has a quiet side that not many people ever see." In that sense, God took the female "side" from the single human being and presented her as a rare gift, a woman whose incredible differences balanced him exactly. Woman is man's perfectly designed companion and equal partner. She was not created from the ground as the *'aadaam* was, but from a physical piece of the *'aadaam*. This "one, yet separate" arrangement is the foundation for the ordinance of marriage. His maleness and her femaleness, so different, but completely suited to one another, brings ultimate stability into the lifelong marriage relationship.

God made the provision of companionship into a special event to show us how carefully He prepared the marriage relationship. Human beings who are living within His blueprint honor the specially designed human relationship between a man and a woman as a priceless gift from the Creator. When we operate outside of the blueprint, we often treat relationships and sex like a new toy, to be used and then indifferently tossed aside. We carelessly cohabit with or marry someone simply because it "feels good." Then, when the good feeling changes or diminishes, as it always will, the relationship fails. However, the cellular imprinting has already taken place, and a divorce decree cannot eliminate the bond.

Humankind was the final and best of God's entire creation. Woman was fashioned out of that best, and 1 Corinthians 11:7 tells us that she is the crown and glory of her husband. Imagine the man's delight when he awoke! As his eyes rested on the beautiful woman God had fashioned to perfectly correspond with him and he realized that he was no longer without human companionship, his shouts of joy must have echoed throughout Eden! This woman was literally the man's own flesh and bone. The closest possible bond existed between them, even though they were now two separate beings. Ephesians 5:28 says, "even so husbands should love their wives as being, in a sense, their own bodies. He who loves his own wife, loves himself."

Isn't God All We Need?

The first woman was taken out of man; every man and woman since has been taken out of woman. One cannot exist without the other (1 Corinthians 11:8-9, 11-12). Men and women are mutually inter-dependent and were designed with differences so that we could relate to each other in a way that balances our unique strengths. This essential inter-dependence is a part of God's design and is why husbands and wives are told to "cleave" or adhere to one another in lifelong commitment, (Mark 10:7-9) and believers are instructed not to neglect "to assemble together with other believers" (Hebrews 10:24-25).

To ignore that inter-dependence with people is to resist the design that God built into us from the first moment of existence. Loners and those who withdraw because of mistrust, hurt, and depression are much more vulnerable to the attack of Satan than those who have the protection and strength found in Godly relationships with other people.

God is the primary source of all that we need, and it is in Him that our deepest needs are met. Our interaction with people is the secondary source of love and affirmation, but in varying degrees, these two resources—God and people—become reversed, and we begin to look to people as our primary source, while having limited or secondary interaction with God. When that happens, our human relationships are damaged and destroyed by the inevitable disappointment and disillusionment.

Nude or Naked: What's the Difference?

Humankind is the only part of God's creation that does not grow "clothing" such as scales, fur, or feathers. Since human beings were crowned at creation with the glory and honor of God, (Psalm 8:5; Hebrews 2:7) it is not unreasonable to suppose that the man and woman were "clothed" in the glory of God—perhaps a light that emanated from them—so that they were not naked. Their lack of self-consciousness came from a focus on their Creator rather than on themselves or their surroundings. The God-designed physical, mental, and emotional differences between the man and the woman were not a source of embarrassment or conflict. But when the man and woman chose disobedience, everything changed.

> And they heard the sound of the Lord God walking in the Garden in the cool of the day, and Adam and his wife hid themselves from the presence of the Lord God among the trees. But the Lord God called to Adam and said to him, "Where are you?" And he said, "I heard the sound of You walking in the Garden and I was afraid because I was naked, and I hid myself."
>
> Genesis 3:8-10

The word *naked* does not only mean "without clothing." There is a difference between nudity and nakedness. If a person is in the shower with no clothing on, he is nude, without clothing but not exposed. But if he is walking down Main Street in his hometown without clothing, he is naked, exposed and vulnerable.

God is not primarily asking the man and woman who told them they were no longer physically covered. The word *naked* is from the Hebrew word *'erom* (Old Testament: 5903) which means "to be or make bare," but is used through the idea of "smoothness" or "to be cunning." It is very closely related to the word *'aruwm* (Old Testament: 6175) used to describe the serpent in Genesis 3:1 as "more subtle and crafty than any living creature of the field which the Lord God had made."[12]

It seems that God is asking them, "Who told you that you can be cunning and crafty and self-sufficient?" By implication, "Who told you that you no longer need Me as your protector and provider?" And because the man and woman were disconnected by sin from the Source of their security and provision, they immediately began to blame each other and their circumstances as they searched desperately for a way to hide their naked inadequacy and vulnerability.

It is God's intent that as we know Him and receive His love, we will live protected by Him and having our needs met through Him. It is only before God that we can be safely vulnerable in our nakedness:

> And not a creature exists that is concealed from His sight, but all things are open and exposed, naked and defenseless to the eyes of Him with whom we have to do.
>
> Hebrews 4:13

Because God's love is perfect and unconditional, being exposed and vulnerable to Him is not threatening or fearful.

Plugged into the Source of Power at Creation

In the marvelous male and female bodies that God designed, *'iysh* and *'ishshah* enjoyed perfect health and vigor because they were designed to live forever. Before they chose disobedience, there was perfect agreement between them and God. He talked with them face-to-face and walked with them each day in the cool of the evening. (Genesis 3:8). There was a peaceful, conflict-free relationship between these two gloriously created human beings and no fear or tension between them and the rest of creation.

But even the first human beings had needs! Because of *The Lie*, we have come to believe that if we were perfect, we would never need anyone or anything. We define "perfection" as the ability to go through life sufficient, comfortable, and entirely satisfied, with no felt needs and no struggle. However, even though Jesus was perfectly sinless, He became hungry and tired, and He felt lonely, rejected, and discouraged.

Read these Scriptures and write the sentence that describes how Jesus felt.

Matthew 26:36-39:

____

____

Luke 22:15-22:

____

____

Isaiah 49:3-7:

____

____

The essence of *The Lie* that Satan brought into Eden is: *if we just know enough, we can be exactly like God in our own knowledge and strength, and we can be complete and satisfactory in ourselves. The Lie* upon which every lie is built is that we can be self-determining and self-sufficient while remaining completely independent of God. Satan has never had to fabricate a new lie because humankind is still accepting the original *Lie* and trying desperately to make it work.

Our Deepest Needs

God designed humankind with some vital and very powerful needs. These needs drive our choices and behavior. How we understand God's ability and willingness to fill these needs determines whether we make choices that honor Him or choices that attempt to get our needs met through the flesh.

1. The need to worship: We are beings created to worship. We are designed to depend with love and reliance on someone greater than ourselves. If we deny or ignore the existence of God, we will be compelled to worship or become dependent upon something else: power, possessions, or people.

   Our need to worship God, who is the only One greater than ourselves, can be met only as we grow in the knowledge that God is absolutely good, and as we understand better that we can worship Him without being afraid that He will take advantage of our helpless dependence upon Him.

   We were not made to live independently of God, but in absolute reliance upon Him. Because worship and intimacy are interrelated, we can only come to know God deeply as we worship Him. Worship of God cannot begin until our human spirit has been made new through regeneration.

2. The need to be loved: This is a basic, deeply felt need. We long to be loved for who we are, not for what we have accomplished. We can only receive this unconditional love from God as we choose by faith to believe that He is always good and always loves perfectly.

3. The need to belong: This need prompts the formation of all kinds of groups, from street gangs to college sororities and church denominations. We deeply desire to be included in a group that agrees with us and affirms us, but no human institution can fully satisfy this need. When our "group" fails to meet our need, the result is divorce, murder, and church splits. Our need to belong can only be fully satisfied in relationship with our Father God, through His Son, Jesus. When we receive our sense of belonging from Him, it becomes possible to enjoy the limited belonging offered by family, marriage, and social groups, even while knowing that at some point we will feel disillusioned and excluded.

4. The need to feel secure: It is God's design and desire that as children we will receive security from a stable home environ-

ment, loved by a male father, a female mother, and our siblings until we are old enough to know that our heavenly Father is our ultimate security. That often does not happen in our sin-broken world, and we struggle with the task of moving beyond faulty human relationships to the Father Who never fails. We can only rest in God's security as we learn to believe that He never changes, even when our unstable world experiences enormous and constant change.

5. The need for significance: Every person desperately wants to be somebody. We want to stand out, to matter! We want to leave a "footprint" that will make a difference in the world and to know that when we die we will be missed.

   In our culture we base our significance on:

   - What we accomplish
   - How well we perform
   - What others think of our performance
   - What we think others think of our performance

   This false sense of value is based only on external things, not internal. But true significance comes from knowing that we are important and we matter because God created us. We have incalculable value simply because we exist. We have immeasurable significance built into us from conception because we are created in the image of the One Who is infinite significance.

6. The need for approval: Approval comes to us in many forms. Children constantly seek parental approval, and if it is seldom given or given only conditionally, a child grows up believing that she is such a failure that God could never approve of her either. The drive for approval is so strong that people will throw away families, health, and all that they have to get approval from someone—anyone—even if for only a few minutes or a few hours.

7. The need for acceptance: Approval and acceptance are not the same though they are closely related.

    - Acceptance is taking or receiving something that is offered.
    - Approval means commendation or sanction.

    Because we confuse these two words, many Christians believe that God cannot accept and approve of our *humanness*; that He only accepts "the Christ in us." Thinking that God must sanction what we *do* in order to receive us drives the false belief that God condescends to only "look at us through the blood of Jesus." Believing that we cannot be approved and accepted until we die and go to heaven leaves us longing for a future that seems hopelessly remote.

    The truth is that God accepts us unconditionally because of what Jesus did on the cross. Our Father does not "see us as righteous, through the blood." Rather, He has declared as an accomplished fact that the blood of Jesus washes us spotlessly clean at salvation, and makes us eternally righteous. He doesn't "see" us as pure and holy; we *are* pure and holy. No blot or stain remains to be "hidden under the blood" (1 Corinthians 6:11; Hebrews 10). We are fully accepted and sanctioned by God from the moment of our new birth. Changes in behavior will follow as God trains us through loving discipline. He is the perfect Father Who loves His children without limit or condition.

8. The need for relationship: We are created to be in relationships; first with God, our Father; then with our brothers and sisters in Christ. The impact we have on the unbelieving world follows as we grow in these first two relationships. In the story of the loving father and his two rebellious sons in Luke 15:11-32, we see how relationships change and mature. Neither of the sons' attitudes or behavior changed their father's response toward them. This parable teaches clearly that there is nothing that can ever change our heavenly Father's love for us, even though

we will experience painful consequences when we make rebellious, self-centered choices.

1. Name two needs from this list that you feel most deeply, most often:

   ____

   ____

2. How have you attempted to get these needs met through people, things or circumstances?

   ____

   ____

   ____

   ____

3. Without using the phrases *trust God*, *love God more*, or *pray more*, describe how you can receive what you need from your heavenly Father. Be very specific.

   ____

   ____

   ____

   ____

The Origin of Discontentment

It was God's desire and design that each time His *'iysh* and *'ishshah* felt any of these needs, they would come to Him to have them met. In Eden, God filled those needs and assured the first man and woman of His love and acceptance as they "walked and talked together in the cool of the evening."

But the serpent came to the woman, whispering *The Lie* that if only they could acquire the same understanding of the knowledge of good and evil that God had, they would be like God out of their own knowledge and ability and would no longer be dependent upon Him.

Satan, through the serpent, began the conversation with the woman by questioning the goodness of God. His question, "Did God really say that?" implied that God was withholding good from them. Satan has never changed his tactic. He still approaches human beings with the intent of convincing us that God is unjust and unreasonable, a harsh, self-centered taskmaster who wants to use the human race to achieve His own objectives.

He also wants us to wonder what we're missing because we don't have *that* car, *that* house, *that* relationship, *that* __________. This is the basis for discontentment and dissatisfaction, even when we have much more than we need.

> And when the woman saw that the tree was good (suitable, pleasant) for food (lust of the flesh) and that it was delightful to look at (lust of the eyes), and a tree to be desired in order to make one wise (the pride of life), she took of its fruit and ate; and she gave some also to her husband, and he ate.
>
> Genesis 3:6-7; 1 John 2:16

The woman believed *The Lie* and was genuinely deceived (2 Corinthians 11:3). The man chose disobedience with her, fully aware that the serpent was lying (1 Timothy 2:14). It appears that he stood by passively without a word of protest while she ate the fruit.

An Idol Is Not Always a Short Little Man with a Round Belly Who Lives in Another Country

The choice the first man made to disobey God along with his wife was the very first instance of idolatry recorded in Scripture. By his choice, the man showed that he placed higher importance on the bond with his created wife than on the bond with his Creator God.

It isn't unreasonable to suppose that because the man loved the woman he didn't want to be separated from her by her disobedience, but his choice shows that he had already begun to believe that God could not be depended upon to protect them and provide for them. Taking matters into his own hands was evidence that *The Lie* was already a part of his thinking. Perhaps he truly believed that he could fix the problem better from the "inside" if he joined her in her wrong choice.

When we set out to rescue someone and meet their needs, our expectation is that they will be pleased and grateful, and reciprocate by meeting our needs. This is actually the model presented by many secular marriage seminars.

But it doesn't work that way. The moment the man ate the fruit offered by the woman, both their eyes were opened, and each immediately realized that the other could not satisfy the deep craving for love, acceptance, and value already crying out for fulfillment. The sinful pattern of idolizing a created being and experiencing immediate disillusionment in them was established.

God called to the man, "Adam, where are you?"

Adam answered, "I heard the sound of You walking in the Garden, and I was afraid because I was naked; and I hid myself."

When God questioned the man about where he got the awareness of his nakedness, he replied, "The woman whom You gave to be with me—she gave me fruit from the tree, and I ate" (Genesis 3:10, 12).

Not only was the man placing the blame for his own failure on his wife, he was also saying in effect, "You are to blame, God, because You gave the woman to me." There was an acknowledgement of sin by the man, but not an acceptance of responsibility for the choice he had made in spite of knowing the truth.

Then the Lord God turned to the woman with the question, "What is this you have done?" And even though Satan was still present, the woman had the courage to say, "It was the serpent. He deceived me. I believed him, and I ate the fruit" (Genesis 3:13).

There is some similarity in the replies of the man and the woman, yet they are very different. They both truthfully admitted that they ate the forbidden fruit. Then they both truthfully admitted the immediate cause. In the case of the woman, it was the serpent, and in the case of the man, it was the woman. The crucial difference is in the remote cause. The man accused God of being the remote cause of evil and sin. The woman accurately identified Satan as the remote cause. Exposing his deception while he was still present suggests that she trusted God to protect her from Satan's anger.

When we point a finger at God, accusing Him of "allowing" sin, or when we say with a sigh, "Well, I guess this (death, accident, rape, etc.) happened for a reason. It must have been God's will because He didn't stop it," we join the first man in accusing God of being the remote cause of evil.

Why do you think the eyes of the man and woman were not opened until the man ate the fruit?

____

____

____

The Illusion of *The Lie*

Every lie is an illusion, created by wrong thinking and sin-twisted imaginations. Even though there is always a bit of truth in every lie, by definition a lie cannot ever be true reality.

Sin is disobedient attitudes and choices produced by accepting The Lie as truth. Sin brought separation from God in the minds of the man and woman as they became afraid and suspicious of God (Colossians 1:21). They no longer had the perfect life of God within them, (Romans 5:12) and they were separated from the glory of God that had covered them so that their nakedness, weakness, and vulnerability immediately became exposed (Genesis 3:6b-7a). Guilt and shame entered their world.

Dry Fig Leaves Itch!

The sin of the first couple was not just the simple act of eating forbidden fruit; it was a treasonous act against the perfect government of God. It was rebellion of such magnitude that we have never been able to fully measure its consequences. But instead of acknowledging the awfulness of the rebellion against their Creator, the man and woman immediately tried to minimize the shame of their failure and hide their embarrassment over their differences with clothing made of fig leaves.

> Then the eyes of them both were opened, and they knew that they were naked; and they sewed fig leaves together and made themselves apron-like girdles.
>
> Genesis 3:7

The fruit of the Tree of the Knowledge of Good and Evil was evident as they came out of hiding wearing the leaves they had substituted for the glory of God in a "self-help" attempt to cover up their own failure. They declared their belief in *The Lie* that they could be just like God, having all knowledge and able to do all things. But the leaves taken from the fig tree quickly became brittle, dry, and uncomfortable. As the man and woman realized the futility of their efforts, their fear of failure grew stronger and gave birth to jealousy, disappointment, anxiety, and dread.

God demonstrated His mercy and goodness toward His disobedient humankind when He killed some of His created creatures to make clothing of skins for them. It must have grieved the heart of the Creator as He caused the first shedding of blood for sin. Out of that first sacrifice, God made clothing of the softest fur and most pliable leather for His beloved humankind.

The Self-Help Lie

There is an entire industry in our culture built upon *The Lie*. Bookstores, including Christian stores, are filled with "self-help" books. These books abound with suggestions that give us new ways to try harder to be what Satan's *Lie* said we could be—gods in our own knowledge and strength. But more of what isn't working still will not work! Self-help advice and effort can only end in greater failure and fear.

Trying to help ourselves is like the salesman who was driving along the road and saw a young boy in front of a barn. There were five targets on the barn with arrows in the bull's-eye of each target. Screeching to a stop, the man walked over to discover how the boy could shoot so well. "Son," he said, "how did you hit all those bull's-eyes?"

"Well, sir," the boy replied, "I take the arrow and lick my fingers like this; then I take my fingers and smooth the feathers like this. I take aim with my hand against my cheek, I let go, and *wherever the arrow hits, I draw a bull's-eye.*"

God set up a "target" at creation, and the "bull's-eye" was that humankind would be like Him as a free gift. Because God's beloved human race is so like Him, He placed us as governors in authority over all of His creation. Men and women are representatives of the sovereign Creator on the colony of the earth.

Satan did not come to the first man and woman with a simple misinterpretation about what God said they could or could not do. Satan entered Eden offering humankind an alternate meaning for life—a completely different target. It wasn't that he simply persuaded them to "make a mistake" in their choices. He changed the entire direction of humankind by convincing them to claim sovereignty for themselves. Our dictionaries have quite a list of words that describe this ongoing attempt to be autonomous:

- Self-appointed
- Self-assertive
- Self-centered
- Self-conceit
- Self-conscious
- Self-defense
- Self-determination
- Self-esteem
- Self-expression
- Self-fulfillment
- Self-governing
- Self-help
- Self-indulgent
- Self-made
- Self-preservation
- Self-reliant
- Self-ruling
- Self-satisfied
- Self-seeking
- Self-serving
- Self-sufficient

This is only a partial list. But no matter how long the list, self-help advice and effort can only end in failure. Since unredeemed humankind is aiming entirely in the wrong direction, there is no hope of hitting the original target, no matter how great the effort. The very best those who are unsaved, and untaught believers can do is draw another target wherever the "arrow" of their effort lands. Our world calls this "barn-art" relativism and insists that if it *feels* right it must *be* right. But no matter how politically correct the title, trying to have confidence in a self-designed god that always ultimately fails only produces fear and frustration.

Our God-given human design means that we are:

- Created in God's actual image and likeness.
- Created to partner confidently with God in His work of ruling over and maintaining His creation.
- Gifted with the permission and authority to have dominion over all of the rest of God's creation.

Humankind is not created to *be* God. We have been fashioned with awareness of our built-in helplessness and vulnerability, and we were designed to have a tender reverence for God Who formed us to live in intimacy and friendship with Him. In all of God's creation, only humankind has been so highly honored and crowned with the glory of God.

The Consequences of Disobedience

It was a terrible moment as the man, the woman, and the serpent stood in the presence of God, already aware of the devastation that had entered their perfect environment because of their disobedience. God's great sorrow must have been clearly evident to them. First, judgment was pronounced upon the serpent:

> And the Lord God said to the serpent, "Because you have done this, you are cursed above all [domestic] animals and above every [wild] living thing of the field; upon your belly you shall go, and you shall eat dust [and what it contains] all the days of your life."
>
> Genesis 3:14

The serpent became a feared and hated outcast. We don't know exactly what the serpent was like before it took part in Satan's rebellion against God; we only know that it was a beautiful and cunning creature that may have stood upright since crawling on its belly was a part of the judgment against it.

No Curse for God's Beloved Humankind

Then the Lord God turned to the woman. He did not curse her as He did the serpent. He told her that there would be hostility and animosity between the serpent and her children but assured her that her descendent (Jesus) would deliver a fatal blow to the head of the serpent (Satan).

God detailed the consequences of her sin, revealing that her sorrow in childbearing would be increased. His words certainly denote physical pain, but they also contain the strong implication that bearing and raising children in a sinful world would be filled with painful, worrisome labor, and the sorrow of watching children grow up surrounded by the pressure and brokenness of sin.

When He added (Genesis 3:16), "Your desire and craving will be toward your husband, yet he will rule over you," God was warning her that sin would distort the relationship between man and woman, so that her built-in desire to nurture and be connected would give her husband opportunity to manipulate, dominate, and contend against her.[13]

God did not command men to have "supremacy" or dominance over women. He was simply making them aware that sin would produce authoritarian and violent behavior in relationships. The teaching that it is the will of God for a man to "rule over" his wife is pointing an accusing finger at God, making Him the remote cause of the evil of control, manipulation, and abuse in relationships.

God's command is that when a man is redeemed and enters into an intimate relationship with the Lord Jesus, he must give up the *sin-created desire to dominate and control*, choosing instead to submit to God's instruction to love and protect his family with kindness and respect.

The husband is given the position of leader. Jesus is the ultimate example of compassionate "servant leader," and His teachings do not give men the right to force their leadership in an authoritarian way. Neither does Jesus's example permit a Christian man to interpret his role of "head" as a position that gives him control over his wife.

Write out Colossians 3:19:

Write out Ephesians 5:25 and 28:

For husbands:

1. Describe a practical way that you can show your wife that you love her.

2. What does it mean to "give yourself up" for your wife?

> Fathers, do not irritate and provoke your children to anger (do not exasperate them to resentment), but rear them (tenderly) in the training and discipline and the counsel and admonition of the Lord.
>
> Ephesians 6:4

3. In what way(s) do you recognize that you provoke your children to anger?

____

____

4. Name three specific things you can do for your children to help them grow in the discipline and counsel of the Lord.

   ____

   ____

   ____

Women are relational and find much of their satisfaction and fulfillment through their interaction with family and friends. God warned the first woman that sin would damage relationships so that sorrow and pain would often overshadow the joy that God intended.

The teaching on submission is difficult for Christian women to accept because of the impact of sin in relationships. Submission is emphasized in Ephesians 5, but the instruction to submit does not start with verse 22: "Wives, be subject (be submissive and adapt yourselves) to your own husbands as [a service] to the Lord." Paul uses the first fourteen verses of chapter five to establish that the husbands and wives he is writing to are indeed "children of the light." He begins the teaching on submission in verse fifteen:

> Look carefully then how you walk! Live purposefully and worthily and accurately, not as the unwise and witless, but as wise (sensible, intelligent people), making the very most of the time (buying up each opportunity), because the days are evil. Therefore do not be vague and thoughtless and foolish, but understanding and firmly grasping what the will of the Lord is. And do not get drunk with wine, for that is debauchery; but ever be filled and stimulated with the [Holy] Spirit. Speak out to one another in psalms and hymns and spiritual songs, offering praise with voices [and instruments] and making melody with all your heart to the Lord, at all times and for everything giving thanks in the name of our Lord Jesus Christ to God the Father. Be subject to one another out of reverence for Christ (the Messiah, the Anointed One). Wives, be subject (be submissive and adapt

> yourselves) to your own husbands as [a service] to the Lord. For the husband is head of the wife, as Christ is the Head of the church, Himself the Savior of [His] body. As the church is subject to Christ, so let wives also be subject in everything to their husbands. Husbands, love your wives, as Christ loved the church and gave Himself up for her.
>
> Ephesians 5:15-25

God's clear instruction is that as each believer—husband, wife, and child—learns what the will of God is and lives with sensitivity toward God and each other, each will choose to exhibit an attitude of submission and consideration toward the other. In order to promote this attitude of submissiveness in the entire church, Paul tells wives to submit to their husbands, husband to their wives, children to their parents, slaves to their masters (employees to their employers); all with the intent of honoring Jesus. This is submission in the sense of *preferring one another and not demanding personal rights.* When this attitude is operating in the body of Christ, the selfless, giving love of Jesus is revealed to the unsaved world.

The Greek word for *submission*, *hupotasso*, is written in the Greek middle voice, which means it is something that an individual imposes upon himself or herself. It means to choose to yield to another, rather than demanding one's own way. Submission is the freewill right of the one choosing to yield. Submission cannot be demanded from another individual. It cannot be imposed upon one person by another. When this occurs, it is no longer *hupotasso*, but domination, an attitude forbidden by Jesus in Matthew 23:11-12: "He who is greatest among you shall be your servant. Whoever exalts himself (with haughtiness and empty pride) shall be humbled (brought low), and whoever humbles himself (whoever has a modest opinion of himself and behaves accordingly) shall be raised to honor."

For wives:

1. What is the difference between Biblical submission (adapting yourself) to your husband, and doing whatever it takes to keep peace?

   ____

____

____

2. How can you show your husband love in a way that may "win him without a word" to obedience to Christ? (1 Peter 3:1-2)

____

____

____

3. In what way(s) do you recognize that you provoke your children to anger?

____

____

____

4. Name three specific things you can do for your children to help them grow in the discipline and counsel of the Lord.

____

____

____

Finally God turned to the man and said, "Because you have listened and given heed to the voice of your wife and have eaten of the tree of which I commanded you, saying, 'You shall not eat of it,' the ground is under a curse because of *you*; in sorrow and toil shall you eat of the fruits of it all the days of your life" (Genesis 3:17).

God was not issuing a command that husbands should not listen to their wives or that wives should not express an opinion. Rather, God is making the man aware of the awfulness of giving priority to people rather than Himself.

Men are fundamentally task oriented and find much of their fulfillment in their work. God explained clearly the ongoing frustration, dissatisfaction, and disappointment that men would experience in their struggle to provide for their families because of sin (Genesis 3:17-19).

In westernized cultures, it has become common for men to give up the struggle and to abandon their families. "Dead-beat dads" is a phrase coined in this generation to describe the abandonment. It was the man who was told "by the sweat of *your* face shall you eat bread." It is significant that the order of things has been reversed so that in many homes the woman has become the sole supporter of the family while trying to nurture as well.

Less Than Human

After their removal from Eden, life became very different for the first man and woman. Their life experience was proof that the serpent lied when he said they would be like God. It quickly became evident that not only were they not more God-like, they were now less than fully human because they were no longer connected to their Creator and Source of life. Because humankind is designed to be intimately related to God, when that connection is missing, we are not fully what God created us to be. *Sin did not make us "more God." It made us less human.*

Instead of living in perfect harmony with the earth and its creatures, the man began to live in frustration and weariness, coaxing a living from the now hostile creation. The woman could only look forward to the prospect of multiplied pain and sorrow and the domination of a husband whose attitudes and behavior were polluted by sin.

Immediately following God's sorrowful description of sin's consequences, we read that the man named his wife Eve. This does not appear to be in response to instruction from God. Naming denotes dominion and authority. Just as *'aadaam* named the animals as proof of God-ordained dominion, now the man named the woman in an attempt to claim sin-driven dominance. Both the activity of naming and the name the woman was given is significant, because God's prediction of the man ruling over the woman was already being carried out. Adam named the woman "Eve" in anticipation of her motherhood. He continued to call himself *'aadaam*—the name given to describe who he *was* (human being)—but gave his wife a title that identified her *by what she would do* ("the mother of those to come.")

There is no indication that the woman protested having her name changed. Perhaps her sense of failure and regret led her to believe she deserved it. God Himself continues to refer to the man and woman as *'aadaam* even as He sent them out of Eden.

In Scripture, all references to Eve are in relation to life and hope,[14] but the two Old Testament references to Adam relate to sin and death.[15] In the New Testament, Paul declares many times that one man is responsible for the fall.[16] Because the entire human race was contained in the sperm of the man, when he rebelled against God, all future humanity was contaminated by his sin.

The sin nature is passed into each generation through the father (Romans 5:17). Jesus's human mother, Mary, was contaminated by the sin passed to her through her human father, but Jesus did not receive the sin nature from her. Because He was conceived in Mary's womb by the Holy Spirit, He escaped the corruption of sin that has affected every descendent of First Adam.

Sin's Rechargeable Batteries

God gave the man and the woman the privilege of making choices, and He placed the Tree of the Knowledge of Good and Evil in Eden to give them the opportunity to exercise the gift of choosing. This ability to choose is a unique characteristic that distinguishes humankind from the rest of creation. *It is in our choices that we become fully established in our human identity.*

There was no "sin poison" in the juices of the fruit of the forbidden tree. The changes that took place in the lord and lady of the earth were the "fruit" or result of the decision they made to disobey God. *'Iysh* and *'ishshah* were spiritually disconnected from God because of sin.

- They were no longer actively involved with the things of God.
- Their thoughts were no longer in harmony with God's way of thinking.
- Their source of knowing that they were loved, accepted, and of great value shifted from their spirit to what they could experience through the senses of their physical bodies.

- Reality and truth became only what they could hear, see, taste, smell, and touch.
- Choices were now being made out of how they felt emotionally and out of their own sin-damaged capacity to reason and understand.

An electrical outlet in the wall has a constant flow of power that is accessed each time a power cord is plugged into the outlet. Some small appliances are designed to run on rechargeable batteries. When the energy from the batteries begins to decrease, the charger has to be plugged into the power source in the wall for the battery to be recharged.

God is the constant Source of power for the human race. Since the very moment that the first man and woman became "unplugged" by sin from their Source of power, their descendents have been trying to get "recharged" through the undependable secondary power source of more, bigger, newer, or faster things and different relationships.

"Addiction" Is Idolatry

A new car brings with it a sense of excitement and power, which fades as the new wears off. A new house ages and needs repair. A new and different relationship carries a feeling of freshness and exhilaration that diminishes as the stresses of everyday living seep in.

Our culture has given the dependence on these things a disease label: *addiction*. Research is constantly being carried on to find a medication that will cure the "disease." But God has a different name for the frantic attempt to find meaning and purpose through this erratic cycle of "power failure" and "recharges." He calls it *idolatry*. We are told that the only permanent "treatment" is to turn away from dependence on unreliable people and things and turn instead to God. He is the ultimate Source for meaning and purpose.

> So kill (deaden, deprive of power) the evil desire lurking in your members (those animal impulses and all that is earthly in you that is employed in sin): sexual vice, impurity, sensual appetites, unholy desires, and all greed and covetousness, for that is idolatry, the deifying of self and other created things instead of God.
>
> Colossians 3:5

The Problem of Disillusionment

When our "idols" fail (people let us down, and our enjoyment of our bigger, newer, faster things diminishes), we become disillusioned. Believing in the illusion of *The Lie* always produces unrealistic expectations. When those expectations are not met, we become disappointed and resentful, blaming other people and God because they didn't do for us what we expected.

Because God is the Father Who loves perfectly, He does not prevent disillusionment from happening. When disillusionment comes we can finally become free from the illusion of *The Lie*. When we truly realize that people and things are not our source of satisfaction, we can at last begin to live in the *truth reality* that only God can fully gratify our deepest needs.

Disappointment indicates that you have believed an illusion. Describe a disappointment you have experienced:

____

____

____

What was the illusion or lie that you believed?

____

____

____

The Effect of Sin on Nature and Humankind

The rebellion of the first couple changed everything. The peaceful, benevolent dominion the first man and woman had over all of creation became only a memory, filled with longing and regret. Through their choice of disobedience, they handed their God-given authority over the earth to Satan. The ravages of sin had an immediate and terrible effect on nature as described in Romans 8:19-23:

> For the anxious longing of the creation waits eagerly for the revealing of the sons of God. For the creation was subjected to futility, not willingly, but because of him (First Adam) who subjected it, in hope that the creation itself also will be set free from its slavery to corruption into the freedom of the glory of the children of God. For we know that the whole creation groans and suffers the pains of childbirth together until now. And not only this, but also we ourselves, having the first fruits of the Spirit, even we ourselves groan within ourselves, waiting eagerly for our adoption as sons, the redemption of our body.
>
> NASU

- Have you ever wondered what a lion or tiger that grazed on grass looked like at the time of creation, before they became carnivorous? The structure of their mouths and teeth must have changed to accommodate their fallen diet of the bodies of other animals.
- We enjoy the singing of birds in the early morning quiet, but the songs we hear are tainted by sin. Our ability to hear the full range of sound created by God is limited by the impact of sin on our bodies. How incredibly beautiful the song of a "pre-sin" mockingbird must have sounded!
- We only know an earth and soil that became poisonous and "anti-humankind" from the moment of sin. In God's perfect creation, every plant grew and produced fruit for the benefit of human beings, with no struggle on their part. The use of those plants as medicinal, health-producing food did not cause side-effects and dependencies.
- As the result of sin, weeds, thistles, and poisonous plants now grow with no effort on our part. If we want beneficial plants, we have to be deliberate in cultivating, weeding, watering, and fertilizing. And even with our best efforts, sin-contaminated, out-of-control weather patterns still often destroy the crop before it can be harvested.

The rebellion of the man and woman had direct consequences in their *bodies* as they immediately became prone to disease, injury, and deterioration. From the moment of disobedience, they began to age and die.

We think of that as normal, but aging, death, and disease were not a part of God's original perfect creation.

In the "new normal" of sin, the earth itself turned against humankind. The soil began to grow plants that were harmful and anti-life. In the same way, the *soul* of humankind (the mind, will, and emotions) also became poisonous and pro-death.

- The *mind* of humankind began to be darkened and confused, (Romans 1:21) "growing" the deadly thoughts of jealousy, bitterness, and self-pity. People continued to accept the twisted doctrines of Satan, which led to increasingly distorted beliefs about God, themselves, and others.
- *Emotions* contaminated by sin became fractured and cruel. As a result, Cain committed the first murder by killing his brother, Abel, in a fit of jealous rage (Genesis 4:3-8). People became depressed, fearful and lonely; filled with guilt and living under the control of out-of-control emotions.
- The *will* became rebellious toward the ways of God, determined to satisfy the selfish demands of the flesh.

Growing a Good Crop

Because of the ravages of sin, we have to deliberately cultivate thoughts that agree with the Word of God, carefully "weeding out" those attitudes and beliefs that are opposed to His Word; generously watering each little seedling of right thinking with the "water" of the Word of God. Even then, we have an enemy who is constantly trying to destroy the crop before harvest.

As the centuries pass, we see the accumulating results of the "weeds" of sinful thinking and behavior as disease, violence, and destruction increases. In our fear and desperation, we identify with Paul's cry, "Wretched man that I am! Who will set me free from this body of death?" (Romans 7:24-25a). And then, when we have accepted the gift of salvation, we can also share Paul's triumphant announcement, "Thanks be to God through our Lord Jesus Christ!" Through a chosen faith in God, individuals are restored to the original relationship with God and are given renewed meaning and purpose for life.

At the Cross, the process of restoration begins. The *spirit* of the saved person is immediately and eternally made new, sinless, and holy. Sin cannot contaminate this new nature, nor can that person ever be taken out of relationship with the heavenly Father. As the process of restoration continues, the soul will gradually be changed. Now it is possible to:

- Renew the mind: training ourselves to think more and more the way God thinks, instead of thinking the way imperfect people in a sinful world taught us to think.
- Strengthen the will to make Godly choices.
- Bring the emotions under the control of the renewed mind.

How quickly we see the results of this process that God promises to complete in us (Philippians 1:6) will depend upon our cooperation with the Holy Spirit. If we refuse a healthy diet of good spiritual food and exercise, our growth will be slow and our spiritual stature stunted and unhealthy. Time spent learning to know God, like beneficial food, will bring good spiritual health and growth.

God's Grace + God's Protection = Banishment from Eden

With our limited human perspective, we often misunderstand the work God is doing because His "equations" are so different from ours and His result doesn't feel or look the way we think it should.

When God sent the man and the woman from the Garden of Eden, it was not to punish them, even though the banishment was surely painful to them and they may have struggled with the feeling that they were being punished. Perhaps they stood as close to the entrance of the garden as possible, gazing longingly at what was once theirs to enjoy.

The Bible tells us clearly that God sent His beloved humankind out of Eden to keep them from eating fruit from the Tree of Life (Genesis 3:22-24). If they had done so after they sinned, they would have doomed themselves and every future descendent to living forever in an eternally depraved condition. Depravity with no end can be described in one word: hell.

But God so dearly loved and highly prized His humankind (John 3:16)! Because of the infinite love of God for the people He had created, as well as love for their yet unborn descendents, God announced His plan to destroy the works of Satan and bring people back into relationship with Himself even before He sent them out of the Garden. In Genesis 3:15, God said to the serpent, "I will put enmity between you and the woman, and between your seed and her Seed (Jesus); He (Jesus) shall bruise you on the head, and you shall bruise Him on the heel." Those who come to God in Christ share in the triumph of Jesus over Satan, sin and death.

> And when this perishable puts on the imperishable, and this that was capable of dying puts on freedom from death, then shall be fulfilled the Scripture that says, "Death is swallowed up (utterly vanquished forever) in and unto victory. O death, where is your victory? O death, where is your sting?" Now sin is the sting of death, and sin exercises its power (upon the soul) through (the abuse of) the Law. But thanks be to God, Who gives us the victory (making us conquerors) through our Lord Jesus Christ.
>
> 1 Corinthians 15:54-57

Chapter 4
Our Beliefs—the Ultimate "Con Man"

A lie is always a mixture of truth and fantasy. Believing a lie as truth ends in disillusionment because:

- We think out of that lie.
- We feel out of that lie.
- We talk out of that lie.
- We choose out of that lie.
- We behave out of that lie.

Disillusionment is inevitable when our life experience is built on the illusion of a lie.

Instinct vs. Beliefs

Because we are created in the image of God, we are distinctly different from plants and animals. A study of belief systems will show us a major area of dissimilarity.

> A belief is an assumption that we accept as absolute truth. A belief is not a passing thought, but one that puts "roots" deep into our way of thinking. As the belief grows and produces the "fruit" of thoughts and choices, it motivates and controls the life of the person who holds the belief.

Birds and animals operate out of a pre-programmed system that we call *instinct*. Each year at a particular time, they engage in a seasonal activity such mating or migrating, not because they have reasoned that it's time, but because something built into them urges them to move. They have no other choice; they cannot think the situation through and choose differently.

Human beings live from an organized structure of beliefs that supports our God-given ability to reason and choose. We have beliefs about everything we think and do, from the smallest detail to the largest event. These beliefs are woven together over time to comprise a grid through which all of our life's experiences are processed. Since this is true, if we are going to enjoy the kind of life the Bible describes as "abundant," our grid must be built on the Biblical thinking that produces abundant living.

"He Said, She Said" and Neither One Is Right!

Snow skiers wear goggles to protect their eyes from the glare of the sun on the snow. A skier wearing bright yellow lenses will see a fellow skier's red overalls as orange. The yellow of the lenses combines with the red of the fabric to make orange. A skier with blue lenses will see the exact same suit as purple—the color produced by combining blue and red. It's the same red ski suit, but two people see it entirely differently because of the color of their lenses.

Each individual belief system is so powerful and pervasive that it "changes the color" of how we perceive everything in our life experience. Our beliefs also affect how we remember a previous situation. Because of the immediate interaction between a current experience and past experiences, memory of any event quickly becomes discolored by our belief system. Memories are filled with inaccuracies. This is one of the reasons why "he said, she said" arguments are so futile. Neither one will remember the incident as it truly happened or sounded.

Ten witnesses to an accident have ten different opinions about how it happened because of the position in which they were standing and the angle from which they viewed the incident, even though they were in the same general place at the same time. Two people involved in a marriage, an argument, a dialog, or even an abusive incident, have very different perspectives of what actually happened, and each one will be absolutely convinced that he or she is right.

Eyes Can't Hear, Ears Can't See

Our eyes cannot hear; they are made to receive light rays, not sound waves. And our ears can't see! They can process sound waves but cannot absorb and process light, even though light rays are all around. In the same way, our belief system will only accept what our life experience permits it to perceive. The things that come through our five senses that are in *agreement* with the system we have created will be received; anything that *disagrees* is filtered out, even though it is the system that is faulty, not the information.

Dead Men Don't Bleed

There was once a family who made an appointment to see a doctor. "Here is the problem, Dr. Smith," they said. "Our brother Michael needs help. You see, he thinks he's dead." It was quickly decided that Michael clearly needed to see Dr. Smith. When he arrived for his appointment the next day, some questioning proved that Michael really believed that he was actually physically dead. So Dr. Smith set out to prove that he most certainly was not a dead man but in fact alive.

Dr. Smith arranged to spend some time each day for several weeks talking to Michael. Each day, he pulled his medical textbooks off the shelves and showed his patient what was written about the functions of a live body, especially the circulatory system. Finally, Dr. Smith said, "Now according to these medical books, if I stick your finger with a needle, you'll bleed if you're alive. Dead men don't bleed, right?" Michael nodded and agreed that according to the textbooks dead men don't bleed.

Dr. Smith asked Michael to sit down, reached into his desk drawer and took out a small needle, telling his patient that he was going to stick his finger to see what would happen. After all, they had just finished reading that dead men don't bleed.

A quick puncture was followed by trickle of blood from Michael's finger. "You see?" said Dr. Smith. "Your finger is bleeding. What do you think now?"

"Well, what do you know?" Michael exclaimed in astonishment. "*Dead men do bleed*!"

This man did what we often do: instead of changing our wrong beliefs to agree with truth, *we twist truth to fit into a sin-distorted system of beliefs*. Remember, a belief is an assumption that we accept as absolute truth. For example, we assume that if "Mom always said it" or "we always did it this way at church," then it must be right, and of course, "everyone should think this way."

The Foundation: Our Belief about God

Our beliefs about God, whether they are Biblically right or wrong, are the foundation on which we build our beliefs about ourselves, other people, and how life should be lived.

The Old Testament account of the twelve spies sent into Canaan is a good example of how a wrong understanding of God resulted in a wrong understanding of themselves, which produced wrong thinking and wrong choices.

> When Moses sent them to spy out the land of Canaan, he said to them, "Go up there into the Negev; then go up into the hill country. See whether the people who live in it are strong or weak, whether they are few or many. How is the land in which they live, is it good or bad? And how are the cities in which they live, are they like open camps or with fortifications? Are there trees in it or not? Make an effort then to get some of the fruit of the land." Now it was the time of the first ripe grapes.
>
> And they returned from scouting out the land after forty days. They came to Moses and Aaron and to all the Israelite congregation in the Wilderness of Paran, and showed them the land's fruit. They told Moses, "We came to the land to which you sent us; surely it flows with milk and honey. This is its fruit. But the people who dwell there are strong, and the cities are fortified and very large." Caleb quieted the people before Moses, and said, "*Let us go up at once and possess it; we are well able to conquer it.*" But his fellow scouts said, "We are not able to go up against the people (of Canaan), for they are stronger than we are." So they brought the Israelites an evil report of the land which they had scouted out, saying, "The land through which we went to spy out is a land that devours its inhabitants. And all the people that we saw in it are men of great stature.
>
> There we saw the Nephilim (or giants), the sons of Anak, who come from the giants; *and we were in our own sight as grasshoppers, and so we were in their sight.* And all the congregation cried out with a loud voice, and (they) wept that night. All the Israelites grumbled and deplored their situation, accusing Moses and Aaron, to whom the whole congregation said, "Would that we had died in Egypt! Or that we had died in this wilderness! Why does the Lord bring us to this land to fall by the sword? Our wives and little ones will be a prey. Is it not better for us to return to Egypt?"
>
> Numbers 13:17-14:3

Remember that these men were part of a people group that had been enslaved for the past 300 years. They were born in slavery in Egypt and had never experienced freedom. As slaves, they were never allowed to look directly at a "superior." They were required to walk through life with their eyes on the ground.

Because their parents, grandparents, and great-grandparents had cried out for deliverance and it had not happened quickly, this entire group developed a belief about God that perceived Him incorrectly as weak and inadequate. As a result, knowing that they were created in His image, they saw themselves as weak and inadequate. Their slave mentality convinced them that they only deserved extermination like grasshoppers. Because ten spies and the people of Israel believed the illusion of a lie as truth, they talked themselves right out of the Promised Land and into the insect kingdom! Then they immediately accused God of being the remote cause of evil in their situation. "It's Your fault, God. You brought us out here simply to die by the sword. Things were much better for us in Egypt." In the discomfort of their new circumstances, their memory of the terrible abuse of slavery in Egypt was already inaccurate.

Joshua and Caleb chose to believe what God said as truth. They had an accurate view of God and refused to live out of the slave and victim mind-set that surrounded them. But the people refused to listen to Joshua and Caleb as they explained the truth about the goodness of God and His ability and willingness to give them what He promised.

> Joshua, the son of Nun, and Caleb, the son of Jephunneh, who were among those who had spied out the land, tore their clothes and spoke to all ... the sons of Israel, saying, "The land which we ... spied out is an exceedingly good land. If the Lord is pleased with us, then He will bring us into this land and give it to us ... only do not rebel against the Lord, and do not fear the people of the land, for they will be our prey. Their protection has been removed from them, and the Lord is with us; do not fear them." But all the congregation said to stone them with stones.
>
> Numbers 14:6-10 (NASU)

The Israelites assumed that the Canaanites thought of them like weak and worthless grasshoppers. But what did the Canaanites *really* think of God's people? Joshua 2:1-11 is the account of Rahab and how she hid the two spies that Joshua sent in forty years later to assess the land, especially Jericho. And this is what she said to them:

> I know that the Lord has given you the land, and that the terror of you has fallen on us, and that all the inhabitants of the land have melted away before you. For we have heard how the Lord dried up the water of the Red Sea before you when you came out of Egypt, and what you did to the two kings of the Amorites who were beyond the Jordan, to Sihon and Og, whom you utterly destroyed. *When we heard it, our hearts melted and no courage remained in any man any longer because of you;* for the Lord your God, He is God in heaven above and on earth beneath.
>
> Joshua 2:9-12 (NASU)

For forty years, the people of Canaan had lived in dread of the arrival of the people of God; their hearts melted in fear when they heard about the power of the God of the Israelites. But during that same time, the people of God were cowering in fear of the Canaanites! Because they believed lies about God and about themselves, they perceived themselves as grasshoppers. Convinced that how they felt emotionally was the truth, they made the assumption that the Canaanites also perceived them as weak.

The Power of Perception

What we assume other people think of us arises out of:

- What we believe about God
- What we believe about ourselves
- How we believe we measure up to our own standards of "should" and "ought"

Assumptions are made when we take our own perceptions, born out of false beliefs and a twisted understanding of God, and impose them on other people.

A Picture Is Worth 1300 Words

People who work in the area of behavioral science tell us that a good communicator speaks at the rate of about 200 words per minute, but *because we think in concepts and pictures*, the communication that goes on in our minds takes place at about 1300 words per minute.

For example, when we hear someone talking about airplanes flying into tall buildings, we immediately have a series of pictures in our minds about a time in our history known as "9/11" that does not require an explanation. In just a few seconds, we see in our minds what would take some extended time to explain verbally.

Our minds never stop thinking. We dream when we are asleep, because our minds are still at work. We are busy commenting in our minds about everything that goes on around us, or what we perceive is going on around us, at 1300 words per minute.

When we observe people or events and evaluate at 1300 words per minute through a lens that is Biblically inaccurate, *we are constantly reinforcing half-truths that keep us in bondage.* And since we are doing it at the rate of 1300 words per minute, no one can speak enough truth words at 200 words per minute to talk us into believing the truth.

The good news is that if we are observing the same people or events through a lens that is Biblically accurate, we are constantly reinforcing truth that will set us free. And since we are reinforcing truth at 1300 words per minute, no one can speak enough half-truth words at 200 words per minute to talk us out of believing the truth. This is why it is so important that our beliefs be based on a careful and accurate understanding of Scripture and the character of God. When we choose to believe that Scripture is the unchanging standard of truth, our perceptions of God, ourselves and others will change.

Why "God Says It, I Believe it, That Settles it" Isn't True

"God says it. I believe it. That settles it!" Christians make this announcement and then point to chapter and verse to prove that what we believe is true. The Bible *is* true, and Scripture *is* enough for us to live in victory and abundance. However, even reading the Bible can be deeply affected by our belief system. Our understanding of what Scripture means is radically affected by what we consider to be "right" and "normal."

Here is an example of how we read Scripture according to our worldview, rather than according to the reality of how it was written. In Luke 11:1-13, Jesus told a parable that seems to indicate that in order to get anything from God, we have to pound on the door and persist so that He will finally, reluctantly say, "Well, okay, if you aren't going to go away, I'll give you some bread."

> It happened that while Jesus was praying in a certain place, after He had finished, one of His disciples said to Him, "Lord, teach us to pray just as John also taught his disciples." And He said to them, "When you pray, say: 'Father, hallowed be Your name. Your kingdom come. Give us each day our daily bread. And forgive us our sins, for we ourselves also forgive everyone who is indebted to us. And lead us not into temptation.'" Then He said to them, "Suppose one of you has a friend, and you go to him at midnight and say to him, 'Friend, lend me three loaves; for a friend of mine has come to me from a journey, and I have nothing to set before him ...'"
>
> Luke 11:1-6 (NASU)

The rest of the sentence (verse seven) is usually read like this:

> And from inside he answers and says, "Do not bother me; the door has already been shut and my children and I are in bed; I cannot get up and give you anything."

The Amplified Bible and New King James Version are the only English versions that have the correct punctuation: *Jesus is asking a question here, not making a statement.* We read this parable through a twenty-first-century, American belief system or worldview. We have telephones and the Holiday Inn Express close by, so it is not a common occurrence for someone to drop in unexpectedly at midnight. In fact, if that happens, we would consider the unexpected guest to be very thoughtless and inconsiderate! We also have freezers, refrigerators, and microwaves, so even if someone did show up without warning, we could come up with something to feed them.

No Convenience Stores in Jesus's World

Jesus is telling this parable to people in an Eastern culture. To refuse hospitality to anyone, even an enemy, was the most insulting thing anyone could do. Any visitor was thought to be a gift from God; an honor bestowed on the household. It was a great privilege to be chosen to share hospitality with a traveler.

Jesus's Jewish listeners would understand both the excitement of having a visitor and the horror of having nothing to offer to a hungry, tired traveler. They didn't have an interstate highway system with well-lighted rest stops and convenience stores. It was extremely dangerous to be walking at midnight because of the robbers hidden along the roadways. For the traveler to be out alone in the middle of the night suggests a serious emergency. When he arrived in the village and knocked on the door, the excited homeowner dashed out of his home to his friend's house.

Again, if we read this through an American perspective, we think of nighttime in our homes where everyone is in bed with windows and doors closed and locked. But Jesus's listeners were people who lived in small villages where much of the sleeping took place on the rooftop or in the courtyard because of crowded conditions and the heat. There was no central air conditioning, and the windows were not closed at night. The next-door neighbor surely knew about the visitor before the knock on his door because the neighborhood dogs began barking at the disturbance from the moment he entered the quiet, sleeping village!

The man does not hesitate to knock on his neighbor's door in the middle of the night because he knows that his friend will understand the wonderful honor of providing for a midnight visitor and he is confident that his friend will be excited to share in that privilege. His knock is persistent and enthusiastic.

Jesus asked the question, "Would any of you have a friend who, if you went to him at midnight with this request, would say to you, 'Do not disturb me; the door is now closed and my children are with me in bed; I cannot get up and supply you with anything?" The implied answer here is, "Of course not!" That would be *unthinkable* in an Eastern culture. Jesus goes on to remind His listeners that even if the friend will not get up and supply him with anything simply because of the friendship, yet because of his shameless, unembarrassed persistence, he will get up and give him as much as he needs.

> So I say to you, ask, and keep on asking and it shall be given you; seek, and keep on seeking and you shall find; knock, and keep on knocking and the door shall be opened to you. For everyone who asks and keeps on asking receives; and he who seeks and keeps on seeking finds; and to him who knocks and keeps on knocking, the door shall be opened. What father among you, if his son asks for a loaf of bread, will give him a stone; or if he asks for a fish, will instead of a fish give him a serpent? Or if he asks for an egg, will give him a scorpion? If you then, evil as you are, know how to give good gifts to your children, how much more will your heavenly Father give the Holy Spirit to those who ask and continue to ask Him!
>
> Luke 11:9-13

The cultural belief or "lens" we are wearing when we read this story causes us to see God as a reluctant neighbor who has to be pestered into giving us what we need. But if we read this parable through the cultural lens in which the story was told, we see that God is enthusiastic about meeting our needs, and that He would never say, "I'm too busy and too tired. Leave Me alone."

In order to enjoy the abundant life that is ours in Christ, the lens through which we view God or read Scripture must be accurate. It is so important that we grow in our understanding of what God is like according to His own account, so that we can trust Him with increasing confidence.

"Con" Words that Describe Our Belief System

Our beliefs deceive us into wrong perceptions and observations. To con means:

- to swindle or trick
- to persuade by deception or cajolery
- a confidence game
- a lie, exaggeration or glib, self-serving talk

Our beliefs are *con*-structed: No one is born with a prefabricated belief system. Beliefs about God, ourselves, other people, and how life should be lived are built the same way a building is constructed: one building block at a time. Each person learns from their social environment how life "should" be lived. Belief systems are constructed from spiritual and family influence; input from books, movies, TV, and music and by the significant relationships encountered outside the family of origin. Our environment and life experience provide the "building material" for our unique belief system .

Our beliefs are *con*-taminated and *con*-fused: The "building material" for our belief system is received from imperfect, sinful people in an imperfect, sinful world. Since each of us comes into the world spiritually separated from God, the pieces of faulty building material are joined together on a foundation of lostness. Confusion is the inevitable result.

Our beliefs are *con*-niving and *con*-trolling: Each of us comes into the world separated from God, but absolutely determined to get our needs met. The life view contained in our belief system is one of the tools we use to manipulate people and circumstances to get what we want, when, where, and how we want it. Choices and behavior are controlled by our beliefs. We don't even notice that our beliefs are dictating what we think and how we choose, because we are so accustomed to them. Daily life has been carrying the building material of this system in and storing it in our "life perception basement" since we were tiny; it's "just how things are," and we don't question it. A belief system is hidden, subtle, pervasive, and powerful enough to control every thought, choice and action.

Our beliefs are very much like the operating system of a computer. When the computer boots up, the operating system logo is the first thing that becomes visible on the monitor. When another program is opened or we go online, the logo disappears. That doesn't mean, however, that the operating system stopped running; if it did, the computer wouldn't work. The system continues to run invisibly, making all the other programs work together. Our belief systems are constantly running "behind the scenes," causing our thoughts, emotions, and decision-making processes to work together in a way that corresponds to the belief system.

Our beliefs are *con*-vincing: Because our belief system is interwoven with our emotions, our beliefs *feel* absolutely normal. We are convinced that our way of believing is right and "if everyone else doesn't believe this way, they should." Emotions are biochemically imprinted in the neurological networks of reasoning in the mind. This means that we can be presented with reasonable, logical, scientifically proven evidence that something is true (dead men don't bleed) and not believe it until the deep limbic system, which is the emotional center of the brain, allows us to feel that it is true. *This is where faith becomes so critically important.*

Faith is choosing to believe what God says in spite of how we may feel or in spite of what our circumstances are like. If we have to wait until our emotions tell us to change our beliefs, it won't happen. But because we are created in the image of God, we are able to make choices that oppose what our wounded, confused emotions tell us to do. As we learn to think differently, our emotions will begin to agree with the new thought pattern, and it gradually becomes easier to think or act in the new way.

Our beliefs are *con*-demned: Because our belief systems are built from birth with faulty material on a faulty foundation, they are clearly condemned from the start. Each individual belief system is stained and disfigured by sin. The damage comes from several sources, though Satan and his desire to destroy humankind lies ultimately at the root:

1. Con-demnation comes from Satan, who actively lies to us. Believing his half-truths always brings destruction and some type of death: physical, emotional, or relational. (Genesis 2:17; 3:3, 19; John 8:44).

2. Con-demnation comes from the world system, which is controlled and manipulated by Satan (1 John 5:19). The world system is pervasive in its invasion of our thoughts. Since thoughts produce behavior, whatever controls our thinking sits in the *driver's seat* of our behavior.

    Keep and guard your heart with all vigilance and above all that you guard, for out of it flow the springs of life. Put away from you false and dishonest speech, and willful and contrary talk put far from you. Let your eyes look right on (with fixed purpose), and let your gaze be straight before you. Consider well the path of your feet, and let all your ways be established and ordered aright. Turn not aside to the right hand or to the left; remove your foot from evil. (Proverbs 4:23-27)

Hear, my son, and be wise, and direct your mind in the way of the Lord (Proverbs 23:19).

God's remedy is to "take thoughts captive" (2 Corinthians10:3-4) and "renew our minds," which is learning to think differently than the unsaved world thinks and urges us to think (Romans 12:1-2).

3. Con-demnation comes from indwelling sin. It is personified in Scripture as an entity that is waiting to slip in the door (Genesis 4:7). It arouses forbidden desires (Romans 7:8; 17-21) and "mates" with selfish cravings, resulting in the birth of sinful behavior (James 1:14-15).

   The Bible tells us that humankind is universally corrupt by nature. This inner corruption (indwelling sin) permeates the entire person—spirit, soul, and body—and becomes evident in all forms of behavioral sin. Regeneration (the new birth) is the total removal of the old sin nature, which is replaced by a new, righteous spirit or nature. *That new nature is the indwelling life of Jesus.*

   This new birth, however, does not result in the immediate removal of indwelling sin in the soul (the mind, the will, and the emotions). Consequently, two conflicting principles reside within the *soul* of the regenerated person: the law of sin, which produces death, and grace, which produces life. The remaining corruption in the soul that we call *indwelling sin* is strengthened when we make sinful "flesh" choices that are carried out through the body. Maturity and right behavior comes from saying *no* more often to indwelling sin from the soul with its destructive behavior, and *yes* more often to the life of Jesus that inhabits and energizes the regenerated human spirit.

4. Con-demnation comes through imperfect people (Hebrews 3:8-10). We make assumptions about how life "should" be lived by watching the adults we grow up with. Adults who know God and are aware of the enormity of their responsibility are conscientious in the example they set before children or grandchildren (2 Timothy 1:5). But even then, we are limited and imperfect in our depiction of the character and love of God. Those adults who don't know God themselves cannot possibly live out an example of who God is.

   As a result, we all receive an understanding of God from the previous generation that is limited and twisted. Our present life experience is built on the entirety of our past. It is not possible to remove or forget that past. It is a permanent, indelible part of who we are in the present. But the hope of the Gospel of Jesus Christ is that *our past does not have to determine our future.* In Christ we are able to take off the old "goggles" and see life increasingly from God's perspective.

5. Con-demnation comes from our own con-taminated thoughts. These old thought patterns, which had their origin in our growing up, often become a treadmill of discouragement and defeat. Even after salvation has occurred and the adults whose influence shaped our lives are gone, their words play like old recordings in the mind. We may take up the refrain, accepting and repeating the half truths we learned to believe until our own thinking becomes as persuasive as the original voices.

Our beliefs can be *con*-verted: The good news established by the life, death, and resurrection of Jesus is that we do not have to live under the power of the old, condemned way of thinking. Our belief systems can be converted or transformed.

When a building has been condemned because of an unsafe foundation, some of what is on the inside can be taken out and reused when the building is reconstructed on a firm foundation. A faulty foundation would not make it necessary to throw away every piece of furniture or office equipment inside the building. God has built truth into each one of us from the moment of conception (Romans 1:19). When we replace the *foundation* upon which our belief system is built, (1 Corinthians 3:10) we can salvage those parts that are Biblically sound and continue to build upon them.

We received a new nature at salvation which makes it possible to begin the process of identifying beliefs that are not in agreement with God's view of life, even though they may feel familiar and right, and to replace them with truth from the Word of God.

Define "belief":

____

____

Identify three beliefs about yourself that feel absolutely true.

____

____

____

How do each of these beliefs agree or disagree with God's truth about you?

____

____

____

Subway System

New York City has a transportation system hidden beneath the city. Over the years, engineers designed and built a network of tunnels for subway trains that carry thousands of commuters to their destination every hour, day and night. The trains are not visible above ground; only where steps descend from the sidewalk into the subterranean system is there a hint of what lies beneath the streets. As long as the trains are running normally, those who use the system don't think about it very often. It is a normal part of their day.

But when there is a malfunction in the system, it quickly becomes noticeable above ground. City streets and parking areas become more congested as people who normally commute by subway drive their own vehicles into the city and try to find parking spaces. Public transportation becomes overloaded, and cabs are scarce and expensive. Businesses suffer because employees are late and deliveries are disrupted. Even though the subway system is not visible, it has tremendous influence on how the city operates, both positively and negatively.

When the subway system breaks down, city planners don't rush to build new streets and parking garages above ground to ease the traffic jams and parking shortages. Rather, they focus on fixing the problem in the invisible, underground system that is the cause of the visible congestion. They know that when the underground problem is repaired, the above-ground problems will ease.

If we only focus on the behavior and emotions that are visible, we will rush to "fix" the problems we're having with behavior modification or drugs. We may pursue new relationships and more things to feel better emotionally.

Most emotional problems or turmoil in our life experience have a spiritual root. The only real and lasting solution is to identify the malfunction in the "underground" belief system. Permanent transformation is accomplished as we bring our beliefs about God, ourselves, and others into agreement with the Word of God.

The Parable of the Garbage

Once upon a time, Bill and Sue bought a lot from a contractor who had promised to fill a new housing addition on the outskirts of the town with lovely, four-story houses. They were the first to purchase a lot and were very impressed by what they saw; the streets were finished, streetlights were shining, and the builder assured them that every single thing they could possibly need to live happily ever after had been provided.

"Well, actually, there is just one small exception," he amended. "Since your house is outside the city limits and is the only house here, the city is refusing to send a garbage truck. You'll have to haul your own garbage."

Bill and Sue decided it would be no problem to load the trunk of the car with garbage bags every week and take them to the landfill. Work began on their house, and eight months later, they moved in.

Several years passed, and the contractor who built their house closed his business and moved away. No other houses were built on the neighboring lots. That was all right with Bill and Sue, who were enjoying their home on the outskirts of town, with no neighbors next door. It was like living in the country, with the conveniences of the city close by.

As Bill and Sue's children were born, their lives became busier. It became more difficult to get to the landfill, but they shrugged and agreed, "It's okay. We aren't using that big basement right now, and the garbage is out of the way. As long as we keep the stairway clear, the garbage won't matter for now."

As the years passed, the garbage piled higher in the basement. Sue loved her home and was an excellent housekeeper. However, she began to notice that no matter how often she swept and scrubbed, there were always flies in the house. She hung fly strips in every room; she swatted flies and even resorted to spray. She killed hundreds every day, but there was no measurable decrease in their numbers.

At the same time, Bill was becoming very resentful toward their friends. "We always used to have people here to eat, play cards, or to watch a movie," he said. "But now if anyone does agree to come, they don't stay long. I just don't understand what their problem is! And another thing, have you noticed when we go to a ballgame or go out to eat and sit next to someone, they give us funny looks and move away? I just don't know what the matter is with people these days. They are getting so 'stuck up!'"

Bill was insulted by the behavior of others and began to withdraw. Sue and the children kept trying to be sociable, but it was difficult when they felt so rejected. People didn't seem to like them or their home anymore.

Moral: If you keep rotting garbage in the basement of your house for years, you'll always have flies. People will not want to be around you because you'll smell like the garbage that surrounds you.

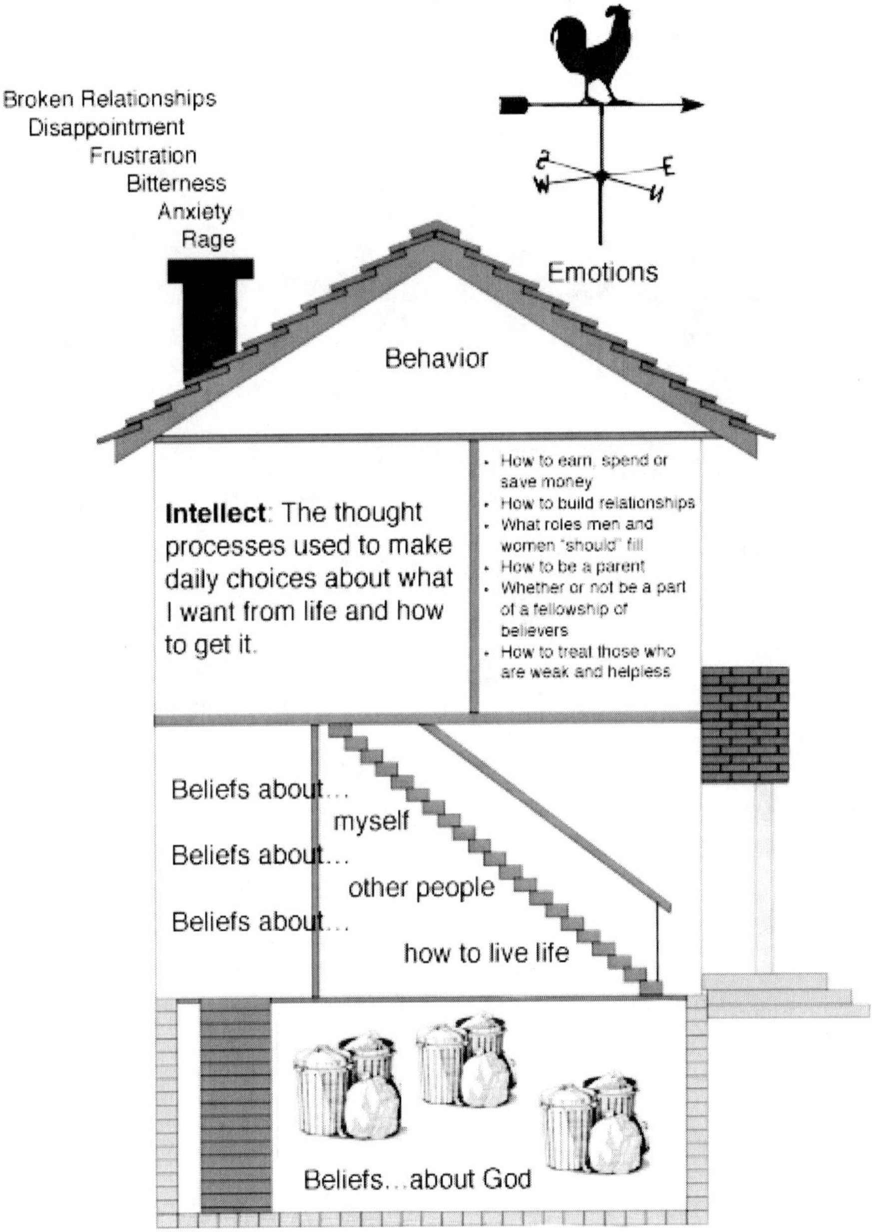
Broken Relationships
Disappointment
Frustration
Bitterness
Anxiety
Rage
S
E
W
N
Emotions
Behavior
Intellect: The thought processes used to make daily choices about what I want from life and how to get it.
• How to earn, spend or save money
• How to build relationships
• What roles men and women "should" fill
• How to be a parent
• Whether or not be a part of a fellowship of believers
• How to treat those who are weak and helpless
Beliefs about... myself
Beliefs about... other people
Beliefs about... how to live life
Beliefs...about God

Basement

The flies that are attracted by the garbage of wrong thinking in the basement are:

- Chemical dependencies
- Sexual promiscuity and immorality
- Violence and abuse
- Excessive spending
- Hoarding
- Eating disorders—overeating and starving, bingeing and purging
- Depression
- Uncontrolled anger
- Anxiety, panic attacks, and phobias
- Workaholism
- Laziness
- Procrastination
- Hyperactivity—avoiding stillness and quietness
- Jealousy and suspicion

This partial list of "flies" will only disappear as we "carry out the garbage" of wrong thinking. This is done through the process of renewing the mind.

When our thinking contains the "garbage" of wrong beliefs about God, it will have a profound effect on the rest of our "house" of life even though we may not be particularly aware that the "basement" exists.

The basement represents the area of thinking where we store beliefs about God that have collected over our years of life. We don't think about it much, and we don't particularly notice the garbage of wrong thinking that is piling up. In fact, we get so accustomed to it that we don't even notice the "smell" of the garbage at all.

We form an opinion of ourselves based on the accurate or inaccurate understanding of God that we have stored in the basement of our thinking. *Since we know that we are created in the image of God, we are going to view ourselves through the same "lens" that we view God.* Our understanding of what God is like also determines what we think He expects of us and how we believe He evaluates our performance.

If we wrongly depend on other people for our sense of worth, how we think "they" value our performance will strongly influence our own evaluation of performance and will dictate our ultimate approval or disapproval of ourselves.

When we mix the truth of Scripture with the untruth of beliefs formed in a sinful world, the result is a poisonous half-truth that can only produce disillusionment and disappointment.

For example:

- If we believe that God only helps those who help themselves, we will be driven to workaholism, fearing that if we don't do enough, God won't do anything for us. We will be critical of anyone who doesn't work as hard as we do. Our thoughts will be a cynical commentary on the incompetence and stupidity of humanity in general. This produces envy and bitterness toward anyone who seems to do less than we do and still receives from God.
- If we believe, because of an angry, demanding parent that God is angry and demanding, we will in turn be angry and demanding of ourselves and of others. The commentary at 1300 words per minute will be negative, critical, and demeaning. This belief produces a victim mind-set that is often expressed in this way: "I've been treated so badly all my life (sigh) ... the world owes me."
- If we have been spoiled as children; undisciplined and given whatever material things we wanted, then our commentary will be a bitter condemnation of anyone who stands in our way. Nothing will ever be enough, and we will think thoughts of self-pity, discontentment, and criticism. We will be angry at God because He doesn't give us what we want, the way we want it, at exactly the time we demanded it.

What's Buried in the Basement? Sorting through the Trash ... Finding the Treasure

It doesn't help to blame someone else for the circumstances in which we find ourselves. However, it can be useful to recognize the influences that surrounded us as growing children, to gain a better understanding of what "planted" the thought patterns that direct the way we live life. As we discover the origin of the corrupted thought and behavior patterns, we can uproot and replace them with Biblically correct ones.

Looking at our past can be compared to cleaning out a waterway. A variety of trash is buried in the muck on the bottom, along with coins and other things of value. The valuable things cannot be retrieved without disturbing the trash and mud. Acknowledging the "trash" as we come to a better understanding of our family is not an attack on them or on ourselves. It is simply a part of God's process to free us from corrupted beliefs. Where there has been outright abuse or physical and emotional neglect, it is necessary to acknowledge the wrong and choose forgiveness.

The following questions will help pinpoint areas where wrong beliefs have been established.

Mother

1. Did my mother hit me (aside from reasonable spanking)? If yes, how often?

    Very often (daily)
    Often (several times a week)
    Once in a while
    Seldom
    Never

2. How did I get along with my mother?

    ____

    ____

    ____

3. Being hugged by my mother made me feel…

4. Was I afraid of my mother when she was angry? If yes, what did I think she would do?

5. In what ways did my mother show anger?

6. When my mother was angry, her voice made me feel…

7. What did my mother like?

8. What did my mother dislike?

9. My mother would always…

10. What did my mother expect from me growing up?

____

____

____

11. Did my mother tease me so that I became hurt and angry with her?

    Yes, often
    Yes, sometimes
    Yes, but not often
    No

12. My mother taught me to ...

____

____

13. Was my privacy respected by my mother when I was growing up? How or how not?

____

____

____

14. Did my mother ever make me promise to keep something a secret? If yes, explain:

____

____

15. Was my mother concerned about her weight? If yes, how did she express her concern?

____

____

16. When my mother was stressed, she would…

17. Three things my mother said to me most often…

18. Three things my mother called me the most often…

19. Did my mother push me to participate or excel in any activities?

20. Did my mother criticize me for participating in activities that didn't interest her?

Father

1. Did my father hit me (aside from reasonable spanking)? If yes, how often?

    Very often (daily)
    Often (several times a week)
    Once in a while
    Seldom
    Never

2. What was my father like?

    ____

    ____

    ____

3. How did I get along with my father?

    ____

    ____

    ____

4. Was I afraid of my father when he was angry? If yes, what did I think he would do?

    ____

    ____

    ____

5. When my father was angry, his voice made me feel…

    ____

    ____

6. When I was alone with my father, I felt . . .

7. How much time did my father spend around the house? Was he there emotionally as well as physically?

8. How did he spend most of his time at home?

9. What did my father expect from me growing up?

10. Did my father tease me so that I became hurt and angry with him?

    Yes, often
    Yes, sometimes
    Yes, but not often
    No

11. Did my father and I talk a lot? If yes, what did we talk about?

12. Did some of the things my father wanted to talk about make me feel uncomfortable? If so, why?

___

___

___

13. Did I ever wish he would talk to my mother instead of me? Why?

___

___

___

14. Was my privacy respected by my father when I was growing up? How or how not?

___

___

___

15. Did my father ever make me promise to keep something a secret? If yes, explain:

___

___

___

16. When my father was stressed, he would...

___

___

___

17. Three things my father said to me most often . . .

____

____

____

18. Three things my father called me the most often . . .

____

____

____

19. Being hugged by my dad made me feel . . .

____

____

20. What did my father like?

____

____

21. What did my father dislike?

____

____

22. Did my father push me to participate or excel in any activities?

____

____

23. Did my father criticize me for participating in activities that didn't interest him?

____

____

Family

1. If there was one word to describe my family, what would it be?

___

2. Five "rules" (spoken or unspoken) for my family were:

___

___

___

___

___

3. Did I have trouble living up to these rules? Which ones and why?

___

___

___

___

4. How did my family respond to real or perceived criticism or disapproval from others?

___

___

___

5. Did one of my parents treat me better than the other? If yes, which one, and in what way?

___

___

___

6. Did the parent who treated me better know that I was being mistreated or neglected by the other? If so, what did he/she do to protect me or to "compensate" for the mistreatment or neglect?

___

___

___

7. I especially remember being hurt by...

___

___

___

8. I felt guilty as a child when I...

___

___

___

9. I believed that I was:

   A bad child
   A good child
   An unwanted child
   A bothersome child
   Other

___

10. Some of the things I swore I would never say or do to my own children were:

___

___

___

11. How did my parents treat me when I misbehaved or disappointed them?

____

____

____

12. How did my parents treat me when I hurt myself, or when I was hurt by someone else?

____

____

____

Church

1. If there was one word to describe the church I grew up in, what would it be?

____

2. Five "rules" (spoken or unspoken) for the church were:

____

____

____

____

____

3. Did I have trouble living up to these rules? Which ones and why?

____

____

____

____

____

4. How did my church respond when I didn't live up to these rules?

____

____

____

5. How did my church respond to real or perceived criticism or disapproval from others?

____

____

____

6. I felt guilty as a Christian when I…

____

____

____

7. I believed God thought that I was:

   A good Christian
   An unworthy Christian
   An unwanted Christian
   A bothersome Christian
   Other

____

When we have identified and gathered the trash of hurt, disappointment and abuse, the next step is a bonfire of forgiveness! First Corinthians 3:10-15 describes the assessment of a believer's works and behavior when we step into the Presence of Jesus. The "wood, hay and stubble" of worthless works is burned up while the "gold, silver and precious stones" survive the fire.

Forgiveness is not saying that the wrongs done "didn't matter" or that the offender is not in any way responsible for the wrong. Forgiveness is not recklessly letting the one who hurt you "off the hook" while continuing to carry bitterness. Forgiveness is not forgetting.

Forgiveness is the "fire" that burns up a lifetime of accumulated trash. It is deliberately choosing to remember that the painful and destructive offenses done against us were paid for by the blood of Jesus at the same time that He paid for our offenses. While we cannot forget what has happened, we can choose to "remember no more" in the same way God does (Hebrews 10:17). He says emphatically that He chooses to *not recall and replay* our offenses against Him. Choosing to "remember no more" sets us free from bitterness and resentment with all the attending physical and emotional problems. (See page 202-203). This acrostic can remind us of what forgiveness is:

F: finalizing
O: offenses
R: rage
G: grief
I: ill will
V: vendettas
E: embarrassment

It can be helpful to make a list of those who have hurt you, specifically stating the offense and the resulting emotion. *Write answers to the first three statements on a separate paper so that it can be destroyed when you finish the exercise.* You may want to use a separate page for each person who has hurt or disappointed you. Say the words out loud as if the person were right there with you. Here are some suggested statements:

1. "I was very hurt when you…" (be specific about the offense)
2. "It made me feel…" (name the specific emotion's you experienced as a result of the offense)
3. What you did has affected my life negatively because…

Commitment of Forgiveness

"I now choose to release the debt you owe. I release you from the responsibility to make everything "okay". I am choosing to trust Jesus as the only true Source for meeting my needs. I believe He is at work right now to bring benefit to me in every detail of my life."

List three ways that you are trusting Jesus to heal you and provide for you emotionally and physically.

____

____

____

"When the memory of this offense comes to mind, I choose to immediately give it to Jesus, thanking Him that He has forgiven me of my many offenses, against Him and other people. I sign this commitment as a reminder that I have released this debt and am choosing to "remember it no more" by not rehearsing the hurt, either in my mind or out loud to someone else."

Signed: ____________________
Date: ____________________

Now shred or burn the lists of offenses, recognizing that you have begun the process of *finalizing* your freedom from the bondage of unforgiveness. It may take some time for your emotions to catch up with your decision to forgive, but as you consistently refuse to rehearse the offenses and instead, recall God's amazing love and mercy for you, the strong emotions will change. Reread this commitment as needed.

First Floor

The next level is the main floor of the house and represents the area of our minds where we learn how to think about ourselves, other people, and how life should be lived. This includes but is not limited to:

- How we judge ourselves compared to other people.
- How we judge other people compared to ourselves.
- How we think we or others should handle money, relationships, and other details of life.
- How we think we or others should dress.
- How we think we or others should talk.

It is on this main floor that the continuous commentary about life and what is going on around us takes place at 1300 words per minute. This assessment arises out of what we have in our "basement" where we hold our beliefs about God.

As we become more aware of the "chatter," we may be surprised by the amount of criticism and negative talk going on in our mind. And because our thoughts produce emotions, when there is a great deal of negative commentary, it is no wonder that we feel so irritated with ourselves, other people, and life in general.

Second Floor

The next "floor" represents the intellect: the processes we use to decide what we want from life and how to get it. These thoughts drive our decisions and produce our emotional responses. Our unique system of reasoning and choosing is affected by the "garbage in the basement" just as an entire house would be affected by odors and flies if the basement was filled with rotting garbage. It is so important that our beliefs about God be progressively more accurate as we grow older. We cannot enjoy a life that is suitable to our wonderful design if our understanding of the Designer is Biblically incorrect.

Third Floor

The top "floor" which is most visible to others, is our behavior. Even though the top of the house seems a long way from the basement, the odor and flies permeate it as well. The wind vane on the top of the house illustrates the instability of emotions, affected by whatever direction the wind happens to be blowing on a particular day.

Emotions and behavior make what is buried in the basement visible. Our behavior is an announcement to the world around us of the beliefs and thoughts we have cultivated over the years. We don't need an LED screen on our foreheads for people to know what we're thinking. Each choice and emotion is a visible announcement of an "invisible" thought.

"Because ... Therefore" Love

Imagine how our life experience will change when we exchange the trash in the basement for the treasure of the truth that:

- God loves us perfectly, not because of who we are, but because of who He is!
- God doesn't love us because of what we do for Him; rather He loves us because it is His nature to love. Our relationship with Him is not based on what we can accomplish, but on what Jesus accomplished on the cross.
- God does not say, "Do this, and I will love you," but rather, "I love you. Now you can be obedient, empowered by My love."

God's love is not "if you do ... then I will love you." Rather, it is "because I love you ... therefore you can!" Because God knows that wrong thinking is deadly, we are instructed in 2 Corinthians 10:5 to "refute arguments and theories and reasonings and every proud and lofty thing that sets itself up against the true knowledge of God; and we lead every thought and purpose away captive into the obedience of Christ the Messiah." Since we cannot take a thought captive until we know it exists, it is critically important that we are aware of what is going on inside our minds.

Our Quick Fix Culture

We *must* know what is in the "basement." We can swat flies attracted by the trash until Jesus comes back, but if we don't haul the garbage out, the flies will continue to swarm through the house. Seeking the excitement of new things and relationships or the quick-fix of drugs are attempts to alleviate symptoms without fixing the problem. It isn't wrong to enjoy new things, but if having more, faster, newer stuff is what gets us out of bed in the morning, we have idols. If we cannot stand quietness and are too hyperactive to be still with the Lord for even a few minutes, then we need to check the anxiety-producing "chatter" coming out of the basement.

Soothing symptoms *will not* fix the problem. The "flies" of anxiety, depression, dependencies, hyperactivity, procrastination, and compulsive behavior, just to name a few, must be dealt with from the inside out, beginning with repentance and salvation. The long-term work of renewing the mind produces spiritual maturity and a stable life.

Dead Sea Theology

From *The Church Snatchers: The Ultimate Identity Theft*
by Dr. Dixie Yoder

The Dead Sea, the lowest point on the surface of the earth, is a mineral rich "soup" of thick water, because it has inlets, but no outlets except evaporation.

American Christians have many spiritual "inlets" including church, Bible studies, and Christian TV, but relatively few believers have "outlets"—regular occasions of evangelism, opportunities to teach or situations where new information is shared and discussed with mature believers in a way that separates correct Bible knowledge from incorrect.

Accurate knowledge of Scripture is declining at an alarming rate. Consequently, as information that *feels* right is received by hearing, reading, or observing something related to spirituality, that piece of information is received as truth and becomes a part of the "theology soup."

As this receiving and mixing process continues, the basic theological framework is constantly changing because of ignorance of Scriptural truth. And since absolute truth has been rejected as a standard by which to evaluate the information that continually comes in, religious concepts from Hinduism, Islam, Mormonism, Christian Science, Naturalism, and Humanism are absorbed with no awareness that it has happened.

The spiritual brew that has collected becomes a poisonous blend of truth and error. Most of this hodgepodge comes through the extensive influence of entertainment and mass communication, including movies, art, video games, contemporary music, sports, and advertising. Some examples are:

- The pantheistic theology in Star Wars
- The occult influence found in the Harry Potter books and movies, along with many cartoons designed for children
- The hedonistic approach to life in Elvis Presley's lyrics "It's now or never, come hold me tight; kiss me my darling, be mine tonight. Tomorrow will be too late—it's now or never, my love won't wait."
- The theory of evolution in the children's cartoon *The Land Before Time* as well as most nature documentaries on TV. These documentaries also teach the foundational belief of Naturalism: that human beings are intruders on the earth, disturbing the flow of nature.

These are only a few of many. If we build our lives on the unstable mixture of inaccurate Bible knowledge and pagan doctrines, the "house" of our life experience will continue to collapse, just as Jesus described:

> So everyone who hears these words of Mine and acts upon them (obeying them) will be like a sensible (prudent, practical, wise) man who built his house upon the rock. And the rain fell and the floods came and the winds blew and beat against that house; yet it did not fall, because it had been founded on the rock. And everyone who hears these words of Mine and does not do them will be like a stupid (foolish) man who built his house upon the sand. And the rain fell and the floods came and the winds blew and beat against that house, and it fell—and great and complete was the fall of it.
>
> Matthew 7:24-27

> In this way laying up for themselves the riches that endure forever as a good foundation for the future, so that they may grasp that which is life indeed. O Timothy, guard and keep the deposit entrusted to you! Turn away from the irreverent babble and godless chatter, with the vain and empty and worldly

> phrases … in what is falsely called knowledge and spiritual illumination. For by making such profession some have missed the mark as regards the faith.
>
> 1 Timothy 6:19-21

Corrupted/Corrected Assumptions

Choose four "corrupted assumptions" from the thirty-five listed that seem true to you. Write the corrupted assumption on the worksheet page 170-172 and evaluate how this assumption has affected your life.

Now write the correlating "corrected assumption." Evaluate how living out of this new assumption will change your responses, behavior, and circumstances.

Corrupted Assumptions About Life

1._____Because I am a Christian, it is my responsibility to always please other people

2._____I can't help but be upset by criticism. It is inevitable that criticism will upset the one who is being criticized.

3._____I need the approval of others in order to be happy and successful. Even if I do a job well, I have not succeeded if other people don't approve of how I did the job.

4._____If people that I care about reject me, it proves that there is something wrong with me.

5._____I need to be loved by another person in order to feel secure and happy. I can only feel about myself the way the significant people in my life feel about me. When they express love, I can feel good; when they don't, I can't help but feel insecure and unhapy.

6._____Being alone or isolated from others will always make me unhappy.

7._____I must excel in at least one thing in order to be valuable and worthwhile. The more I excel, the more value I have.

8._____I must be a useful, productive and creative person, or life will have no purpose or meaning.

9._____If I do not perform as well as other people, it means that I am inferior, and a failure. I have to continually try harder until I measure up to others. I can't help but feel like a failure when I make a mistake.

10._____If I do not set and reach the highest possible standards for myself, I will only be a "second rate" person.
11._____If I strongly deserve something, I have good reason to expect that I will receive it.
12._____I cannot help but be angry and frustrated if I do not get what I want.
13._____If I am a good husband or wife, then I can expect my spouse to love me and make me feel good about myself. If my husband or wife makes me miserable, or doesn't do for me what I need, it means that I am not being a good spouse.
14._____If I put other people's needs before my own, then I can depend on them to help me when I need them.
15._____I am responsible for how the people close to me feel and for the choices they make.
16._____In order to be a good, worthwhile and moral person, I must help everyone who needs help, no matter what the circumstances.
17.____I can expect others to treat me the way I believe I have treated them.
18._____Because I am a Christian, I should be able to control how I feel.
19._____I cannot control my temper or my moods. Moods are created by things that are beyond my control; my past, my body chemistry, my hormone cycles and other people.
20._____My happiness is dependent upon what happens to me in my external circumstances.
21._____I am sure that those who look good and "have it all together" are happier than I am.
22._____Because I am a Christian, I must keep the peace, no matter what it costs.
23._____Because I cannot change the past, I am trapped by it. I cannot change.
24._____I have to be independent to protect myself from the untrustworthiness of others.
25._____I must not reveal or acknowledge any weakness.
26._____I must never be silly or spend time foolishly. "Idleness is the devil's workshop."

27._____People who know me well should know what I want and need without me having to tell them.
28._____Pain is always bad. I must avoid pain at all costs.
29._____I must not ever think negative thoughts. If I think positively enough, everything will work out the way I feel like it should.
30._____My feelings have to change before I can make different choices.
31._____I must concentrate on the negative and expect the worst so that when it happens, I won't be disappointed.
32._____When I am right and of course, I usually am, people should take notice and acknowledge that I am right.
33._____I have the right to justice and fairness. Justice and fairness are right, so I know that justice and fairness will always win out in the end.
34._____I feel guilty, so I know that I must have done something wrong or bad. If I feel guilty, I know that I must be guilty of something, even if I'm not sure what it is.
35._____As God's child, I will know that I have sinned when the Holy Spirit convicts me and I feel "real" guilt from God as opposed to "false" guilt from Satan.

Corrected Assumptions About Life

1. I want to be pleasing to God first. When I do my best, it is the choice of others whether they are pleased or not. God simply tells me to "walk in a manner worthy of the Lord; to please Him in all respects (Colossians 1:10)
2. Criticism may hurt my feelings, but if my desire is reach my full, God-given potential, I can choose to evaluate criticism and use it as a tool to make necessary changes.
3. Jesus never gained the approval of the religious leaders, but was absolutely successful in His life's work. The approval or disapproval of other people does not guarantee either success or failure.
4. Rejection by imperfect people is an unavoidable part of life in a sinful, imperfect world. Jesus was rejected even though He

lived His earthly life without sin. God says I am His beloved child and He will never leave me or reject me. Faith is choosing to believe what God says about me in spite of how I may feel about myself.

5. Even those who love me best will fail me at times. This can prompt insecurity. True security comes from knowing and depending on God, Who is faithful and unchangeable and will never let me down. I will choose to think about myself the way God thinks and feels about me, and my emotions will eventaully follow.
6. Aloneness is a fact of life on earth, occasionally or frequently. Aloneness is necessary to the process of spiritual growth and is a part of life that I can choose to accept and use as an opportunity to grow in intimacy with God.
7. It is God Who has declared my value, based on the fact that He created me and redeemed me. Nothing that I do can increase or decrease my value. It is a free gift, not based on my performance.
8. The purpose for my existence to be loved by God, to love Him in return and enjoy Him forever. The means to do this comes from Him. I choose to agree with His plan, His time and His place. My life has meaning and purpose simply because He loves me.
9. God promises to work all things together for my good (Romans 8:28), so failure in behavior is not just failure, but an opportunity to learn and grow. The way God measures success or failure is very different than our world's assessment. Mistakes are inevitable and are an important part of the learning process. I can choose to be upset, or I can choose to trust God in the middle of failure..
10. There are no "second rate" people in God's Kingdom. God's grace and mercy, not performance, is the qualifying standard for acceptance.
11. This kind of expectation will inevitably lead to disappointment. Expectations are often part of the power struggle that happens when I want to control or change someone else. If I deserve something and do not receive it, I can choose to give

that expectation to God and trust Him while He meets the need in the way He knows as best.

12. Anger and frustration indicate a blocked goal or expectation. I can choose to stay angry and frustrated, or I can choose to take my disappointment to the Lord and receive what I need from Him.
13. If I am being a "good" spouse in order to get what I want, then I am being manipulative. I am to love my mate simply because God loves me and wants me to share that love. My spouse's responses are between him/her and God.
14. This is an expectation that will often not be met. If I serve others so that they will serve me, I am being manipulative. Jesus gave Himself to me in love with no strings attached. His new commandment is that we are to love others in that same way.
15. I am only responsible before the Lord for my own thinking and for the choices I make. Except in the case of training young children, I am not responsible for the thoughts, feelings and choices that others make.
16. This is assuming responsibility for everyone, which becomes slavery rather than service. God calls us to help certain people at certain times, because He provides for the needs of people through other people. But my priority must be to work in partnership with God, not to be a one-person "first responders" team for everyone. If I rescue someone without first hearing from God, I may interfere with the work God wants to accomplish in them through their difficulty.
17. Manipulation, performance and power struggles are all involved in the expectation that people will only treat me the way I treat them on my best day. What about the days that my own responses are thoughtless, selfish and angry? God wants me to treat others with kindness and consideration, no matter how they respond.
18. Feelings will always respond to my thoughts. Emotions are neither good nor bad; they simplymake me aware of what I am thinking. Because I am God's child, I can choose to take my thoughts captive to the obedience of Christ (2 Corinthians 10:5); renew my mind (Romans 12:2); and set my mind on things above

(Colossians 3:2). As I do, my emotions will come increasingly under the control of my renewed mind.

19. God enables me to choose my behavior (Ephesians 4:26). Moods may be magnified by chemistry, hormones and other people, but believing that I cannot control moodiness denies the victory that Jesus won over all things, including moodiness. If my moods are controlling me and causing those around me to suffer, I need to choose to take responsibility for my physical health as well.
20. Happiness is indeed external. But because I am in Christ, circumstances do not have to control my sense of well-being. Joy comes from the inside as my relationship with God becomes more intimate. That joy cannot be taken away, no matter how unhappy my external circumstances may become.
21. "Looking good" may be covering up a lot of hurt, disappointment and anger. While there is nothing wrong with looking the best we can, a certain kind of look does not change the fact that we all have needs and pain.
22. As a believer, I am to be a peacemaker not a peacekeeper. Peacekeepers often avoid conflict until an explosion takes place. Peacemakers face conflict as it arises, even though it may be painful.
23. It is true that I cannot change or eliminate the past, but in Christ, I no longer have to be controlled by it. I am a new creation in Christ (1 Corinthians. 5:17). I am now free to make choices out of my present relationship with God, and out of the knowledge of what my future with Jesus holds.
24. Depending either on myself (independence) or depending on other people (dependency) will only produce disappointment and disillusionment. My dependence must be in God so that when people let me down, I can trust God to be at work in the hurt and disappointment.
25. Trying to never show weakness is fear of being vulnerable or taking a risk. God says that it is in my weakness that His strength is made perfect (2 Corinthians 12:9).

26. There is a big difference between the silly foolishness of a fool and the childlikeness that allows us to play and relax. Constant intensity and seriousness will end in burnout.
27. God gave us the ability to communicate with one another, not the ability to read one another's minds. Mind reading is trespassing; communicating is exercising a gift from God that expresses our likeness to Him.
28. Pain is an inescapable part of life, and is used to benefit me when I allow it to push me deeper into Father's arms. The constant attempt to avoid pain always leads to addictions and avoidance of risk and intimacy.
29. I am created in the image of God, with the ability to make choices, which involves analytical thought processes. In order to think a situation through, I must acknowledge and discuss the negative aspects as well as the positive. Pretending the negative does not exist is not faith, it is fear.
30. My emotions are an important part of me, but they serve me by making me aware of my thoughts. I do not serve or obey my emotions. I obey God, and He directs my thoughts and my behavior as I communicate with Him and listen to Him.
31. Concentrating on the negatives and expecting the worst will not protect me from disappointment; it will only lock me into a negative, pessimistic and critical mindset. It also denies the sovereignty of God over all of my life, including those things that look negative or feel painful.
32. Always insisting on being right is an indication of insecurity and fear of punishment. God is always right, but He does not force His rightness on me. He allows me to choose to accept or reject Him. I cannot force my "rightness" on others, even when I am truly right.
33. Life on this earth is contaminated by sin, so it cannot be fair. In a sin contaminated world system, justice will always be tainted. There are things I can do to make certain situations more fair, and I can combat injustice wherever I see it, but no one can bring about perfect fairness and justice on earth until sin is completely eradicated.

34. I may have been "programmed" to feel guilty so that I will assume that "it's my fault" no matter what the situation really is. Because of this guilty mindset, it is very possible for me to feel guilty when I have done nothing sinfully wrong at all.
35. John 16:8 says that the Holy Spirit convicts the unsaved world, not believers. John 16:13 tells me that the Holy Spirit will guide me into the truth—truth about Who God is; who I am and how my thinking and behavior needs to change. Conviction and guilt are for sinners. Knowledge of truth and sorrow for sin are for God's children.

1. Write out the corrupted assumption:

How has this corrupted assumption affected you?

Write out the correlating corrected assumption:

How will living out of this new assumption change my responses, behavior, and circumstances?

2. Write out the corrupted assumption:

How has this corrupted assumption affected you?

Write out the correlating corrected assumption:

How will living out of this new assumption change my responses, behavior, and circumstances?

3. Write out the corrupted assumption:

How has this corrupted assumption affected you?

Write out the correlating corrected assumption:

How will living out of this new assumption change my responses, behavior, and circumstances?

___

___

___

4. Write out the corrupted assumption:

___

___

___

How has this corrupted assumption affected you?

___

___

___

Write out the correlating corrected assumption from the right column:

___

___

___

How will living out of this new assumption change my responses, behavior and circumstances?

___

___

___

Chapter 5
Riding the Emotional Rollercoaster with Your Hands Up!

God's Design for Emotions VS Sin's Design for Emotions

GOD'S DESIGN FOR EMOTIONS:	REFERENCE	SIN'S DESIGN FOR EMOTIONS:	REFERENCE
To show us what we're thinking.	Psalm 22 Psalm 32	To lock us into a wrong mindset.	Judges 14:1-3
To aid us in motivation and performance.	Matthew 14:14 Psalm 119:67 2 Corinthians 5:14	To motivate us to sinful choices and behavior.	Acts 5:1-2 1 Kings 3:1-4
To make God visible to others.	Ephesians 4:23-24, 32 Ephesians 5:8-9	To make the flesh and sin visible to others.	Mark 14:66-72
To make us aware of the needs of others.	Matthew 15:32	To keep us focused on selfish needs.	2 Samuel 11:1-4
To motivate us to make choices in agreement with God's Word.	Philippians 1:21-25	To motivate us to control circumstances and other people.	1 Samuel 28:4-20

Emotions: in just an instant, they can carry us to the height of joy or drop us to the depths of despair.

Emotions are a part of the soul, along with the mind and the will. Because emotions are so powerfully felt, and because American culture places tremendous emphasis on how we *feel*, unstable emotions have been given a place of such authority that we live life on a rollercoaster ride of emotional ups and downs.

Have you ever wondered why we were given emotions as a part of our design? There are times that are so painful:

- When we have been betrayed by a friend.
- When a death has occurred.
- When we have received a fearful diagnosis from the doctor.

These times make us not want to feel anything at all! But emotions bring color and light into our life experience, like watching a movie on a sixty-inch high-definition plasma TV. Life without emotions would be colorless, lifeless and dull, like watching a documentary about the Grand Canyon on a twelve-inch black-and-white screen.

Our emotions are a gift from a loving Creator. God's nature is perfect love, joy, anger and peace. God doesn't *have* emotion. He *is* emotion in its completeness. Because we are created in His image, those aspects of His nature are reflected through us. Scripture tells us that God experiences and expresses:

- Grief (Genesis 6:6; Ephesians 4:30)
- Anger (Psalm 78:38)
- Joy and excitement (Zephaniah 3:17)
- Love (John 3:16-17)
- Compassion (Isaiah 30:18)
- Hate (Malachi 2:16)

As we read this list, we might say, "Well, this makes God sound too much like a human being!" But remember that our emotions are patterned after His. God's responses are not like ours! Human emotions have been tainted by sin, so that we become moody and unreasonable. Because sin cannot contaminate God in any way, His emotions are perfectly pure and sinless. *God does not have moods!* His perfect hatred of evil and sin is proof that His righteousness is also perfect.

For God to express hatred may seem like a contradiction to us because we think of love and hate as opposites. However, an opposite is actually anything that neutralizes something else. For instance:

- Heat neutralizes cold; it becomes warm or cool.
- Light neutralizes dark; it becomes twilight or light.
- Energy neutralizes inactivity; it becomes motion.

First John 4:17 says that love neutralizes fear, not hate. So the opposite of love is actually fear rather than hatred. God does not fear; He is perfect love. God has no contradiction in His nature.

Faked Fossils?

Years ago when fossil evidence was first presented as "proof" that the theory of evolution is scientifically true, many churches responded with the attitude, "We know that evolution is not true; therefore, the fossil evidence must not be real. Someone must have faked it."

Over the years, there certainly has been evidence of forgery in the attempt to find the nonexistent "missing link." One clear example: in 1921 geologist Harold Cook found a single tooth in Snake Creek Quarry in western Nebraska. From this one tooth he and some other evolutionist "experts" believed they had found unmistakable evidence of humankind's evolutionary ape-like ancestors in America. *The Illustrated London News* of June 24, 1922 published articles, drawings, and "a pedigree of the human family" to show that this tooth proved that humans had evolved from ape-like creatures. But it was all fiction. When more excavations were done and more of the same type of tooth were unearthed, it was realized that the tooth was from a type of pig! It had nothing at all to do with humans or evolution. But "Nebraska Man" is still presented as a "fact."

However, by rejecting all evidence as false, the church missed a wonderful opportunity for many years to show how real fossil evidence agrees with the Bible. *It isn't the evidence that is problematic but rather the perspective from which the evidence is viewed.* As believers look at the same fossil evidence from a different perspective, our conclusions are completely different from one who believes there is no God.

As modern scientific research continues to develop, it is showing us more clearly what happens in our brains and bodies as the result of our responses to circumstances. MRI scans, CAT scans, X-rays and other lab tests reveal the fact that the human body is made up of two systems:

- The endocrine (chemical) system
- The nervous (electrical) system

There is no question that drugs, both legal and illegal, are misused. But if we reject the genuine information about our biochemical makeup in a "knee-jerk" reaction to the plethora of chemical "solutions" presented by the American medical system, we will miss another wonderful opportunity to show how this real and measurable information about the workings of the human body agrees with what God says in the owner's manual He has written for us. As we see affirmation of how wonderfully and intricately we are made, our confidence in God's solutions will increase.

Here again, it is not the evidence presented by scientists that is problematic; *it is the perspective from which the evidence is viewed.* As we look at the same evidence, but through a Biblical perspective rather than a strictly physiological or psychological paradigm, our conclusions about solutions to life's challenges will be very different than those presented by our culture.

Medicated Brain or Renewed Mind

According to the American Institute of Stress, 75-90 percent of visits to primary care physicians result from stress. Research shows that around 87 percent of illnesses can be attributed to our thought life; only about 13 percent to diet, genetics, and environment.[17] When our thought life is not in agreement with the Word of God, emotions rage out of control and produce migraines, high blood pressure, irritable bowel syndrome, strokes, cancer, infections, and allergic reactions. Studies also point to a direct correlation between anxiety and an irregular heartbeat.

Researchers have acknowledged for years that rage, depression, anxiety, and other negative emotions play a large part in producing physical health problems. The twenty-first century response is to develop pharmaceutical drugs aimed at trying to change the brain chemistry so that we will feel good as quickly as possible. God's solution is to *take thoughts captive* (2 Corinthians 10:5); *set our mind on heavenly things* (Colossians 3:2); and *renew our mind* (Romans 12:1-2) so that long-term, permanent changes are made in the mind and, as a result, in our emotions and body. There is a vast difference between a medicated brain and a renewed mind.

The Physical Anatomy of Thoughts and Emotions

How we feel emotionally is a major roadblock we encounter in the process of taking thoughts captive and renewing the mind. Thoughts produce emotions, choices, and behavior. A thought or memory cannot ever be separated from the emotions that are biochemically connected to it, which makes it very difficult to act differently than we feel. In fact, *apart from the power of the Holy Spirit, it is not just difficult, but impossible to set aside wrong thinking and make choices that oppose the emotions connected to that thought.* This is the reason that chemical "solutions" are not successful long term.

A thought resembles a tree in the brain. These "trees" are made up of neuron cells that are electrically stimulated. Each tree has a trunk and many branches called dendrites. Dendrites are highly complex nerve structures which enable cells to communicate. Each person has around 100 trillion of these trees in their brain, each one capable of growing up to 70,000 branches. This means we have approximately three million years of storage space in our brains. The brain's ability is so great that it is impossible to use it up in a lifetime.[18] Believing the cultural lie that "Forty means I'm over the hill and I can't think or remember anymore" short-circuits much of what God wants to accomplish through us throughout our lifetime. Most of our difficultly remembering or thinking clearly is caused by inadequate nutrition, too much stress, and poor sleeping habits. This results in mental apathy and the failure to exert the effort required to concentrate.

Intentional concentration and memorization is necessary for the development of dendrites. Without concentration, dendrites won't develop and function efficiently even though they are continually receiving and integrating the information that comes into the brain through the five senses. The more we choose to pay attention, the more numerous the dendrite branches become. As a result, thoughts become more intelligent and accessible, and memory improves. It logically follows that a child who is not trained to concentrate will be unable to process information and will grow into an adult who, without the effort of retraining the mind, won't be able to think clearly or remember what he has just said, heard, or experienced. We blame it on old age and too much information, but the problem is predominately a diet of processed foods that are high in starches and sugars and low in nutrition, combined with lazy concentration habits. Ritalin and Adderall are sad substitutes for a nutritionally healthy brain and a mind that is trained and disciplined God's way.

The Bible teaches that as we change our habits of thought and the choices we make, our emotional responses also change. In time this leads to our feeling better. But advanced research on the brain shows that our thought habits and choices can also change our brain's structure and function over time.

In their book *Will Medicine Stop The Pain?* authors Elyse Fitzpatrick and Dr. Laura Hendrickson, M.D. highlight the findings.

> Many of us don't realize that a large body of research in the field of *neuroplasticity* shows that even adult brains change throughout life as a result of the things we learn and the thought habits we practice. When we return to college after our children leave home, or we take up a new activity, our learning produces measurable changes in the brain that reflect our new knowledge or skill. *Even people who have suffered brain damage in adulthood due to injury or stroke have been able to "retrain" the healthy parts of their brain to take over functions lost by the injured part of the brain.*
>
> As we practice Biblical principles, we introduce changes in our lives that spring from a changed heart and can result in measurable changes in our brain function. *This is very different from feeling better because a medicine has altered our brain's function by changing its chemicals* in the absence of genuine heart transformation. Medicines can't teach us to think differently; they can only suppress the feelings we have in response to our thoughts.[19]

The information received and integrated by the brain's dendrites is translated into electrical impulses and transported across synapses (small chemical gaps) between the neuron trees. Whether toxic or beneficial, each thought and its attending emotion are represented in the body as electrochemical reactions that occur in the emotional center of the brain, called the *deep limbic system.* This system encompasses a group of structures that work like a chemical factory. This "factory" includes:

- thalamus
- hypothalamus
- pituitary

- hippocampus
- amygdala (uh-MIG-duh-la)

The amygdala is central to the expression of negative emotions. It is an almond-shaped neuro-structure that stores and activates emotional perceptions each time a memory is built.

The amygdala responds to nonverbal signs of anger, avoidance, defensiveness and fear in other people. It directs behavior such as the freeze reaction, sweaty palms, tense-mouth display, and gestures such as flexing our arms or leaning away from whatever is upsetting us. If the amygdala is surgically removed, growls, screams, angry voices or facial expressions, and other negative signs may lose their meaning and become incomprehensible to the central nervous system so that there would no longer be a fear response to a threatening situation.

The amygdala mediates the bloodstream, which is our chemical nervous system. Working through the hypothalamus, the amygdala releases excitatory hormones, such as adrenaline, into the circulating blood, which disrupts the control of rational thought.

The inside of the amygdala is like a huge library that stores the emotional perceptions developed during the building of memories from time in the womb until the present. For example, if a child constantly heard a parent yell, "You can't do anything right," that memory is stored in the amygdala. Thereafter, every time the person sees similar body language, hears that tone of voice or hears someone (even his own voice in his mind) say, "You can't do anything right," he will re-experience the same feelings of shame, hurt and fear because that information passes through the amygdala, "opening the book" of that particular negative emotion.

The response from the amygdala is reactive. It is unreasoning and strong enough to override any coherent, reasoning elements that might be in a thought about the current situation. There are more connections going from the amygdala to the cortex (which is the center of decision making) than from the cortex to the amygdala. This means that the amygdala dominates the cortex, preventing reasoning from automatically taking control. *Reasoning is a response that has to be deliberately chosen.*

The cerebral cortex is the part of the brain that we call the *will.* It controls intelligence and personality and manages how we interpret what comes into the brain through the five senses. It determines motor function, planning and organization. Whenever we see, hear, touch, smell or taste something, information from our senses converges on the lower part of the cortex. From there, the information goes into the thalamus, which relays the information to the "neuron trees" in the cortex where memories are stored and activated. This performs an alerting function to prepare the brain for the incoming information. This is the first place that thoughts begin to activate an attitude.[20]

If a negative memory is alerted and "switched on," a negative attitude is activated. The emotional response carried to the thalamus will be one of negativity or stress. The information then passes back through the thalamus and hypothalamus, activating the release of chemicals in response to the emotional state.

Whatever the internal feeling—happiness, peace, excitement, anger, guilt, greed, jealousy, fear or insecurity—the chemicals released will correspond to that emotion. The positive chemicals produce and support a sense of well-being and enhance the quality of life; negative chemicals produce physical illnesses and erratic mood swings. All of these cerebral parts are interconnected and play a role in creating a biochemical representation of a thought, processing that thought, and building memory.

In our brains, the imagination is where we create. We create "movies" of the past and the future in our imaginations. We call these movies *regret* and *worry*. As directors and actors in these movies, we try to be what *The Lie* said we could be—gods apart from God. In our imaginations we see ourselves as the star of a tragic imagination "movie" in which our spouse abandons us, or we develop cancer or become bankrupt and lose our home. As the movie plays in our imagination "theater", our body registers the movie fantasy as truth. And even though we get up in the morning, still married, without cancer and with a job, the actual chemicals flowing into our body are the same poisonous biochemical reactions we would have to actual sickness or tragedy.

Biochemical Imbalances

In this sense, medical scientists are correct when they maintain that there is a biochemical problem in the brain when anxiety or depression or out-of-control emotions are present.

The problem is that if the negative progression is not stopped at its foundation (the imagination and thought processes), then medication is only a temporary, weak solution at best. Hyperactivity in children that is not caused by a specific brain injury is most often the body's response to too much stress and sensory stimulation. This happens in homes where verbal or physical abuse is common or where the atmosphere of the home is tense and anxious. Where abuse does not exist, the stimulation often comes through overexposure to television and video games. This physiological and emotional disturbance cannot be healed by "ADHD" drugs.

When adults struggle with anxiety caused by abuse, neglect or abandonment, the problem cannot be eliminated by simply taking any of the myriad of anti-anxiety drugs. They only temporarily soothe symptoms. Antidepressants and relaxant-type drugs change how we feel without changing how we think about difficult circumstances. *Drug-induced feelings that don't match our thinking or circumstances produce greater confusion* as our complex systems try to reconcile the discrepancy. The medicine enables us to *ignore the need to change our minds for a time,* but if we don't change our thinking, sooner or later we'll need different or stronger medicine to maintain the same level of "feeling better."

Pharmacological compounds are synthetic imitations of the biochemicals that *our bodies produce naturally when we are thinking in a way that is Biblically correct.* These synthetic replacements are recognized by the body to be foreign matter. The body goes into protection mode as it tries to reject the foreign substance, producing a new set of symptoms that we call "side effects."

Emotions: Roadblocks to Change

Learning how thoughts and emotions are chemically and electrically imprinted into the very cells of our bodies helps us understand why it is so difficult to act differently than we feel. We frequently refer to someone who acts differently than they feel a *hypocrite*. We may say:

- "She is such a hypocrite. I know she hates me, but she is so nice to my face."

- "I know how bad he feels, but he always puts on a happy face. It seems hypocritical and dishonest to me."

The Bible has a different viewpoint. For example, if we make the choice to be kind to someone who has hurt us, even when we really feel like getting even, the Bible calls that response obedience, not hypocrisy.

Acting Differently Than You Feel Is Obedience, Not Hypocrisy!

Hypocrisy has to do with identity, not emotion. *Hypocrisy is acting like someone we are not.* The word hypocrite comes from the Greek word *hupokrites* and describes a stage player acting under an assumed character. The Greeks loved drama and the arts, but a woman was not allowed on stage. When a woman was needed in a play, a man dressed as a woman and played the part. This man who pretended to be a woman was called a *hypocrite*, one who was acting like something he was not. It had nothing to do with how he felt.

We are instructed to choose obedience out of our new nature in Christ, *who we really are*, rather than out of how we *feel*. Emotions are not a good authority, because so many things have an impact on them:

- Emotions are affected by weather. The number of violent crimes is known to increase when a low-pressure system is moving in. When high-pressure is in place and the sun is shining, violent crimes decrease.
- Emotions are affected by a change in hormonal balances. A decrease or increase in estrogen, testosterone, thyroid, or insulin has a tangible impact on how we feel emotionally.
- Emotions are affected by tone of voice, facial expression, or body language. An encounter with another person that seems negative can have an adverse effect on the rest of the day, while an experience that feels good has a positive impact.
- Emotions are affected by memories. Remembering pleasant things produces good feelings. Remembering hurtful, sad, or disappointing events produces painful feelings.

If we let our emotions determine how we are going to respond to life:

- We will be happy one moment, unhappy the next.
- We will be up one day and down the next.
- We will be satisfied in our relationships one week and dissatisfied the next.
- We will be pleased with our job in the morning and disgusted with it that afternoon.

Jesus and Emotions

Jesus is God and eternally exists with His Father. He continued to be God during the thirty-three years He spent on earth. He is God now, seated at the right hand of the Father. He has never, and will never, cease to be God because God cannot cease to exist.

But Jesus lived every day fully human, in the way we were *designed* to be human. His life on earth is the complete model of how we are to live life after we receive salvation and are spiritually restored. Jesus did nothing during His time on earth out of His God nature (Philippians 2:5-8). He deliberately chose to set aside His right to act as God during His time on earth, living only out of His fully human nature.

- He was born into a human body. As a baby, He cried when He was hungry or cold or when His swaddling clothes were wet. The song "Away in a Manger" is incorrect when it says "no crying He makes." He was a fully human, fully helpless baby. He had no other way to make His needs known. Of course He cried!
- He grew as a human toddler. He had to be potty trained. He had to learn to feed and dress Himself. He was not born knowing how to do these things.
- He was a growing child in a family with a mom, dad, and siblings. He played, teased, wrestled, and cried in frustration. We know this because Hebrews 2:16-17 tells us "so it is evident that it was essential that He be made like His

brethren in every respect, in order that He might become a merciful, sympathetic, and faithful High Priest."

- As the eldest brother, He had opportunity to be bossy, controlling or mean, but we know that He chose not to act in that way, because He was human without ever sinning (Hebrews 4:15).
- He had opportunity to be disrespectful and disobedient to Mary and Joseph, but we know that He chose obedience instead (Hebrews 5:8).
- We don't read anything about Joseph after the incident when Jesus was left behind at the temple at age twelve. Husbands were often significantly older than their wives in this culture, so Joseph may have died while Jesus was still a teenager. As the eldest son, Jesus would have been responsible to provide for the family.
- As a teenager and young adult, Jesus was sexually tempted. Hebrews tells us that He was tempted in every way, which means He also faced the temptation of homosexual behavior. Possibly the greatest temptation in that area would have been with John, His close friend with whom He had a strong emotional bond. This does not imply in any way that either Jesus or John had homosexual tendencies; only that temptation to any wrong sexual behavior often begins with emotional closeness. But because He was sinless in His behavior, we know that He said *no* to all sexual temptation.
- When Jesus began His public ministry, people recognized Him as "the carpenter from Nazareth." He was a well-known businessman. As a businessman, He faced the temptation to overcharge, to take money-saving shortcuts, and do less than His best because of time pressure.
- Jesus was tempted to be discouraged. In Isaiah 49:1-7, we find a conversation between God the Father and Jesus that is prophetically recorded by Isaiah. The New American Standard Bible is the only English version that capitalizes the personal pronouns. This is important because if the capitalization is missing we may mistakenly read it as a conver-

sation between God and Isaiah, instead of between God the Father and Jesus the Son.

> Listen to Me, O islands, and pay attention, you peoples from afar. The Lord called Me from the womb; From the body of My mother He named Me. He has made My mouth like a sharp sword, In the shadow of His hand He has concealed Me; And He has also made Me a select arrow, He has hidden Me in His quiver. He said to Me, "You are My Servant, Israel, In Whom I will show My glory." But I (Jesus) said, "I have toiled in vain, I have spent My strength for nothing and vanity."

When would Jesus have experienced such deep discouragement? Possibly after a day of conflict with the religious leaders or perhaps after one of the times that His disciples just didn't seem to "get it." They could not seem to understand who He was or grasp the real purpose of His human life. However, Jesus didn't stay focused on the frustration. As soon as He expressed His feeling of discouragement to His Father, He shifted His focus onto what His Father had promised to accomplish in Him and through Him:

> "Yet surely the justice due to Me is with the Lord, And My reward with My God." And now says the Lord, who formed Me from the womb ... it is too small a thing that You should be My Servant to raise up the tribes of Jacob and to restore the preserved ones of Israel; I will also make You a light of the nations so that My salvation may reach to the end of the earth ... kings will see and arise, princes will also bow down, because of the Lord Who is faithful, the Holy One of Israel who has chosen You. (NASU)

- Jesus was faced with the opportunity to use drugs to numb the sharp edges of reality as He hung on the cross. (Mark 15:23). He refused because He trusted his Father to support Him and meet His needs in that time of horrendous pain.

We can accept that Jesus was fully human in these things, but confusion begins when we read the accounts of Him:

- Walking on the water (Matthew 14:25-27)
- Stilling the storm (Matthew 8:24-26)
- Calling up a fish with money in its mouth (Matthew 17:25-27)

We immediately think, “This is Jesus being God, right?” No! Since we know that He set aside His right to accomplish the Father’s will as God, then we know that He did these “miraculous” things as a fully human man, taking the authority over nature that God gave to humankind from the very beginning.

> God said, Let Us (Father, Son, and Holy Spirit) make mankind in Our image, after Our likeness, and *let them have complete authority* over the fish of the sea, the birds of the air, the (tame) beasts, and over all of the earth, and over everything that creeps upon the earth.
>
> Genesis 1:26

When First Adam chose rebellion against God in the Garden of Eden, all of humankind lost the privilege of living in a loving relationship with the Creator, and of exercising wise authority over all creation. In order to win back for humankind what a human being (First Adam) threw away, Jesus was incarnated as Last Adam, a fully human man (Romans 5:17). During His life on earth, Jesus modeled for us what it means to be in relationship with our Father (John 5:19). He also showed us what happens when we listen to what Father says and exercise authority over nature. He did not still every storm, but when His Father said, “Tell this storm to be quiet,” He spoke to the storm, and it was instantly calm. He took human authority over nature when He walked across the water and when He spoke a blessing into five small loaves of bread and two little fish so that five thousand men and their families ate with plenty left over. He was able to heal the sick, raise the dead, make deaf ears hear and blind eyes see by listening to what His Father wanted Him to do and letting the power of the Holy Spirit work through His choices, His hands, His feet, and His voice.

"Yes, But That Was Jesus ..."

Jesus is not the only human being who modeled the miraculous.

- Elijah took authority over the weather, and neither dew nor rain fell for three and a half years (James 5:17).
- Elisha took authority over an axe head, and iron floated on the top of the water (2 Kings 6:4-7).
- Moses and Elisha both took authority over water and commanded it to divide so they could pass through on dry land (Exodus 14:21 and 2 Kings 2:14).
- Joshua took authority over nature, and the sun stood still (Joshua 10:12-13).
- Elijah multiplied flour and oil for the widow and her son (1 Kings 17:9-16).
- Elijah raised a child from the dead (1 Kings 17:19-22).
- Elisha's bones brought life into a corpse (2 Kings 13:21).
- Peter spoke a word and a man crippled from birth could walk (Acts 3:4-8).
- Paul was not affected by a poisonous snake bite; he laid hands on the sick and they were healed (Acts 28:3-9).

These people were all human beings just as we are! The miracles that Jesus did are not Jesus acting as God. He did and said everything as a fully human man with a sinless human nature, empowered by the Holy Spirit and in relationship with God the Father.

This same description belongs to the believer. We are fully human. When we are born into God's family by the Holy Spirit, we are given a sinless human nature (new man) in exchange for the sin nature (old man) with which we were born. We are empowered by the same Holy Spirit and in relationship with the same Father God. The Bible describes the differences between the old man: First Adam and his body, which is humanity in rebellion against God, and the new man: Last Adam (Jesus) and His body, the Church. This is humanity reconciled to God.

At creation, God announced that the human design was very good. Jesus did not come to earth to deliver us from being human. Rather,

He came to earth, fully human, *to redeem us from the sin* that contaminated God's wonderful human creation when First Adam chose to disobey. When we live in sin, we are less than fully human, less than God designed us to be. Jesus decisively defeated sin and Satan on the cross so that we no longer live under the power of evil. Jesus, our Head, ascended to the throne, giving us, His Body, the mandate that we find in Matthew 28:16-20:

> Now the eleven disciples went to Galilee, to the mountain to which Jesus had directed and made appointment with them. And when they saw Him, they fell down and worshiped Him; but some doubted. Jesus approached and, breaking the silence, said to them, "All authority, all power of rule, in heaven and on earth has been given to Me. Go then and make disciples of all the nations, baptizing them into the name of the Father and of the Son and of the Holy Spirit, teaching them to observe everything that I have commanded you ..."
>
> Mathew 28:16-20

As His hands and feet; eyes, ears and voice, we are to do whatever Jesus modeled for us by the example of His earthly life. He commands us to go as His Body, in the authority of His Name, and by His power, do the good works He began as Jesus of Nazareth. His plan is to accomplish and complete His will on earth through us.

> Most assuredly, I say to you, he who believes in Me, the works that I do he will do also; and greater works than these he will do, because I go to My Father. And whatever you ask in My name, that I will do, that the Father may be glorified in the Son. If you ask anything in My name, I will do it.
>
> John 14:12-14 (NKJV)

Jesus and the Other Garden

In the Garden of Gethsemane, as Jesus prepared to die for the redemption of humanity, He told His disciples that His "soul was grieved to the point of death." We read these words casually, but Jesus is expressing fear, anxiety, and grief that was so heavy, He felt like He was going to die before He got to the cross. The Amplified Bible explains:

> Then He said to His disciples, "My soul is very sad and deeply grieved, so that I am almost dying of sorrow."
>
> Matthew 26:38

In our vernacular, we might say, "I was scared stiff" (indicating death or being paralyzed by fear), or "I was so terrified, I thought I was going to die." Jesus was so stricken by anxiety that He had great clots of blood oozing out of the pores of His skin (Luke 22:44). This is a condition known as *hematohidrosis,* a well recognized condition in which a human being sweats blood when suffering extreme levels of stress.

Dr. Frederick Zugibe, Chief Medical Examiner of Rockland County, New York says,

> There have been many documented cases of this condition. It happens like this: around the sweat glands, there are multiple blood vessels in a net-like form. Under the pressure of great stress, the vessels dilate to the point of rupture. The blood goes into the sweat glands. As the sweat glands are producing copious amounts of sweat, it pushes the blood to the surface, coming out as blood mixed with sweat. [21]

In Gethsemane, Jesus was under such intense pressure of dread and anxiety that His blood vessels were bursting. His disciples had abandoned Him emotionally, and He was lying on His face on the ground pleading, "Please Father, if there is any other way to do this, I don't want to do it this way!"

And yet, as a fully human man, Jesus was able to override the emotions with His will and agree with His Father that if this was the only way to complete what they planned together before the earth was created, He was willing (Luke 22:42).

The question is sometimes asked, "Would it really have been possible for Jesus to say no to the cross?" We find the answer in Matthew's account of Jesus's arrest. Soon after Jesus came to wake His disciples from their exhausted sleep, Judas arrived, leading a group of religious leaders and soldiers into the garden to arrest Jesus. Peter bravely lashed out with his sword, cutting off the ear of the high priest's servant. Jesus said to him, "Put your sword back into its place, for all who draw the sword will die by the sword. Do you suppose that I cannot appeal to my Father, and He will immediately provide Me with more than twelve legions (more than 80,000) of angels? But how then would the Scriptures be fulfilled, that it must come about this way?" (Matthew 26:52-54).

Scripture indicates that Jesus could have chosen not to go through with the crucifixion, and it does not say that God the Father would be displeased and would disown the Son. Jesus could have refused without condemnation and would have escaped the cross. But if He had acted out of how He felt, we would have been left with no means of reconciliation to our loving Creator, and the Bride that Jesus loves so tenderly would not have come into existence. In spite of how Jesus felt emotionally, He chose obedience to God, and God "exalted Him, giving Him a name that is above every name" (Philippians 2:8-9).

Emotions: A "No-brainer"

Our emotions are closely tied to our belief systems. Every event that either forms or reinforces a belief is tied to the emotions that occurred at the time of the event. Certain music, sights and scents, such as perfumes or bread baking can stir up memories and emotions. Even though our memory of an event is never fully accurate, it will feel true and real. This is why emotions are not a good basis for making choices about how we are going to talk or act.

We are going to use five *B* words to help us understand emotions better:

1. barometer
2. bewildered
3. buried
4. brain
5. balance

1. Barometer: Our emotions are like a barometer, an instrument that measures changes in atmospheric pressure. We cannot see air pressure, but we can observe changes in air pressure by noticing whether the liquid in the glass is higher or lower. The liquid

in the glass makes invisible atmospheric pressure "visible." *In the same way, emotions make our invisible thoughts visible.*

- If our emotions are constantly sad, we can be sure our thoughts are set in a sad pattern.
- If we are continually feeling anger in our emotions, we know the mind is busy with angry thoughts.
- The same is true of any other emotion.

Our emotions could also be compared to the warning lights that we find on the dashboard of a car. These lights are neither good nor bad. They simply give us information about what is going on underneath the hood in places we can't see. And we don't have to be an experienced mechanic to know that if a picture of an oil can comes on and we keep driving, the problem is not just going to go away. If we ignore the light, the engine will soon be damaged beyond repair.

Our emotions are neither good nor bad, even though some may feel better than others. Emotions are morally neutral, and as we learn to identify the emotions we experience, we can use them as an indicator of what is going on in the mind in places we cannot see.

Thoughts produce emotions. An emotion cannot exist without an underlying thought. Our thought patterns are so deeply ingrained and familiar to us that we often don't even realize a particular thought pattern has begun to play. This can be illustrated by the way music is burned onto the surface of a CD. When the disc is placed in a CD player, whatever music has been recorded will be audible through the speakers. If country music is recorded there, contemporary Christian music will never come through the speakers, no matter how often the disc is replayed.

Our thought patterns begin to be "burned" into our minds from the moment we are born into our family environment. An *event* is the "play button" that starts a particular thought process. *Emotions* and *choices* are the "speakers" that make our thoughts audible and visible to others through our behavior.

When an event takes place, our old familiar thought patterns start spinning without any effort on our part. If the thoughts are filled with frustration, joy will not come out in our behavior. If they are envious and critical, love and peace will not be displayed. In the same way that the CD can only play what has been recorded, our emotions and behavior can only exhibit what has been recorded into our minds. Renewing the mind (chapter eight) is the only way to change the "recording" in order to enjoy permanent changes in emotions and behavior.

Emotions are a visible expression of the inner working of our minds. An emotion is simply a tool to give us an awareness of our thoughts. When we feel a particular emotion (for example, frustration or impatience or fear), we know that a specific thought pattern is playing. As we recognize it, we can begin the process of replacing it with a new thought that agrees with God's Word.

2. Bewildered: A major problem with our emotions is that they are bewildered. Our emotions have been trained by environment and repetition to respond to certain situations, sights, sounds, and smells in a particular way. Because this training was done in an imperfect, sinful world by imperfect, sinful people, our emotions have become confused and often out of control.

3. Buried: We can bury our emotions, but we need to know that we are burying something that is alive and will stay alive. *Emotions that are "buried alive" destabilize the natural chemistry of the brain.* By their very design, emotions are made to be felt and expressed. The more we try to hide them, the more they will make themselves known, usually through physical symptoms such as constipation or diarrhea, nausea and vomiting, ulcers, irritable bowel syndrome, fertility problems, muscular tension, and brittle bones. Synthetic chemicals further suppress emotions, setting us up for a greater problem as time goes on.

4. Brain: We live in a culture that has given ultimate authority to the emotions. This is dangerous because emotions do not have a brain for reasoning. Consider what happens to our emotions when we watch a "tear-jerker" movie. The hero dies, and his beautiful girlfriend mourns, tears flowing down her cheeks. We find ourselves grieving with her as tears flow down *our* cheeks. Why? It's just a flat picture on a flat wall. It's an

imaginary story that is being acted out by people who are alive and well. Why would our emotions respond as though it's a real death happening to real people? Because emotions cannot think! Emotions cannot recognize the difference between reality and fantasy or between accurate and inaccurate memories. Consequently, emotions will respond to fact and fantasy, lies and truth in exactly the same way.

Emotions cannot assess a situation and make a rational decision about what needs to be done. They can only react in the way they have been trained by environment to react to the immediate sights, sounds, and conditions. Memories aroused by the current conditions become a part of the mixture. As a result, we often experience a response to a situation, a comment, or facial expression that is totally out of proportion to what is actually happening at the moment.

5. Balance: Since our emotions don't have a brain and cannot think, it is critically important that we take back the authority we have given to them and turn instead to our ultimate authority, God and His Word. This is accomplished as we sort through our belief systems and renew the mind. The result is a healthy balance between a renewed mind, a will that is being strengthened and emotions that are being brought under the control of the mind and the will. As we practice, practice, practice, we grow in our ability to relax and enjoy the pleasurable emotions and become better at hearing the warnings the uncomfortable or painful emotions send.

1. What emotions were considered "acceptable" when you were growing up?

____

____

____

2. What emotions were considered "unacceptable" when you were growing up?

____

____

____

3. What are the physical "red flags" that warn you of an unexpressed emotion?

____

____

____

God, David, and Emotions

Our culture tells us that emotions are our authority, and how we feel is how we should act. We are given two basic ways to handle our emotions:

1. The first is to *bury* all of the hurt, anger, or frustration down inside and literally become a walking garbage can. This only postpones the inevitable explosion that will come as the pressure builds. "Stuffers" experience health problems because our bodies are not designed to be storage containers for toxic emotion.
2. The second option is to *blow up* and vent all of the emotion on the nearest person, whether that person is a part of bringing the emotion to the surface or not. Children or those who are smaller or seem weaker are usually the victims of these tirades.

Neither of these options is helpful or good. If we bury an emotion, it builds pressure that will eventually explode. On the other hand, continually venting our emotions on others hurts them, because no human being is designed to be someone else's garbage can.

Believers have a third option that many Christians either don't know about or would not dare to take advantage of because of a distorted, fearful view of God. This third option is to acknowledge our emotions and pour them out on God. Of course, if we believe that He is angry or distant and uninterested, we are not going to take emotions to Him that we believe will make Him angrier or cause Him to like us less.

We can learn how to avoid painful consequences by reading about David's life experiences and taking his admonitions to heart. Psalm 55 is a clear illustration of how to take our emotions to the Lord. Knowing the context and history behind this psalm will help us not to shrug and say, "David was king, and had all the money and power he could ever need. I don't think his struggles were real, at least not as complicated as mine."

David wrote this psalm at a very difficult time in his life. His oldest and favorite son, Absalom, was attempting to overthrow his throne and become king in David's place. David had a friend named Ahithophel, who was his closest friend and political advisor. We discover in 2 Samuel 11:3 and 2 Samuel 23:34 that Bathsheba was the daughter of Eliam, who was the son of Ahithophel. Ahithophel was Bathsheba's grandfather!

The sordid story of David's affair with Bathsheba and the subsequent murder of her husband, Uriah, is found in 2 Samuel 11-12. At some time, perhaps rejected by friends because of his circumstances, David came to trust Ahithophel completely.

Absalom's rebellion took place about twelve years after David and Bathsheba were married. Psalm 55:20-21 indicates that Ahithophel held bitterness against David during that time; perhaps he loved Uriah and blamed David for Bathsheba's trouble. Ahithophel may have been bitter about the death of their first baby—his great-grandson. Whatever the cause, he was deeply embittered against David but buried it and hid it well for some years.

Absalom planned to turn the hearts of the people away from David and toward himself by sitting in the city gate and undermining the people's confidence in David (2 Samuel 15). When he gathered an army and began marching against Jerusalem, David fled in fear for his life.

At this crucial time, Ahithophel betrayed David by joining forces with Absalom, while still giving advice to David. Second Samuel 16:23 says that "the counsel of Ahithophel in those days was as if a man had consulted the Word of God; so was all Ahithophel's counsel considered both by David and by Absalom." Some of the advice Ahithophel gave to Absalom at this time was to take David's concubines and have sex with them on the roof of the palace, in full view of the people of Jerusalem. It was a way of showing the ultimate disrespect toward David (2 Samuel 16:20-22).

So while David was still dependent upon Ahithophel for information and advice, Ahithophel was encouraging Absalom to greater rebellion, stirring up increasing strife and mistrust between the father and son. It was in this agonizing time of fear and hurt that David wrote Psalm 55, expressing a full range of emotions to God.

Verses 1-2: David expresses anger toward God: "Why aren't you listening to me, God? Stop hiding Yourself from me!" The implication from David is that if God had been paying attention, this situation would not have happened.

What time in your life did you feel anger toward God for "allowing" something to happen?

____

____

____

Verses 3-5: David tells God what is happening and that he is terrified. What situations in your life are most likely to make you feel afraid?

____

____

____

Verses 6-8: David tells God that he wants to escape from it all when he says, "If only I had wings like a dove, I would fly into the wilderness and be at rest."

What have you wanted to escape from?

____

____

Verses 9-12: David accuses his enemies, Ahithophel, Absalom, and their armies, of violence, fraud, and deceit. He is angry at the betrayal and wants God to destroy their schemes.

Describe a time that you felt betrayed by someone you trusted.

Verses 13-14: David expresses the deep hurt that he feels from the rejection and betrayal of a son and an intimate friend. "We had sweet fellowship together, and we used to walk in the house of the Lord together," he laments.

Describe a time that you felt betrayed by a fellow believer.

Did the hurt feel deeper because he/she was a believer? If so, why?

Verse 15: As he thinks about the betrayal and his frustration grows, David goes from wanting God to destroy the *schemes* of his enemies to wanting God to destroy *them*! "Haul my betrayers off alive to hell—let them experience the horror, let them feel every desolate detail of a damned life" (from *The Message*). David is expressing a murderous rage that wants his enemies to live forever, suffering the torments of hell.

Describe a time that you wanted God to "get" someone when they hurt you.

What belief do you have that makes you think God wants to "make them pay" for what they've done to you?

Is your belief supported by Scripture that you have learned or heard about? If yes, list the Scripture or write the general idea of the Scripture as you understand it.

Verses 16-17: David makes a deliberate decision to call on the Lord for help and strength.

Describe a time that you prayed for God to help you and give you strength.

Did it seem to you that God heard you or ignored you? Why?

Verses 18-19: Even though his situation has not changed, David is beginning to express confidence in God. "He has redeemed my life in peace from the battle that was against me; God will hear and humble them, even God who sits enthroned forever." What is the significance of David's recognition that God is "enthroned forever"?

____

____

Verses 20-21: David reminds God again of how devious and hypocritical Ahithophel has been.

Why was it necessary for David to tell God again how badly he had been treated?

____

____

Verses 22-23: David reminds himself to take his burdens to the Lord and expresses confidence that it is the Lord who will "bring down the wicked."

What is the difference between David's attitude here and in verse 15?

____

____

____

Why Tell God? I Thought He Already Knew Everything

God was not shocked or horrified at David's expression of anger. He knew long before David did that the hurt of betrayal was going to grow into that tremendous, murderous rage. In Psalm 51:6 David says that God "desires truth in the innermost being." This is not because God needs information about what is going on, but because when we become honest about the emotion seething inside, then God can do the work in us that needs to be done.

God does not deal with hurt and rage in the same way. Where there is hurt, He brings healing; where there is rage and bitterness, He guides us into a different way of thinking and forgiveness.

It was important that David expressed his emotions to God rather than to Ahithophel. If David had confronted Ahithophel and told him that he wanted him to go alive to Sheol, there would likely have been a fight, leading to the death of one or both since they were trained soldiers. Because David knew God, he entrusted the outcome of his situation to Him.

In the middle of the revolt, Ahithophel advised Absalom about how to fight against his father's troops. Another commander named Hushai disagreed and gave advice to Absalom that made more sense to the young rebel. When Ahithophel saw that his advice was not being taken, he realized that he had lost control over Absalom. He saddled his donkey, went home, put his house in order, and hung himself (2 Samuel 17).

The armies of David and Absalom met to settle the attempted overthrow, resulting in the death of 20,000 men. When the battle turned against Absalom, he acknowledged his failure, mounted his donkey, and fled. As he rode under a low-hanging tree, Absalom's head was caught in the fork of two branches. As he hung helplessly, the commander of David's army killed him, bringing an end to the rebellion (2 Samuel 18:1-17).

Just Get Over It

Why does the healing process take so long? Why can't people just "get over it"? In spite of how often we use this phrase, we know it is not an easy task to move beyond emotional hurt, disappointment, rage and fear. In fact, it's impossible if we don't make some very deliberate choices about our thinking.

"Collateral damage" is a phrase that came out of the Gulf War. When a Scud missile was fired, where it landed was the center of the damage. Any other damage away from the direct hit was called collateral damage.

In 1995, the Alfred P. Murrah building in Oklahoma City was severely damaged in a domestic terrorist attack against the U.S. government that claimed 168 lives and injured over 800 people. The wreckage of the Federal building was eventually torn down and hauled away, but before the new building and the Oklahoma City Memorial Park were built to replace the damaged area, collateral damage was visible for blocks around the center of the explosion. There were broken and boarded windows, cracks in the walls of nearby buildings, and scars on walls still standing. Hidden damage extended down into the foundations of some adjacent structures.

- The initial impact took several seconds.
- The rescue of the survivors took several days.
- The finding of all the bodies took several weeks.
- The cleanup of the rubble took several months.
- The repairing of the collateral damage took several years.
- The building of the memorial on the site of the old Federal building took more than seven years.

While the cleanup and rebuilding was taking place, Timothy McVeigh was tried for the crime, found guilty, and sentenced to death. He was executed in 2001. The families of the dead and injured spent days facing the results of the tragedy and making decisions that either moved them forward into a "rebuilding" of emotions or kept them stuck in the horror of April 19, 1995.

When our emotions have taken a direct hit through abuse, neglect, or any of the myriad hurts that we face, the process of cleaning up often does not begin as immediately as it did in Oklahoma City. Hidden damage can be extensive. Very often, the pain is so great that the one who is injured begins to "board up" the damage with attempted forgetfulness, sometimes because it hurts too much and sometimes because we are told that Christians are supposed to be "like God" and forget.

Forgiving and Forgetting Are Not Conjoined Twins

God isn't forgetful! An attribute that is a part of His infinite nature is omniscience: knowing all things at all times without having to learn what He knows. If God ever forgot anything, He would not be infinitely all-knowing. We are created in His image, and even though our ability to recall things is finite, we can't "just forget it" either.

This confusion about forgiveness comes from Jeremiah 31:34 and Hebrews 10:17 where God says, "I will forgive their iniquity, and I will remember their sin no more." *Forgetting* describes a loss of information over time, a meaning that is not found in the Biblical definition of forgiveness. *Forget* is an American-English misinterpretation of the phrase: "remember no more." The word *zakar* (zaw-kar') means to mark, so as to be recognized; by implication, to mention. A more accurate understanding of God's statement is that God deliberately chooses not to recall our offenses. He refuses to mention or think on our transgressions. To do so even once would dishonor the blood sacrifice of His Son.

Since emotions are produced by what we think, if we continue to focus on our hurts and disappointments, replaying them over and over again, our emotions will stay in turmoil. On the other hand, if we try to ignore the hurts and disappointments by "just forgetting about them," the buried emotions become a festering sore.

Because we are being formed into the likeness of God's Son, (Romans 8:29) we too can *choose not to dwell* on offenses done toward us. Forgiveness is "releasing a debt." To "remember no more" like God means that when a suffered offense comes to our mind and we're tempted to repeat the details either to ourselves or someone else, at that moment we *choose to refuse* to dwell on it or talk about it. Instead, we *choose to rehearse the truth* that the wrong done to us was washed away by the blood of Jesus. Choosing to recount the hurt discredits the price Jesus paid to cleanse not only our sins, but the sins of those who offend us in some way. It is *not* possible to forget; it *is* possible to remember no more. (See page 156-157 for forgiveness worksheet and "Commitment of Forgiveness.") Forgiveness is the only vehicle that will haul away the rubble of resentment, bitterness, and revenge. When the rubble is cleared, we can rebuild our joy and freedom, even if a relationship is not restored. Using the Oklahoma City bombing illustration:

- The explosion of the bomb is the offense done against us.
- The rubble is the cover-up of denial.
- The consequences of denial are ulcers, addictions, rage, and eating disorders. This is like sorting through the rubble looking for bodies after all hope of finding survivors is gone.

- Hauling away the rubble is recognizing the hurt and choosing to forgive.
- Renewing the mind is remembering the offense differently and rebuilding. There will probably always be some scars and reminders, even years after, but they no longer control life.
- The Bombing Museum in the old Journal Record building illustrates how we recount the hurt repeatedly, keeping the memory alive. This keeps people stuck in the pain of the past.

Isaiah 43:18: "Do not (earnestly) remember the former things; neither consider the things of old." Again, the idea expressed is not the loss of information, but refusing to replay hurtful events over and over again.

Summary

To help us summarize, here are six *a* words that describe emotions:

- Emotions are easily *aroused.*
- Emotions are *argumentative.*
- Emotions are *assertive.*
- Emotions are *announcers, not authority.*
- Emotions must be *arrested.*
- Emotions must be *allayed.*

The acrostic O-V-E-R describes how we "get over" emotional hurt:

O - observe
V - verbalize
E - evaluate
R - resolve

1. O - Observe which emotion you are experiencing. Is the emotion hurt? Is it envy? Or rage? Frustration? Christians may try to define an emotion (anger) by one that seems more acceptable (hurt). It is important to be honest with ourselves about what we feel. This takes practice, *and is for our benefit, not for God's information.*

2. V - Verbalize to God first, not people. If we take our emotional reaction to people first, the explosion will cause damage. If we go to God first, release our emotions on Him and receive what we need from Him, we are far less likely to explode on people when the time comes for discussion.

3. E - Evaluate what your emotions tell you about your thinking. *Remember that thoughts produce emotions.* Emotions make invisible thoughts visible to others. As you become aware of your thoughts and listen to what God has to say about the situation, He will enable you to change any thought patterns that are Biblically wrong and harmful. Describe the thinking indicated by your emotions.

4. R - Resolve or determine to make decisions about your situation according to what you hear from God, not according to how you feel. Look for Scriptural support for what you are hearing from God. Be careful not to use just one verse, which can lead to proof texting, but find overall attitudes and instruction from the Word of God.
   What is your decision concerning your current situation?

What Scripture helped you to make this decision?

____

____

____

A Biblical View of Depression

Those suffering from the debilitating effects of depression and anxiety may defensively insist that they need medication "because the physical symptoms are real." But it isn't a question of whether the physical symptoms are real; they undoubtedly are. The question that needs to be answered is, "*Why do the symptoms exist*?" For the believer, the pressing question should not be "Which new drug will relieve my symptoms?" but "How does my thinking need to change so that I am able to live freely the way God designed me to live?"

The Bible tells us this freedom can be ours no matter what our circumstances are like when we are in Christ and are being changed into His likeness, from the inside to the outside. Romans 12:1-2 specifically instructs believers not to "be conformed to this age, fashioned after its external, superficial customs, but be changed by the entire renewal of your mind, by its new ideals and its new attitude."

The world is crying out for answers to the overwhelming concerns that are a part of life on this sin-wrecked planet. God has promised that His children can experience joy rather than sadness, peace instead of anxiety, and hope in place of despair through His Son, Jesus. God's Word tells us how to joyfully endure when our life experience isn't what we want it to be.

Because we are created in the image of God, we cannot know ourselves and experience joy, peace, and hope apart from knowing Him. Just as a light bulb has no function or purpose apart from electricity, humankind has no reason for existence apart from God.

Our "before Christ" separation from God produced the sense of rejection and abandonment that defines the fallen human condition. The human spirit becomes fully alive at the moment of conception, so we are spiritually aware of the separation long before the brain is rationally able to process that fact. Consequently, even in infancy we are already contaminated with fear, loneliness, and the desperate need to be accepted. These needs are so deep they cannot be adequately met by anything or anyone but God. The futile attempt of the human race to find meaning and purpose apart from God only magnifies the hopeless emptiness and frustration.

Even after receiving salvation, anger continues to be a very real and often misunderstood part of the lives of Christians. Believers frequently feel guilty about anger because we've been taught that Christians should not feel that way. Ephesians 4:26 acknowledges that anger is a part of life but admonishes, "In your anger, do not sin." We typically define sinful anger as yelling, foul language or violence, and that certainly qualifies as wrong behavior. But what about sinful anger that is expressed quietly as anxiety, depression, resentment, or apathy?

Write out Philippians 4:6:

____

____

____

In John 14:27, Jesus's instruction to His disciples at a very stressful, fearful time, just before His crucifixion, was straightforward and clear:

> Peace I leave with you; My (own) peace I now give and bequeath to you. Not as the world gives do I give to you. Do not let your hearts be troubled, neither let them be afraid. (Stop allowing yourselves to be agitated and disturbed; and do not permit yourselves to be fearful and intimidated and cowardly and unsettled.)

Grumbling, fretting, and living in continual anxiety is an audible expression of the sin of unbelief which ends in depression. Solomon, the wisest man who ever lived, tells us that "anxiety in the heart of man causes depression" (Proverbs 12:25).

When we allow ourselves to be "pressed into the mold of this age," we will accept the cultural solutions for life's problems almost without question. But either the Bible is truth, or the world's wisdom is truth;

we cannot have it both ways. James gave clear instruction about how to think concerning trials. His description of the double mindedness of the church of his day accurately describes the American twenty-first-century church as well:

> Consider it wholly joyful, my brethren, whenever you are enveloped in or encounter trials of any sort or fall into various temptations. Be assured and understand that the trial and proving of your faith bring out endurance and steadfastness and patience. But let endurance and steadfastness and patience have full play and do a thorough work, so that you may be (people) perfectly and fully developed (with no defects), lacking in nothing. If any of you is deficient in wisdom, let him ask of the giving God (who gives) to everyone liberally and ungrudgingly, without reproaching or fault-finding, and it will be given him. Only it must be in faith that he asks with no wavering (no hesitating, no doubting). For the one who wavers (hesitates, doubts) is like the billowing surge out at sea that is blown hither and thither and tossed by the wind. For truly, let not such a person imagine that he will receive anything (he asks for) from the Lord, (for being as he is) a man of two minds (hesitating, dubious, irresolute), (he is) unstable and unreliable and uncertain about everything (he thinks, feels, decides).
>
> James 1:2-8

Expectations

An expectation is the assumption that something we are looking forward to will take place. We build expectations primarily through three avenues: (1) comparisons of ourselves with others; (2) spoken or implied commitments from others; (3) our God-given needs to be loved, accepted, secure, and of value.

The expectations we hold concerning ourselves, other people, and what life should be like are developed in the context of our unique belief system. When these expectations, both realistic and unrealistic, are not fulfilled in the ways that we believe they should be, the emotional result is anger, disappointment, and the sense that "life isn't fair."

The words *should, ought*, or *shouldn't* always denote an expectation.

If we live life expecting others to do things the way we believe they should or shouldn't be done, the following pattern will develop:

1. We expect too much of imperfect people in an imperfect world.
2. We don't get what we expect.
3. We become angry and frustrated.
4. We demand what we expected.
5. We still don't get what we expected.
6. We become passively or aggressively angry.
7. We begin to threaten and manipulate through violence or silence.
8. We attack: verbally, physically, or by withdrawing.

Even our most unrealistic expectations feel realistic to us. Here are some guidelines to assess where our expectations may fall on a scale of 1-10—one being realistic; ten being very unrealistic. An expectation may be reasonably realistic if:

1. The other person *is able* to give you what you are asking for.
2. The other person *wants* to give you what you are asking for.
3. Giving you what you want *does not consistently take away* from what the other person wants or needs.
4. Giving you what you want *does not make the other person feel disrespected, ashamed, or guilty.*

The reality is, even when an expectation is realistic, there is no guarantee that we will get what we want or need, how and when we've asked for it. When we expect "a lot" and don't know how to give the expectations to the Lord, we live under the burden of constant disappointment. As we learn to accept that life is seldom what it "should" be—rather, "it is what it is"—we will more often find enjoyment in life *as it is* while waiting on the Lord to make the needed changes.

Sometimes people believe if they "expect nothing at all," they will avoid disappointment. But thinking this way doesn't *avoid* expectations, it simply produces a negative mindset that always expects the worst to happen. This inevitably ends in bitterness and resentment and produces a whining, complaining attitude that destroys relationships.

The lasting solution is to take each expectation, especially those that are unfulfilled, to the Lord and receive from Him what is needed. Medicating the physical symptoms produced by depression and anxiety will not solve the problem. In fact, temporarily alleviating symptoms may actually make the person physically comfortable enough that the spiritual root of resentment and bitterness will not be confronted.

Physical and emotional healing is accomplished over time as expectations are expressed to the Lord, perhaps many times a day at first. As the choice is made to receive from God, needs are met in the way He sees best, and the believer depends less on imperfect people in an imperfect world to get needs fulfilled. This diminishes the likelihood that we will manipulate people and circumstances to feel the way we want to feel.

This is simply choosing to trust God instead of people and circumstances, looking to Him as the only real source of contentment, joy, and security. When expectations, disappointment, and anger are not settled Biblically, we descend a "staircase" of emotional chaos, at the bottom of which lies depression. This is not a chemical imbalance *originating in the body*, but *hopeless despair that germinates and grows in the mind*, producing physical symptoms.

Expectations Evaluation

Complete each statement in just a few words or a sentence.

1. God is …

____

____

2. God will always …

____

____

3. God will never …

____

____

4. God should . . .

5. I am . . .

6. I will always . . .

7. I will never . . .

8. I should . . .

9. Other people are . . .

10. Other people always . . .

11. Other people never . . .

____

12. Other people should ...

____

____

13. Christians are ...

____

____

14. Christians always ...

____

____

15. Christians never ...

____

____

16. Christians should ...

____

____

Eight Steps to Depression

Expectations and Anger:

Eight Steps That Lead to Depression

Expectations are assumptions built on valid needs, verbal or implied commitments and comparisons made by ourselves and others.

Disappointment and anger are the emotions that arise when expectations are not fulfilled, or are not met in the way that we wanted them to be.

Grief is the sense of bereavement that comes when something we were looking forward to does not happen, or when someone we depended upon is no longer available to us either physically or emotionally.

Bitterness is associated with wrath, slander and malice (Ephesians 4:31). It is a toxic poison that contaminates everyone it touches. Forgiveness is the only antidote for this destructive toxin. (Hebrews 12:15).

Revenge is the desire to "get even." Revenge comes with an attitude of malice (anger which is hardening into rage and hatred). "Getting even" is an attempt to make things "fair"—according to our own personal definition of fairness. The problem is that each of us has our own idea of fair; what I believe is fair will inevitably seem unfair to someone else.

Resentment and ingratitude: When we cannot make things turn out "fair," we become more indignant and offended, developing an ungrateful attitude, coupled with selfishness, arrogance, disobedience and rebellion. (2 Timothy 3:2-4)

Agitation, restlessness and the inability to enjoy life: This condition stems from a persistent attitude of irritation, annoyance and ingratitude. Repentance from unbelief and complaining, and deliberately cultivating a heart that is grateful for the underserved grace of God is the only remedy for this miserable condition.

Depression, physical illness and death: Wounded, out-of-control emotions have a powerful effect on physical heath (Psalm 38:6-8; 102:3-7). To avoid or eliminate depression and to enjoy improved physical health, hurts, disappointments and wounded emotions must be taken to the Lord for healing.

The first three steps (expectations, disappointment, and grief) cannot be avoided. Because we are created in the image of a perfectly just God, it is impossible even for the unsaved to live without expecting goodness and justice. And because we live in a sin-poisoned world where imperfect people behave imperfectly, anger, disappointment, and the grief of loss are inevitable. However, the first three steps are not the cause of depression. Depression is the end result of continuing to walk down the "staircase" by choosing to live in unforgiveness, resentment, self-pity and ingratitude. We can't stop people from letting us down, but we can choose Godly responses in the hurt that follows. For example, Ephesians 4:31 describes how we are to respond verbally when someone hurts us:

> Let all bitterness, indignation, and wrath (which are passion, rage, and bad temper), resentment, (which is anger and animosity), quarreling (which is brawling, clamor, and contention), and slander (which is evil-speaking, abusive or blasphemous language) be banished from you, with all malice (spite, ill will, or baseness of any kind).
>
> Ephesians 4:31

The words *be banished* describe a violent personal action, as if throwing off a filthy or contaminated piece of clothing. God does not take away our sinful attitudes; we choose by His power to put them away. We walk back up the "staircase" by choosing to forgive those who hurt us, releasing them from our own personal expectations and demand for repayment. If restitution needs to be made, we defer the right to make it happen to God. He says He will take care of it (Romans 12:17-19).

This Thing Called Anger

Anger is an unavoidable part of life. It is both an emotional and a physical response to circumstances

Jesus expressed great anger toward the injustice and dishonesty that was being carried out in the temple when He drove out the moneychangers (John 2:14-17) and when He verbally scourged the Pharisees for their hypocrisy (Matthew 23:23-33). The anger that Jesus expressed was not a selfish defense of His own agenda. His anger was aroused because religious leaders were taking advantage of sincere people who wanted to come to the temple to worship God. We know that Jesus was without sin; therefore, we know that it is possible to express anger in a Godly way.

We have identified the underlying cause of anger as unmet expectations, both realistic and unrealistic. Defining some commonly used words gives a clearer understanding of what anger is and what it is not.

1. Anger (the physical response): Anger in the body is a physical condition that prepares us to respond to a crisis. This physical readiness always takes place in the face of fear, hurt, or frustration. Anger is *physical power* as the body goes into high alert; more adrenaline is secreted, more sugar is released into the bloodstream, the heart beats faster so that blood pressure rises and the pupil of the eye opens wide. *Anger* is sometimes used to describe turbulent waves or dark, threatening clouds. These things do not have an emotion, so in that sense we can understand anger as *a neutral state of power* that can be used constructively or destructively.

2. Anger expression: This is behavior that follows the physical readiness. The emotional expression of anger needs to be considered separately from the physical state, because while the response of the body to fear, hurt, or frustration is unavoidable, each individual is personally responsible for how that anger is expressed.

3. Aggression: This is a response too often chosen in the physical state of anger. The intent of aggression is to intimidate and threaten another person's sense of security or value. Aggression is used to inflict injury on people or objects. The injury may be caused by words, fists, or weapons of various types, but however it's done, aggression intends to punish or force compliance with the aggressor's wishes. The long-term consequences of aggression are always negative, even if short-term advances seem to be accomplished.

4. Assertiveness: This response involves the firm, direct expression of feelings, opinions, or needs *without aggression*. Because assertiveness offers great potential for positive change in relationships, the long-term results of practicing assertiveness is always constructive.

5. Hurt: This is the emotional pain that occurs when another person treats us in a way that causes a sense of rejection or disappointment.

6. Frustration: This is the feeling of helplessness or powerlessness that follows hurt.

7. Fear: Fear comes from being threatened physically or emotionally. It is a feeling of anxiety, agitation, or apprehension caused by the nearness of danger, evil, or pain.

8. Hostility: This is an attitude that develops over time as unresolved resentment continues to be deposited in the mind. Hostile people are disillusioned and antagonistic. Their thinking is pessimistic, and they rarely expect positive changes in themselves or others.

9. Bitterness: Bitterness is hostility that has hardened into malice and spite. The embittered person will go to almost any length to avoid or "get even" with someone who has caused an offense. Hostile, vengeful people suffer from headaches, stomach problems, colitis, and high blood pressure. People will go out of their way to avoid them.

What Prickly-Pear Cactus and Bitterness have in Common

In the Southwestern landscape, a prickly pear cactus in full bloom is a beautiful sight. The flowers are a bright yellow against the green of the plant, and where blossoms have matured and fallen, pink fruit adds its own splash of color. But if a hiker gets too close or is careless when picking the fruit, long sharp thorns as well as tiny hair-like stickers diligently protect the plant, and whatever comes in contact with the cactus will come away from the encounter full of painful reminders. Bitterness, like cactus thorns, hurts everyone who comes in contact with it, even those who may be innocent of any wrongdoing in a situation.

When the invisible root of bitterness is established, it produces the visible "thorns" of vengefulness, discouragement, irritation, anxiety and depression. Some areas of this person's life may look good from a distance, but all relationships will be affected. The bitter person is unable to establish intimate relationships because anyone who tries to get close will be repulsed by the complaining and criticism. As the animosity pushes them away, they are added to the list of those who have been a disappointment.

Bitter people will never be satisfied, no matter how much others do to help, protect, or to make past wrongs "right." The spiral downward to depression continues as they focus on every disappointment and the pain of each unmet need. Because they keep a detailed mental record of how badly they were treated, their energy and attention stays focused on the failure of others. Constant blame-shifting keeps them from making necessary personal changes, and it becomes extremely difficult for them to see how God could possibly meet their needs. Trusting expectations to the Lord is the only hope for lifelong emotional stability and healing:

> As it is written, Behold I am laying in Zion a Stone that will make men stumble, a Rock that will make them fall; but he who believes in Him [who adheres to, trusts in, and relies on Him] shall not be put to shame nor be disappointed in his expectations.
>
> Romans 9:33

> May grace (God's favor) and peace (which is perfect well-being, all necessary good, all spiritual prosperity, and freedom from fears and agitating passions and moral conflicts) be multiplied to you in (the full, personal, precise, and correct) knowledge of God and of Jesus our Lord. For His divine power has bestowed upon us all things that (are requisite and suited) to life and godliness,

through the (full, personal) knowledge of Him Who called us by and to His own glory and excellence (virtue).

2 Peter 1:2-3

Lean on, trust in, and be confident in the Lord with all your heart and mind and do not rely on your own insight or understanding. In all your ways know, recognize, and acknowledge Him, and He will direct and make straight and plain your paths. Be not wise in your own eyes; reverently fear and worship the Lord and turn (entirely) away from evil. It shall be health to your nerves and sinews, and marrow and moistening to your bones.

Proverbs 3:5-8

Slowness to anger makes for deep understanding; a quick-tempered person stockpiles stupidity. A sound mind makes for a robust body, but runaway emotions corrode the bones.

Proverbs 14:29-30, (MSG)

Chapter 6: Who Are You? Tramp? Bag Lady? King's Kid!

Our New Identity in Christ

"Ten Thousand Ways That Don't Work"

One of history's sharpest minds belonged to Thomas Edison, the great inventor. Despite only three months of formal schooling, Edison and his inventions changed the world forever. His secret? "One percent inspiration and ninety-nine percent perspiration," as he put it, and he proved his definition by working days at a time, obsessed with his projects, and stopping only for short catnaps. Failure never seemed to discourage him. When nearly 10,000 experiments with a storage battery failed to produce results, a friend tried to console him. "Why, I've not failed," Edison quipped. "I've just found 10,000 ways that won't work." What he *thought* about his efforts enabled him to keep trying when his circumstances were not what he wanted them to be.

Of all his inventions, perhaps the most famous is the electric light. He spent two years looking for the right filament, sending associates to the jungles of the Amazon and to the forests of Japan. He even tried strands of red hair from a friend's beard. Finally, he utilized carbonized thread, and it worked! The world gained electric lights.

Light bulbs are made of three parts. There is the glass itself: the bulb that surrounds the filament. Inside the bulb is a mixture of gases, and in the center of the bulb is the filament. The filament is made of a very tough metal, and when electricity flows through it, it becomes very hot, about 4,500 degrees, making it glow and give off light.

Incandescent bulbs bear a fascinating resemblance to human beings. There is the outside covering: the body. Inside, like invisible gases within the bulb, is the soul: the mind, the will, and the emotions. And at the very center of it all is the "filament": the human spirit that is intended to glow and shed light into the darkness of our sinful world.

Unredeemed humanity is very much like a light bulb that has burned out. The filament is broken, and it is unable to fulfill the purpose for which it was designed. When we receive the life of Christ at salvation, the Bible says "the old has passed away, behold, the new has come." What has become new? It's immediately obvious to us that our bodies haven't changed, and we quickly realize that the mind still thinks many of the old thoughts, emotions still surge out of control, and the will still makes wrong choices. The soul is not brand-new either.

It is in the "filament" of our spirit or human nature that we have become new. This change guarantees a new identity that sheds light into our world. However, it takes some time for that newness to become evident in our thinking, emotions, choices, and behavior.

New Identity in the Witness Protection Program

The United States Department of Justice has a program that is designed to protect a witness who might be threatened by defendants. While a witness may only require protection until the conclusion of a trial, some are provided with an entirely new identity and live the rest of their lives under government protection.

The Witness Security Program is designed to create total anonymity for witnesses and help them blend into a new city where they are least likely to be recognized by old acquaintances. Following the acceptance of a witness into the program, the Marshals Service creates a new identity and locates a new city for the witness, his family, and any endangered associates.

An important rule of the program is that witnesses must break contact with former associates or unprotected family members and agree not return to the town from which they were relocated. According to the Marshals Service, no witness who has followed these rules has ever been killed.

Witness Protection Program provides:

- New location
- New name
- New birth certificate and social security number
- New career, which often includes training in a new field
- New history—participants must become so familiar with the story of their new family and new history that when anyone questions them, they answer confidently out of their *new identity*, not out of their old history.

When we receive our new identity as the result of salvation:

- We are moved out of the old life of darkness into the new life of light (Ephesians 5:8)
- We are given a new name (Isaiah 43:1).
- We receive a new birth certificate (1 John 3:10).
- We receive a new history; all that Jesus accomplished is now ours (Galatians 2:20).
- Our past transgressions are completely erased (Hebrews 8:12).
- We begin a new spiritual career as ministers of the Gospel of Christ (2 Corinthians 5:18).
- We are protected from intimidation by the enemy (Ephesians 6:10-18).
- Through study, we become so familiar with the account of our new family that when anyone asks us questions we answer out of our new identity, not out of our old "before salvation" history (1 Peter 3:15).

Our name identifies who we are. At the time of our physical birth, we received our names from someone who had authority over us. Anyone who knows us and calls us by our first name or nicknames has access into our lives that strangers do not and should not have.

Naming and Authority

Our name can be used to show us love and affection, or, when misused, names can be used to hurt. A name is an identity that is assigned by one in authority. God named His creation. He called darkness *night*; He called the light *day*. He is the authority over His creation, and He declared His authority by assigning identity.

The *'aadaam* was given authority over God's creation. This God-given authority was established in part by naming the animals. The animals were named according to their traits and characteristics, which showed the *'aadaam's* full understanding of what each species was like.

Our parents named us at birth with the name that is on our birth certificate. But that is not the only name we received. Throughout our lives, other people named us as well, not Jane or Bob or Mary or Bill, but sentence names such as:

- "I wish you had never been born!"
- "You are so precious!"
- "Why can't you do anything right?"
- "Wow! Look at you!"
- "Why aren't you like ... ?"
- "You'll never be as good as ... "

"Sentence names" were very common in Bible times. Daniel and his three friends are examples:

- Daniel means *God is my judge*. Every time Daniel's mother called him, she was saying, "Come here, little God is my judge."
- Hannaniah means *Yahweh has been gracious*. When his mother called him in to eat, she said, "Lunch is ready, little Yahweh has been gracious!"
- Mishael means *Who is like God*? When his dad played ball with him he said, "Way to go, my son, who is like God!"
- Azariah means *Yahweh has helped*. Whenever he helped his grandma, she said, "Thank you for helping, little Yahweh has helped."

These four Jewish boys were named by parents who desired that their children grow up knowing God, able to stand firm in their faith in Him. These children were reminded of the power and love of God each time someone called them by name.

When they were about fourteen years old, the Babylonians captured Jerusalem. Many of the leaders and residents were killed, but Nebuchadnezzar had the brightest and most gifted children of Jerusalem's leaders brought to him so they could be trained to be leaders in his kingdom. When Daniel and his three friends arrived in Babylon, the very first thing king Nebuchadnezzar did was to assign new names to each of them.

- Daniel was given the name *Belteshazzar*, which means "Bel will protect his life." Bel (Marduk) was one of the king's favorite gods.
- Hannaniah was given the name *Shadrach*, which means "commanded of Aku." Aku was the moon god of the Babylonians.
- Mishael was given the name *Meshach*, which means "who is like Aku is!"
- Azariah was given the name *Abed-Nego*, which means "servant of Nego." Nego is a variation of the Babylonian name of the god Nebo. Nebo, son of Bel, was the Babylonian god of writing and vegetation. He was also known as Nabu. Nebuchadnezzar's name contains the name of this god.[22]

Nebuchadnezzar clearly understood the principle of naming and of coming under the authority of the one who does the naming. Daniel and his three friends also understood that if they accepted the new names containing the names of Babylonian gods and if they ate the food from the king's table that had been offered to those pagan gods, they would be in covenant with them and subject to them. Daniel appears to be the spokesman for the young Hebrew men. He uses his own Hebrew name, Daniel, sixty-eight times in writing this book, indicating that they did not accept the pagan names.

The Bible tells us that God has called us by a new name. Being named by Him shows we are recipients of His love and are under His righteous authority.

> But now, thus says the Lord, your Creator, O Jacob, and He who formed you, O Israel, "Do not fear, for I have redeemed you; I have called you by name; you are Mine!"
>
> Isaiah 43:1

Our New Name

We received a name from God at our new birth:

- Beloved of God: 1 Thessalonians 1:4
- Precious in His sight: Isaiah 43:4-5
- Righteous one: 2 Corinthians 5:21
- One who has the mind of Christ: 1 Corinthians 2:16

It is clear that if we live out of the name God has given us, we will live in freedom and victory. But throughout our lives, we receive "name changes" as our enemy, Satan, deceives us into believing that we are still under his authority since our thinking, emotions, and behavior are not perfect.

In order to keep us in the bondage of fear and failure, Satan works through people and our own thinking to cause us to use the names he has given us instead of the name God has given us. Consequently, we believe that we are:

- "Too stupid to learn anything," and we stay in the bondage of "I can't learn." This name keeps us from increasing in our knowledge and understanding of Scripture.
- "I wish you had never been born," and we stay in the bondage of self-hatred. This keeps us from loving other people.
- "Why aren't you like your sister or brother or the neighbor's kids?" and we stay in the bondage of fear of rejection and criticism. This keeps us from enjoying the success we do achieve because it never feels like it's enough.
- "I'm getting old, and I'm so tired," and we stay in the bondage of thought-induced weariness and apathy. This mindset keeps us from reaching our full potential as God's sons and daughters. It hinders the work of God's kingdom and limits our heavenly rewards.
- "We'll never be as good as ..." and we stay in the bondage of fear of what other people are thinking about us or what we think they may be thinking. This keeps us in discontentment, constantly dissatisfied with ourselves and with others.

Avoiding Identity Theft

Identity theft is rapidly becoming the most costly crime of our culture. Identity theft happens when someone steals another person's name and personal information and uses it for their own benefit. When Satan replaces the name God gave us with another name and uses it to manipulate, control and destroy, it is the *ultimate identity theft*. We have to actively stand against his attempt to steal from us. Here are some practical suggestions to avoid theft, both financially and spiritually:

1. Periodically go through your wallet or purse and remove rarely used credit cards, receipts and other items that contain personal financial information useful to a thief. Carry no more than you absolutely need for everyday use.

   The spiritual correlation to this is to get rid of all extra "baggage" that you don't need. Don't carry thoughts of bitterness, anxiety, and discontentment. Second Corinthians 10:3-4 tells us to take every thought captive to the obedience of Christ.

2. Memorize all passwords and PIN numbers. Don't carry any record of these numbers in your wallet or purse. Ask your bank, long-distance company, and creditors to require a password before responding to inquiries or making changes to an account.

   The obvious spiritual correlation is to memorize the Word of God.

3. If you keep a lost-and-found tag on your key ring, don't use your home address. Ask that they be mailed to a post office box or to your bank. If your keys are stolen, reduce the thief's access to your personal property and information by replacing the locks on your home and car.

   Don't think of this present world system as your permanent home! Recognize that your home address is with the Lord. Replace the locks on your important spiritual information by making sure that Jesus holds the combination to your treasure; for where your treasure is, there your heart will be also.

4. Keep photocopies of your driver's license, credit cards, Social Security and insurance cards, and other contents of your wallet or purse, and other personal financial information in a secure place in your home. You will need this information if your identity is compromised. Shred all such records before throwing them away. Do not make them easily accessible to a burglar.

   Memorize, memorize, memorize! Keep photocopies of the Word of God in your wallet, in your car, on the walls of your house. Keep it in a secure place in your heart (Psalm 119:11—I have hidden Your Word in my heart).

As we grow in our understanding of who we really are—God's beloved sons and daughters—what people do and say will have less control over how we live life. Knowing who we are at the deepest core of our being will make us less concerned about what people think or even what we *think* they are thinking. Relationships will change. We become progressively:

- Less defensive.
- More often kind than unkind.
- More accepting of others and their differences.
- More likely to put on tenderness and mercy in place of criticism and rejection.

"Know Thyself" Is Not an Optional Extra

Knowing our true identity (our real name) is absolutely essential for developing healthy, loving relationships in our homes, church families, businesses, and communities.

Knowing who we are is essential for living the abundant life that Jesus died to give us. His life in us frees us progressively from fear of failure, humiliation, and rejection. Knowing our new identity in Christ is not an optional extra that we can choose to believe if we feel like it; it is a foundational truth that impacts every area of life.

It is the covenant with our Father, sealed in Christ that gives us our new name. We were accepted into that covenant at the moment of our new birth. Our identity comes from *who our Dad is*, not from the earthly things around us. Our world wants to identify us by:

- Who we know.
- What we wear.
- What we drive.
- How much money we make.
- How many right things we do.
- How many wrong things we avoid.

In Christ, we are identified as:

- God's beloved son or daughter.
- A joint heir with Jesus.

Identical to Jesus

Jesus identified with the human race and became what we are: fully human (Philippians 2:5-7; Hebrews 2:11-18). Webster's dictionary defines identification as "to become identical to." Jesus became identical to us in our humanity and became just like we are, but never choosing to sin. When we accept the gift of salvation we become identical to Jesus in our essential nature. We receive His life and become like Him, fully able to choose obedience rather than sin.

> By this, love is perfected with us, that we may have confidence in the day of judgment; because as He is, so also are we *in this world*. (Now, not when we die and "go to Heaven"!)
>
> 1 John 4:17

> Seeing that His divine power has granted to us everything pertaining to life and godliness, through the true knowledge of Him who called us by His own glory and excellence. For by these He has granted to us His precious and magnificent promises, in order that by them you might become partakers of the divine nature, having escaped the corruption that is in the world by lust.
>
> 2 Peter 1:3-4

Jesus knows that we are now like Him and is not ashamed to call us His next of kin!

> For both He who sanctifies (making men holy) and those who are sanctified all have one (Father). For this reason He is not ashamed to call them brethren.
>
> Hebrews 2:11

Because we are identified with, or identical to Jesus and because we have the *same* nature, the *same* Father, and are Jesus's brothers and sisters in the *same* family, we now also have the *same* life, the *same* power, the *same* authority, the *same* privileges and the *same* work that Jesus has, right now, during our lifetime in this world.

"Cultivated" Does Not Mean "Fake"

A good farmer knows that an important part of raising a healthy crop is cultivation. A specially designed implement is used which opens up the soil around the plant, so that oxygen and water flow freely into the root system. It also kills weeds that have sprouted and are coming up close to the row. If cultivation is neglected, the plants will be yellow and stunted, and the harvest will be minimal.

In the same way, a healthy relationship with God does not happen without care. It must be cultivated. The seed is planted at salvation; the warmth of God's love sprouts the seed. Roots are established, and the plant grows. But to enhance its growth, the "soil" of what we surround ourselves with has to be stirred so that weeds of wrong thinking are killed and so that the food, oxygen, and water of the Word of God reach the roots.

At salvation, we are made new, righteous and holy in our human spirit. That's what gives us the characteristics that make us who we are at the core of our being. The better we understand who we are, and the more we cultivate truth in our thinking, the less often we will make decisions out of the flesh.

But if we neglect or refuse to cultivate truth, the weeds of *The Lie* will grow in our minds, and we will make decisions out of the flesh. When we believe Satan's lies and half truths, we think wrong thoughts, we have wrong attitudes, and we make flesh decisions, so that we behave in wrong ways. "Flesh" is defined as: "I want what I want, when I want it, how I want it—give it to me right now!"

Nothing But the Truth

What is absolutely true about us is what God says:

- Not what we think about ourselves on our own.
- Not how we feel about ourselves.
- Not what other people think or feel or say about us.

What God says is always absolutely true:

> See what (an incredible) quality of love the Father has given (shown, bestowed on) us, that we should (be permitted to) be named and called and counted the children of God! And so we are! The reason that the world does not know (recognize, acknowledge) us is that it does not know (recognize, acknowledge) Him. Beloved, we are (even here and) now God's children; it is not yet disclosed (made clear) what we shall be (hereafter), but we know that when He comes and is manifested, we shall (as God's children) resemble and be like Him, for we shall see Him just as He (really) is. And everyone who has this hope (resting) on Him cleanses (purifies) himself just as He is pure (chaste, undefiled, guiltless).
>
> 1 John 3:1-3

Now here is another part of the challenge: it is often easier to think God's thoughts about ourselves than to think God's thoughts about our brothers and sisters in the Church. Consider a fellow believer named Harry. If we are focusing on the things about Harry's personality or behavior that are irritating or truly wrong instead of focusing on what God is doing in Harry, or perhaps doing in us through Harry; we will be antagonistic, rejecting, and bitter. It's ironic that we often end up doing to Harry, in a little different way, what we are upset at him for doing to us!

When John was receiving the revelation of Jesus the Messiah, he wrote of the time that Jesus first appeared to him:

> Then I turned to see the voice that was speaking with me, and His face was like the sun shining in its strength. When I saw Him, I fell at His feet like a dead man. And He placed His right hand on me, saying, "Do not be afraid; I am the first and the last."
>
> Revelation 1:12-18 (NASU)

Notice that He said, "do not be afraid," not "do not worship Me." Because He is Lord, He received John's worship.

Later, as John is continuing to receive the revelation, he describes meeting with another heavenly messenger:

> And I, John, am he who heard and witnessed these things. And when I heard and saw them, I fell prostrate before the feet of the messenger who showed them to me, to worship him. But he said to me, "Refrain! You must not do that! I am only a fellow servant along with yourself and with your brethren the prophets and with those who are mindful of... the truths contained in the messages of this book. Worship God!"
>
> Revelation 22:8-9 (NASU)

This messenger identified himself as "a fellow servant," along with John. This seems to be a glorified saint, one who had died physically, and now, living in the presence of Jesus, is carrying out His work. Why would John fall on his face to worship a glorified human being? Because the glorified saint looked so much like Jesus, Who had appeared to John earlier, that John could not tell them apart, even though he was Jesus's close friend during His time on earth.

That is what we are like on the inside. If we will choose to look past the prickly, moody emotions and the behaviors that offend us, we will see the likeness of Jesus that is in the spirit of every believer. Seeing that likeness will cause us to treat one another differently, with acceptance and genuine love instead of rejection and frustration.

The key is realizing that we are responsible to cooperate with God (cultivation) to make the changes needed in order for maturity to develop. The changes in another person are between that person and God unless God specifically gives us instruction about how we are to be involved. Otherwise, we are to love, accept, encourage and admonish, speaking the truth in love, not irritation.

Saint or Sinner?

To say we are "King's kids" is the ultimate humility, because we are simply saying, "Yes, God, You're right. This is who You made me to be. Thank You."

God has declared that His children are no longer sinners, but saints. To think, talk, and live as though we are "tramps" or "bag ladies" sounds humble, but is ultimately pride because we're telling God that He doesn't know what He's talking about. The Bible clearly describes the difference between self-centered pride and the true humility we receive from Jesus:

> Think of yourselves the way Christ Jesus thought of Himself. He had equal status with God but didn't think so much of Himself that He had to cling to the advantages of that status no matter what. Not at all! When the time came, He set aside the privileges of deity and took on the status of a slave. He became human! Having become human, He stayed human. It was an incredibly humbling process. He didn't claim special privileges. Instead, He lived a selfless, obedient life and then died a selfless, obedient death — and the worst kind of death at that: crucifixion.
>
> Philippians 2:5-8 (MSG)

This teaching about humility becomes a half truth when we define humility as "putting ourselves down" or never accepting a compliment without a disclaimer about why the compliment can't really be true.

If we were to wear a nametag that says "(your name): Saint," fellow believers would look at us with some degree of disdain, demanding, "Who do you think you are?" But if we wore a nametag that says "(your name): Sinner, saved by grace," many would nod and agree, "Yes, she is a sinner, but isn't grace a wonderful thing?"

The problem with that response is that it disagrees with what God says about us in His Word. It is pride to disagree with God, but we do it because of how we feel. When we are having a bad day—and sometimes, even on a good day—it just doesn't feel true that we are saints.

All through the New Testament, when Paul addresses the churches, even when he is chastising the Corinthians for their sinful behavior, he does not refer to them as sinners. Look up the following references and notice what word or phrase Paul uses to describe believers in Corinth, Ephesus, and Galatia.

1 Corinthians 1:2

____

2 Corinthians 1:1

____

Ephesians 1:1

____

Galatians 1:1-2

____

You see, if we believe we are still sinners with a sin nature, we will continue to do what sinners do best: sin! But if we believe as truth what God says about us, we will accept that we are saints, and will increasingly choose to do "saint things." Our thinking, choices, and emotions will reflect more accurately *who God has made us to be* through salvation. *We are saints who still sometimes choose to sin.* But even when we make wrong choices, we can confidently agree with God:

- I am a saint.
- I am righteous.
- I am holy.
- I am blameless in my spirit.

This is true, not because we have done "enough" right or have managed to avoid "enough" wrong. We are who God says we are because He washed us clean, and declared that we who have received the life of Christ are saints.

Remember the illustration in "Belief Systems" from Luke 11 that showed how our western worldview about hospitality can change how we read that parable? In the same way, our evangelical view of pride and humility changes how we understand what God declares to be true about us. For example, Psalm 8:4 asks the question "What is man that You should be mindful of him?" If we stop reading there, we are left thinking that we're just "worms" or are less than nothing in God's sight.

But if we finish reading what David wrote, we discover his breathless excitement as he announces who we are. Keep in mind as you read that David is sitting outside, seeing stars that we will never see because of the "light pollution" around us. He is observing creation and worshiping the awesome goodness of God.

> O Lord, our Lord, how excellent (majestic and glorious) is Your name in all the earth! You have set Your glory on [or above] the heavens. Out of the mouths of babes and unweaned infants You have established strength because of Your foes, that You might silence the enemy and the avenger. When I view and consider Your heavens, the work of Your fingers, the moon and the stars, which You have ordained and established,(I ask the question)"What is man that You are mindful of him, and the son of (earthborn) man that You care for him? Yet You have made him but a little lower than God—Eloheim—(or heavenly beings) and You have crowned him with glory and honor. You made him to have dominion over the works of Your hands; You have put all things under his feet—all sheep and oxen, yes, and the beasts of the field, the birds of the air, and the fish of the sea, and whatever passes along the paths of the seas. O Lord, our Lord, how excellent, (majestic and glorious) is Your name in all the earth!
>
> Psalm 8

David rejoices that humankind is created so extraordinarily in the likeness of God that even a tiny, nursing human baby has authority to silence Satan. He expresses his sense of amazement at the wonderful honor and privilege God placed on men and women. There is no hint of the "wormy worthlessness" that is far too prevalent in evangelical Christianity.

The Authority of the Believer

"It is not so much what we don't know, but what we *think* we know that obstructs our vision."[23]

The obstacle of *what we think we know and believing that we know it correctly* is far greater than the obstacle of not knowing a thing at all.

In His life on earth, Jesus showed us what completely restored humanity could and should be like. He walked on this earth confidently, fully human, with authority over all things. When He ascended the throne of God, that same authority was made available to each one who believes in His name for all eternity. Taking a closer look at *what we think we know* will expand our understanding of the incredible position we have in Christ.

Repainting God's Self-Portrait

We are conceived by sinful, imperfect people (Psalm 51:5). Our view of God is distorted from birth onward as we're taught by people who are imperfect in their knowledge of God. This sin-distorted view causes us to repaint the beautiful self-portrait of God found in His Word. Selecting colors and textures from the world and the people around us, we paint over the portrait until we have a picture that looks very like the adults who were significant in our lives as children. For example:

- Where God says of Himself in Exodus 34:6, "The Lord, the Lord God, compassionate and gracious, slow to anger, and abounding in loving kindness and truth," we look at an earthly mother that was quick to anger and we cover God's patience and tenderness with mom's impatience.
- Where God declares that it is impossible for Him to ever be untruthful with us (Numbers 23:19; 1 Samuel 15:29), we remember the times that dad promised things that never happened, and we "paint over" the absolute faithfulness of God with the faulty promises made by an imperfect dad.

Because we begin to do this immediately at birth, these ways of thinking feel so normal to us, they become the things we *think we know correctly*.

Even though these beliefs are not true, they feel true, and sound true, so we live as though they are true. Many of us enter young adulthood with the mistaken belief that God basically dislikes us, even though we may have memorized all of the "God so loves ... " verses.

We know that we are made in the image of God. We will, therefore, become *like we believe God to be.* To walk in the power and authority given to us when Jesus ascended to His throne, we must recognize God *as He is* rather than how we have perceived Him to be.

Romans 12:2 (TEV) tells us "do not conform yourselves to the standards of this world, but be transformed inwardly by a complete change of your mind. Then you will be able to know the will of God—what is good and is pleasing to Him and is perfect." Our thinking about God will change as we replace what we learned in an imperfect world from imperfect people, with the truth from God's Word. As our thinking conforms to God's truth, what He tells us about the privileges, responsibilities, power, and authority He has given us will become as real to us as the half truths were before.

When God created the earth as the habitation perfectly suited for humankind and placed the first people in Eden, He gave them complete authority over His marvelous creation.

> Then God said, "Let Us make man in Our image, according to Our likeness; and let them rule over the fish of the sea and over the birds of the sky and over the cattle and over all the earth, and over every creeping thing that creeps on the earth." And God created man in His own image, in the image of God He created him; male and female He created them. And God blessed them; and God said to them, "Be fruitful and multiply, and fill the earth, and subdue it; and rule over the fish of the sea and over the birds of the sky, and over every living thing that moves on the earth."
>
> Genesis 1:26-28

Genesis 2:15 goes on to say that "the Lord God took the man and put him into the Garden of Eden to cultivate it and keep it." The word *keep* is shamar (shaw-mar'), and is defined by Strong's Concordance as to hedge about (as with thorns), to guard; generally, to protect. The *'aadaam* (humankind) was to keep the Garden free from the intrusion of sin. Because of his relationship to God, he had the authority to keep Satan out. God gave him the right to use that authority just as if *'aadaam* was God Himself.

However, when Satan came into the Garden using the body of the serpent, the man and woman chose to believe Satan rather than God. They transferred their allegiance and God-given authority over the earth to Satan. In effect, they gave Satan the right to use the gift of authority God had given to them. The Bible says that as a result of their disobedient decision, "the whole world lies in the power of the evil one" (1 John 5:19). Jesus called Satan "the ruler of this world" in John 14:30 and did not argue with Satan when he told Jesus, "I will give you all this domain and its glory; for it has been handed over to me, and I give it to whomever I wish" (Luke 4:6). Because Adam was the one who handed the earth over to Satan, a member of Adam's race had to be found who could take the lost heritage back from Satan.

But the sin of Adam made every human being a slave to Satan, and since slaves have no legal standing in a court of law, a member of the human race who had not endorsed Adam's rebellion had to be found. Jesus came to earth, fully human, as an authentic member of the human race, but because He was conceived by the Holy Spirit rather than a human father, Satan had no claim on Him. Jesus, Last Adam, walked and ministered on the earth as the First Adam had been created to do.

Although Jesus had the infinite resources of deity at His disposal, He met Satan in this decisive battle purely as a human being. Jesus knew that He could only recover what First Adam had thrown away by going through death on the cross. He resisted the temptation to regain what had been lost by worshipping Satan. He withstood temptation by standing on the Word of His Father. That same Word of Truth is available to all humankind.

Jesus was the first faultless man. He fulfilled the Law perfectly by:

- Living a sinless life.
- Shedding His blood to wash away our unrighteousness. He restored the authority to humankind that had been stolen through First Adam's rebellion.

In His life on earth, Jesus did what humankind was originally created to do. When He was baptized in the Jordan River, the Holy Spirit came upon Jesus to empower Him for His earthly ministry, and He began to do things that astounded those who saw them. The authority Jesus claimed and exhibited was obviously extraordinary to those who heard Him:

> And they were amazed at His teaching; for He was teaching them as one having authority, and not as the scribes (Mark 1:22). And amazement came upon them all, and they began discussing with one another saying, "What is this message? For with authority and power He commands the unclean spirits, and they come out."
>
> Luke 4:36

Jesus was confident in His position as God's Son. He spoke with authority to those who were sick, and they were healed. He spoke with authority to the wind and the sea, and it became calm. His disciples were amazed and said, "What kind of man is this, that even the wind and the sea obey Him?" (Matthew 8:27). Jesus went to the cross fully human, and having paid the penalty of sin by His death, He disarmed Satan and every demon. He debilitated them by taking away the right to use their power against God's sons and daughters.

> When He had disarmed the rulers and authorities, He made a public display of them, having triumphed over them through Him.
>
> Colossians 2:15

> Since then the children share in flesh and blood, He Himself likewise partook of the same, that through death He might render powerless him who had the power of death, that is, the devil.
>
> Hebrews 2:14

Jesus, Last Adam, took back the keys of authority that First Adam surrendered through his disobedience, and then He gave the keys back to humankind:

> I will give you the keys of the kingdom of heaven; and whatever you bind (declare to be improper and unlawful) on earth must be what is already bound in heaven; and whatever you loose (declare lawful) on earth must be what is already loosed in heaven.
>
> Matthew 16:19

The authority that we have been given as believers comes from our identification with Jesus. This is the same authority that was modeled by Jesus and is grounded in the same power of the same Holy Spirit. It is the God-given right and privilege of the believer to receive and use God's power as it flows from the indwelling Holy Spirit.

The basis of this authority is our position in Christ, not our feelings or our accomplishments, and this is where many believers have difficulty. Because Satan is defeated and the authority is now ours, the only way he can keep us in bondage is through deception. Satan and his demons use our emotions and circumstances to try to convince us that they still have the upper hand. But the key to living life in the bold assurance that the power of God and the right to use it is indeed ours, is *to simply believe what God says is true, in spite of how we feel and no matter how our circumstances appear.*

Because this power and authority has been entrusted to us by God, we do not own it. Just as we are to be stewards of the earthly things He has given us, so we are simply to be stewards of the authority He has given us. We are to be diligent in our use of this mighty power, treating it as a precious gift and carefully seeking God's wisdom to use it for the purposes for which it has been given. We have an example of an attempted misuse of God's delegated power when James and John wanted to call down fire from heaven and burn up those who had insulted Jesus.

> And they did not receive Him, because He was journeying with His face toward Jerusalem. And when His disciples, James and John saw this, they said, "Lord, do You want us to command fire to come down from heaven and consume them?" But He turned and... severely censured them. He said, "You do not know of what sort of spirit you are, for the Son of Man did not come to destroy men's lives, but to save them from the penalty of eternal death." And they journeyed on to another village.
>
> Luke 9:53-56

Notice that James and John didn't ask Jesus to call the fire down; they said, "Do you want us to command fire to come down?" James and John knew their authority. They obviously knew that they *could* call the fire down, and Jesus didn't argue with their statement. However, because they were confused about when and how to use the power and authority they had been given, Jesus corrected them. Jesus also faced opportunities to misuse His authority but always refused.

> And the Pharisees came out and began to argue with Him, seeking from Him a sign from heaven, to test Him. And sighing deeply in His spirit, He said, "Why does this generation seek for a sign? Truly I say to you, no sign shall be given to this generation."
>
> Mark 8:11-12

Because the authority we have is through our identification with Jesus, not from ourselves, we must guard against the tendency to presume upon God. While we have authority over the same things Jesus did, it never gives us the right to command God to do our will. Jesus did only those things that the Father instructed Him to do (John 5:19; 8:28), and He never tried to convince His Father to change His plans. In Gethsemane, He clearly told God that He would rather do it another way but humbly submitted to "not My will, but Yours be done" (Matthew 26:43).

One way we may try to manipulate God is by making our own plans and then expecting Him to bless them. The underlying wrong belief is that "God wants me to be happy, so if I tell Him what I want and believe Him for it, He will have to respond to my faith and give it to me."

Sometimes, in our pride, we may believe that we are the only one who really understands what God wants to accomplish in a given situation and refuse to consider the wisdom of other believers. This can cause us to misuse our God-given authority by promoting a personal agenda that makes us feel good, rather than what God wants to have accomplished.

Any misapplication of our God-given authority will result in spiritual pride. If we focus simply on the results we see, we may feel that we are especially gifted, or maybe even indispensable to God! Remember the reactions of the twelve disciples after Jesus gave them power and authority over demons and to heal diseases. They came back, astonished and rejoicing and amazed at what "they" had been able to do (Luke 10:17). But Jesus very quickly helped them get their perspective back in balance when He reminded them that it was their relationship to God that was most important.

> Nevertheless do not rejoice in this, that the spirits are subject to you, but rejoice that your names are recorded in heaven.
>
> Luke 10:20

Fortunately, God does not wait until we are perfect in our use of His authority to give it to us, but He certainly wants us to grow up! Our reason for drawing on the authority entrusted to us will become less selfish as we mature spiritually. Building relationships with spiritually mature and growing believers is an important part of growing up. God designed us to function as a body. *Believers who live as isolated cells or body parts cannot grow and will never become healthy and strong as long as they remain detached from other believers.*

God's truth declares that every believer shares complete identity with Jesus. According to the Word:

- We are crucified with Him (Galatians 2:20).
- Buried with Him (Romans 6:4).
- Raised with Him (Colossians 2:12).
- Exalted with Him (1 Peter 5:6).
- Enthroned with Him (Romans 6; Ephesians 2).

We can accept that Jesus is exalted and enthroned; it is harder for us to believe that we have been exalted and enthroned with Him. Yet it cannot be otherwise if 1 Corinthians 6:12 is true when it says "he that joins himself to the Lord becomes one spirit with Him." If all things have been put under the feet of Jesus and we are His Body, then all things are under *our* feet. Just as the body cannot function without its head, so our Head, (Jesus), by His own choice does not function apart from His Body of redeemed humankind. Through salvation we share His life;

therefore, His victory over darkness is our victory. He seized the keys of death and hell, and we share in that triumph. He ascended to His throne and is seated in the heavenly realm. Because we are joined to Him, we are exalted with Him (Ephesians 2:1-7).

When Jesus sat down at the right hand of God, it was an announcement of Satan's total defeat. Satan was stripped of his authority over the earth, and the infinitely superior power of God neutralized every weapon he uses against humankind. When Jesus exploded out of death and ascended to the throne, all believers were raised and seated with Him for all eternity. This is true right now, even though we are at the same time still occupying our place on earth.

In his book *The Authority of the Believer*, John McMillan writes:

> Christ, having conquered for man, sits as his representative in the seat destined for him when redemption is fully manifested. In the interim, the wonderful provision exists that man shall be considered completely in Christ, and shall, to the limit of his spiritual understanding and obedience, be endowed with the authority of His name. Often we realize that aspects of our circumstances are the working of the enemy. We cry to God to rebuke the enemy, and to alter things. Through the teaching of the Word, He replies, "My children, rebuke the enemy yourselves. The authority over him is yours. It's a responsibility I have committed to you. I desire you to learn in these things to prevail. I have purposed a high and holy ministry for you in the coming age. This is for you the time of testing and preparation."[24]

This truth from God's Word is reality, not a spiritual theory. We are not fearful, cringing slaves, because everything God gave to Jesus is ours as well (Romans 8:17). In His triumph, Jesus has given us the weapons we need: His power and His authority.

There is a vast difference between knowing this as a vague spiritual "hope" and believing it as an essential, practical part of everyday living. As the *knowing* becomes *believing* and we continue the work that Jesus began, we will do what He modeled in His earthly life. What we call "miracles" are simply normal events to those who believe that the power of Jesus flows from the Head into His Body. Believing involves us regularly in *other normal events* such as:

- Physical healings
- Loving the unlovable
- Deliverance from the power of darkness
- "Important" people serving "unimportant" people
- Having authority over weather
- Forgiving the guilty
- Angelic protection
- Refusing to worry
- Guidance and revelation through words of knowledge and wisdom
- Refusing to be bitter
- Refusing to take revenge
- Choosing not to seek worldly prestige and honor

Such things are only miracles to those whose definition of *normalcy* is tied to the earth. May we learn to judge normalcy by Jesus's standards. [25]

Jesus, Son of God

Son of God:	Mark 1:1; Luke 1:35; John 3:16
Raised to new life:	Acts 2:23-24
Loved by God:	Matthew 17:5
Precious to God:	1 Peter 2:4
Empowered by the Holy Spirit:	Luke 3:22
Sent into the world by God:	John 3:16
Light of the world:	John 8:12
All things given to Him:	John 3:35
Given the responsibility to judge:	John 5:22
Given all authority by God:	Matthew 28:18
Speaks the words of God:	John 3:34
Jesus's words bring life to mankind:	John 6:63
Jesus's words have eternal value:	Matthew 24:35
Jesus intercedes for the saints:	Hebrews 7:25
Jesus was accused of being crazy:	Mark 3:21; John 10:20;
Received whatever He asked of God:	John 11:21-22
Jesus crushes Satan under His feet:	Genesis 3:15
Jesus is triumphant over death:	Romans 6:9
Jesus reigns over all things forever:	Revelation 11:15

Believers

Sons and daughters of God:	Romans 8:14; Galatians 3:26; 4:6
Raised to new life:	Romans 6:4
Loved by God:	John 17:23
Precious to God:	Isaiah 43:4
Empowered by the Holy Spirit:	Acts 1:8
Sent into the world by Jesus:	John 17:18
Light of the world:	Matthew 5:14
All things given to us:	Romans 8:32; 1 Corinthians 3:21-22
Given the responsibility to judge:	1 Corinthians 6:2-3; John 7:24
Given all authority by Jesus:	Matt.9:8; Luke 9:1-5; 2 Corinthians 10:8
Speak the words of God:	John 17:8, 14; 1 Corinthians 2:13
Our words bring life to mankind:	Proverbs 15:4; Proverbs 18:21
Our words have eternal value:	Matthew 12:36-37
We intercede for the saints:	1 Thess. 5:25; 2 Thess. 1:11; James 5:16
We will be accused of being crazy:	John 15:20; Acts 26:24-25
Receive whatever we ask in Jesus's name:	John 14:13-14; John 16:23-24
Satan is crushed under our feet:	Romans 16:20
We are triumphant over death in Christ:	Romans 5:17
We will reign forever with Jesus:	Revelation 22:1-5

Chapter 7: Chains of Law, Wings of Grace: Legalism, Grace, and the Holy Spirit

We live in a pressure cooker world. There is pressure to conform, succeed and measure up; the pressure to be perfect and never fail. But we do fail, and as we look at those around us who seem not to fail, at least not as often as we do, we drag ourselves to our feet and start the "try harder" cycle all over again.

What drives this compulsion to be "better than" those around us? Why do we always feel that we should be "more than" we are?

Let's review what happened in the Garden of Eden. Satan approached the woman through the serpent and convinced her that if she could only acquire the same knowledge of good and evil that God has, she and the man could be just like God in their own knowledge and power. They would no longer need God. They would be God.

The woman believed *The Lie*; the man chose to accept *The Lie*, even though he knew the serpent was lying. When their eyes were opened, they immediately dressed themselves in fig leaves; a feeble attempt to cover the shame they felt as they realized they could not be God. In fact, they had become less than fully human because they were no longer connected with God Who gave them life. Humankind is designed to be bonded to God; without that connection, we cannot be fully what God created us to be. *Sin did not make us "more God." It made us less human.*

However, since that first terrible act of treason against God's perfect plan, every generation has tried to make *The Lie* work. We think we can make it work if we:

- Try hard enough
- Do enough
- Know enough
- Earn enough
- Please people enough
- Please God enough

Enough, enough, enough. But no matter what we do, "enough" is never enough. Sometimes it's not enough, because we actually didn't do what we were trying to do, the right way. Or maybe, we did it the right way, but someone was displeased because it wasn't what they expected. The disapproval can make us try harder for a while, but after a time, we get tired and discouraged and we sink into: "I give up. What's the use? I can't do it right anyway. Why try?"

Proverbs 29:25 describes the problem and the solution:

> The fear of man brings a snare (like a hook in the nose), but whoever leans on, trusts in and puts his confidence in the Lord is safe and set on high."

In the Old Testament, the Assyrians were frequently a sharp thorn in the side of the Israelites. God often brought His people out of idolatry and back into relationship with Himself through attacks by this pagan nation.

Assyria did not take many prisoners of war when they conquered another nation. Only those who would benefit the Assyrian agenda were kept alive. And to make sure that the prisoners would not try to escape and would go where they were told, the Assyrian soldiers would pierce the septum of the nose and put a ring through the hole. A cable was attached, held by a soldier on horseback. The prisoner, following on foot, was obligated to go wherever the soldier directed him by pulling on the cable. If he hesitated, he would lose part of his nose.

Proverbs 29:25 explains that when we are afraid of what people think of us, or what we *assume* they may be thinking, we are like a prisoner of war with a hook in our nose. Whichever way we get "pulled" by the expression on someone's face or tone of voice is the way we feel obligated to go. This wrong focus on people puts us in terrible bondage. But when we focus on the Lord; when our confidence is in His acceptance of us, we are controlled less and less by the disapproval (real or perceived) of people.

The Bondage of the Law Opposes the Freedom of Grace

In the Old Testament, the Law was a unique code of ethics and behavior given by direct revelation from God to instruct His people in their relationship to Him and in their social and personal relationships with each other. Romans 7:12 describes the Law as "holy, righteous, and good."

Legalism is a misuse of the Law. It is a method of trying to get greater acceptance from God by doing more "good" and less "bad." Legalism attempts to achieve righteousness before God by keeping our own particular interpretation of the "shoulds" and "oughts" of the God-given Law.

While legalism is trying to find acceptance with God, *standards* are the attempt to find acceptance with people by keeping a set of *man made* rules.

Jesus warned His disciples on several occasions to "beware of the leaven of the Pharisees." In Matthew 16:12 and Luke 12:1, Jesus defines "leaven" as hypocrisy, deceit, and the teaching of the Pharisees and Sadducees. Leaven is symbolic of evil in the Old Testament, and in the New Testament, it is used to describe malice and wickedness (1 Corinthians 5:6-8).

Religious externalism constituted the leaven of the Pharisees (Matthew 23:14, 16, 28). Jesus warned the multitudes who followed Him, that while they were to do all that the Pharisees taught, they were not to do what the Pharisees were actually doing because "they preach, but do not practice."

Legalism or religious externalism always ends in bondage to performance; either to please God or to please people. Those held in the bondage of legalism constantly work at renewing their *efforts* rather than renewing the *mind*.

The Law Is a Mirror

Each morning all over America, people stumble sleepily into their bathrooms, rubbing their eyes as they gaze into the big mirror on the wall. The mirror can't speak out and say, "Look at yourself! You really need some shampoo!" But our reflection shows us the tangles and gel buildup. The mirror has now "told" us that our hair needs to be cleaned. It would be foolish to pull the mirror off the wall and start rubbing our hair with it, hoping the mirror could make our hair clean. The mirror does not exist to wash our hair; it exists to show us that our hair needs to be washed.

God's perfect, righteous and holy Law is our spiritual mirror. God places it in front of those who don't know Him to show them how desperately soiled and helpless they are apart from His righteousness. When unbelievers or believers pull the Law "off the wall" and attempt to wash themselves clean by trying to keep it "more," it is a misuse of the Law. The Law does not exist to make us righteous. It exists to show us our need for cleansing and points us to Jesus, the only true Righteousness. First Timothy tells us very clearly that the Law is not for the righteous (saved), but the unrighteous (unsaved).

> Certain individuals have ... wandered away into vain arguments and discussions and purposeless talk. They are ambitious to be doctors of the Law, but they have no understanding of the words and terms they use. Now we recognize and know that the Law is good if anyone uses it for the purpose for which it was designed ... the Law is not enacted for those who are in right standing with God, but for the lawless and unruly, for the ungodly and sinful, for the irreverent and profane, for those who strike and beat and [even] murder fathers and mothers; for impure and immoral persons, those who abuse themselves with men, kidnapers, liars, perjurers — and whatever else is opposed to wholesome teaching and sound doctrine as laid down by the glorious Gospel of the blessed God.
>
> 1 Timothy 1:6-11

Galatians 3:19, 21-25 emphasizes the purpose of the Law.

> What then was the purpose of the Law? It was added after the promise, to disclose and expose to men their guilt ... and to make men more conscious of the sinfulness of sin; and it was intended to be in effect until the Seed (Jesus) should come ... Is the Law then contrary and opposed to the promises of God? Of course not! But the Scriptures (picture all mankind as sinners) shut up and imprisoned by sin, so that blessing which was promised through faith in Jesus Christ (the Messiah) might be given ... to (all) those who believe in and rely on Him. Now before the faith came, we were perpetually guarded under the Law, kept in custody in preparation for the faith that was destined to be revealed (unveiled, disclosed), so that the Law served ... as our trainer (our guardian, our guide to Christ), to lead us until Christ (came), that we might be justified (declared righteous, put in

> right standing with God) by and through faith. But now that the faith has come, we are no longer under a trainer (the guardian of our childhood).

The meaning of the word *guardian* is weakened by the use of the words *schoolmaster* or *trainer* in some English translations. The Greek word is *paidogogos*, which means "child disciplinarian." In Greek culture, a person was hired by parents to accompany their children to school. If the child wondered from the path, the *paidogogos* would swat the child with a long stick. If the *paidogogos* was hired to take a group of children to school, they were literally driven like a herd of cattle. But when the children arrived at school, the task of the *paidogogos* was done.

Like the *paidogogos,* the Law drives us to "arrive" at righteousness. Its demands seem unreasonable and cruel because there is no way we can ever measure up to the righteousness of God. The task of the Law is accomplished when we are compelled to accept righteousness as a gift from God. Placing ourselves back under a system of "shoulds" and "oughts" after we have received that gift puts us again under bondage to the Law, and we quickly re-experience the self-righteousness of trying harder, and shame of giving up.

In Romans 3:20-24 the purpose of the Law and the righteousness of Jesus is contrasted.

> For no person will be justified (made righteous, acquitted, and judged acceptable) in His sight by observing the works prescribed by the Law. For the real function of the Law is to make men recognize and be conscious of sin (not mere perception, but an acquaintance with sin which works toward repentance, faith, and holy character). But now the righteousness of God has been revealed independently and altogether apart from the Law… namely, the righteousness of God which comes by believing with personal trust and confident reliance on Jesus Christ (the Messiah). (And it is meant) for all who believe. For there is no distinction, since all have sinned and are falling short of the honor and glory which God bestows and receives. All are justified and made upright and in right standing with God, freely and gratuitously by His grace (His unmerited favor and

> mercy), through the redemption which is [provided] in Christ Jesus.

God never intended for us to gain righteousness by keeping His perfect and holy Law! It is clearly impossible. However, because God's instruction in the Law gives us information about ethics and behavior that keep order in society, our obedient response to the love of God, empowered by His Holy Spirit, includes *not* murdering, *not* stealing, *not* slandering, *not* committing adultery, *not* coveting, even after we are set free from the Law. The practical, daily application of the Law's moral intent is not to *gain* righteousness, but to *make the righteousness we've received from Jesus, now written on our hearts, visible* through our obedient choices and behavior.

The Consequence of Legalism Is Spiritual Abuse and Bondage

Spiritually abusive systems routinely use guilt, fear, and intimidation as the means for controlling their members. Leaders promote dependency by focusing on submission, loyalty, and obedience. While it is made to sound as if the submission, loyalty, and obedience are toward God, it is actually demanded for the gratification of the person or system. The demand for "holy living," usually defined as strict adherence to the legalist's understanding of God's Law, becomes an end to itself, rather than a Spirit-filled walk through life with God.

Systems that promote legalism have several very noticeable characteristics:

1. Focus on performance: This comes from the belief that how people act is more important than who they are in their spiritual identity and performance is more vital than spiritual maturity. Keeping certain standards gains acceptance in the system, but because the standards are manmade, they constantly change. A focus on performance creates perfectionism which produces:

    - Giving up without trying or doing only those things that one does well

- Inability to admit mistakes
- Procrastination
- Inability to ask for help
- Inability to rest, even when exhausted
- Inability to have fun without feeling guilty
- A strong sense of self-righteousness
- A strong sense of guilt
- Unrealistic demands of others
- Always expecting the worst from others
- Living a "double life": feeling like failure inside while always trying to appear perfect on the outside.

2. Shaming: Shame constantly belittles, comparing people by asking the questions, "What's wrong with you? Why aren't you like . . . ?" The intent is to encourage someone to shun evil and do good, but shaming always forces change for the wrong reasons: to escape the anger and condemnation. Shaming produces a negative attitude expressed as "I'm stupid" and "I'm no good." Recipients of shame will go on to shame others.

3. Manipulation: Spiritual manipulation uses powerful rules that are usually unspoken. It's important that they remain unspoken, because when verbalized, the foolishness of the rule becomes obvious. For example, no one is likely to say out loud, "What people think of us is much more important than really being right on the inside." People who manipulate also use "code-talk," an indirect way of communicating that prevents anyone from saying, "You said this . . . what did you mean?" It also includes forceful body language: frowns, clearing the throat, silent treatment, or disconnecting from a conversation by pointedly looking away. Another way of avoiding direct communication is sending a message through another person. A manipulative approach makes it impossible to deal with people honestly and directly. A person trained in manipulation constantly reads "deeper" meanings into the words and actions of others and has a profound mistrust of people and God.

4. Focus on fault and blame: When someone fails to perform in the expected way, reaction toward the failure is quick and severe. A performance-based system believes that every failure must be punished. Blame has to be established so that whoever failed can be made to pay. Shame is piled on so that the person will "never" act that way again. Instead, shaming produces rationalizing, lying, blaming, and criticism of others. A person who is a part of this kind of system will have difficulty forgiving, and finds it nearly impossible to receive the love and forgiveness of God. Focus on fault and blame ends in bitterness.

5. Exclusion and avoiding "sinners": The Pharisees were experts at "cleaning the outside of the cup" but had no understanding of how to receive cleansing on the inside. Legalists seek "cleansing" through a doctrine of avoidance. "Don't go there, don't touch that, don't be seen with… don't… don't… don't." Condemnation is expressed through shunning, ignoring, and excluding people who don't measure up to the system. This produces negativism and self-righteousness.

6. Pride: Pride happens when a person or system measures worth by success or being "right." However, the good feelings seldom last long. At the first hint that failure might happen or disapproval is expressed, the "good" feelings disappear and are replaced by fear and shame.

7. Avoidance of risk: Risk avoiders are unwilling to be involved in anything that might not succeed. They don't reach the potential God has given them because they only involve themselves in what feels "safe." They stay in a comfort zone that doesn't allow for anything new, settling for comfort and convenience. Anxiety levels rise because it's impossible to maintain a comfort zone that never changes. Risk avoiders try to ease the pain of failure by abusing chemicals, sex, food, sleep, and entertainment to escape, at least temporarily, from their sense of failure and inadequacy.

8. Making the system more important than individuals: Many have been rejected or punished because they didn't obey a particular interpretation of nonessential doctrine. This is often done under the guise of "defending God's reputation," but God does not need our defense! Putting a system above God and people produces resentment. Discouraged, frustrated people walk away, determined to avoid anything that reminds them of God.

9. Making a relationship with God into a formula: Legalists insist that too much teaching about grace presumes on God, and will lead to uncontrolled behavior. But it is actually the legalist, with his insistence on "right" actions, restrictions, and rules who misuses the grace of God. A legalist often uses "formulas" to "force" compliance from God. An example is the ritual of taking a particular verse, praying it repetitively, believing that God "has to respond" to that kind of "faith."

10. Using God as a threat to force obedience to the system: "God will punish you for that. Remember, God is always watching you. You make God so sad. After all He's done for you, how could you act that way?" are commonly used warnings. If we believe all-powerful God is hostile toward us, there is no way we can accept grace from Him. We will live in unreasoning terror of God, avoiding Him at all costs. This is one cause of atheism: a determination to believe God doesn't exist at all.

Jesus expressed great anger toward religious leaders who promised people a connection with God then, when they responded, piled up such a heavy burden of "dos" and "don'ts" that no one could possible qualify.

> Then Jesus said to the multitudes and to His disciples, "The scribes and Pharisees sit on Moses' seat (of authority). So observe and practice all they tell you; but do not do what they do, for they preach, but do not practice. They tie up heavy loads, hard to bear, and place them on men's shoulders, but they themselves will not lift a finger to help bear them. They do all their works to be

> seen of men; for they make wide their phylacteries … and make long their fringes … and they take pleasure in and (thus) love the place of honor at feasts and the best seats in the synagogues, and to be greeted with honor in the marketplaces and to have people call them rabbi.
>
> Matthew 23:1-7

"Bait and switch" is a form of fraud that lures customers by advertising a product or service at an unprofitably low price, later revealing that the advertised product is not available but a higher priced substitute is. Legalism is a religious bait and switch scheme. It promises relationship with God, but the moment the seeker reaches for what is promised, a demand for performance is exchanged for relationship with God.

Measuring the "Legalism Quotient"

1. God would be more pleased with me if I could….

   ____

2. God would be more pleased with me if I would…

   ____

3. God is disappointed with me when I….

   ____

4. God would like me better if I could change this one thing about myself….

   ____

Your answers indicate areas in which you have not yet accepted the grace from God that is yours in Christ.

Write out Colossians 1:22

____

Write out Romans 8:1

Write out Ephesians 1:6-7

Death by Antifreeze

From *The Church Snatchers: The Ultimate Identity Theft*
by Dr. Dixie Yoder

Ponca City, Oklahoma: In 1998, a sentence of life in prison was handed down to Dennis Heller, a fifty-three-year-old man who pleaded guilty to killing his wife with soft drinks laced with antifreeze. Hellar was first charged with first-degree murder, which was later reduced to first-degree manslaughter. Prosecutors alleged that he slipped antifreeze into Carol Hellar's drinks over a period of eight months. Mrs. Hellar died June 12, 1995, on the eve of her first wedding anniversary. Mrs. Hellar, who was in her early fifties, made twenty-eight trips to hospitals and reported various ailments during the year of her marriage. The only month she did not go to the hospital was in April 1995, when her husband was jailed on a theft complaint, prosecutors said. Investigators recovered a half-full gallon jug of antifreeze from the Hellars' apartment in Perry, sixty miles north of Oklahoma City. Investigators said antifreeze, which tastes sweet, causes the kidneys to shut down.

Prosecutors believe Mrs. Hellar was poisoned because Hellar had a girlfriend and wanted his wife's Social Security income. Assistant District Attorney Mark Gibson said Hellar had been a suspect all along, but that the case took a long time to prove. A state medical examiner ruled the cause of Mrs. Hellar's death was consistent with "ethylene glycol intoxication."

Russell Busby, chief investigator for the Eighth District Attorney's Office serving Kay and Noble counties in Oklahoma, helped solve the three-year-old poisoning murder case. It took more than three years for the investigators to sort through thousands of pages of medical records and to find a forensic toxicologist from Virginia who was familiar with the effects of antifreeze poisoning. They obtained the use of an undercover ex-girlfriend to get a confession that resulted in Dennis Hellar's arrest for first-degree murder.

What made it possible for Mr. Hellar to use antifreeze as a murder "weapon" is its sweet taste. The flavor was so like the sweetener in his wife's diet soft drink that she could not detect its presence; yet in spite of the similarities in flavor, the effect was deadly.

The world system that surrounds us is governed by Satan, the bitter enemy of the human race. Because he is consumed with hatred for humanity and is determined to inflict as much damage as he possibly can, he continually infuses our thinking with "anti-truth" thought processes that are poisonous and will cause sickness and death in some form if they are absorbed. Most Christians have at least heard that Satan poisons the minds of the unbelieving through darkness and confusion and may suspect that he is trying to poison believers as well, but because many of the thoughts have a "sweet taste," it can be difficult to distinguish between truth and untruth. Certainly the effects of the poison are evident: divorce continues to increase in Christian families, there is a rising percentage of believers who struggle with depression and anxiety, the same percentage of believers rely on medication to control their moods as unbelievers. Instead of the absolute certainty of sin, there is now a pervasive confusion among Christians about whether behaviors such as abortion or extra-marital sex are always really wrong. In the confusion, we are often unable to identify where the toxins are coming from.

The small amounts of antifreeze in Mrs. Hellar's soft drinks

> were not noticeable because it didn't have an offensive flavor, but if she had known it was there, she would have refused to drink it, not because of the flavor, but because of the effect it would have on her body. She certainly would not have agreed to drink undiluted antifreeze straight from the container. Mr. Hellar knew that and carefully infused small amounts into a normal part of her daily routine, drinking a diet soda. In the same way, Satan has infused the poisonous thinking from the world around us into our normal daily routine. One "sip" at a time, it has become so much a part of what seems "normal" to us that we don't notice that it is there until tremendous damage or even death has occurred from the accumulated effects of the poison.[26]

Now that we have received salvation and are born into God's family, we are His children. How do we live in a world that often does not acknowledge that our Father is relevant or even real? Knowing the truth about God, ourselves, and Satan's schemes is the only way to resist "drinking" the little drops of poison that infiltrate every moment of life.

Circuit Breakers and the Holy Spirit

Every building wired for electricity has a breaker box with circuit breakers. They are simple but essential safety devices that protect us and keep the electrical systems from damage.

There are three main reasons why a circuit breaker will flip and shut off the power:

- Overload to the circuit. This can be caused by a surge of electricity; either from a faulty piece of equipment in the building, a surge from the power grid, or too many items plugged into one circuit. When this occurs, we can flip the breaker on and continue to use the equipment. If the circuit is overloaded, the switch will occasionally continue to flip off until more circuits or a bigger breaker is added.
- Short circuits. This is the result of a live wire touching another wire. When this happens, the breaker will not reset.

It will not allow restoration of power until the short circuit is repaired.

- Ground or earthing faults. "Earthing" of electrical systems is required to ensure the safety of people near the system and to prevent damage to the system in the event of a fault. It provides a low resistance path for fault current so that the circuit protective devices disconnect the supply. The purpose of a ground, besides the protection of people and equipment, is to provide a safe path for the dissipation of lightning strikes and static discharges.

Before we are born into God's family, we are not "grounded." There is no protection from the overload of the world, so we have to find ways to protect ourselves. Our world calls these techniques "coping mechanisms." They include:

1. Disengagement: Disengagement occurs when someone mentally "flips a switch" and *suddenly* cuts off involvement with people or a lifestyle that is believed to be creating the stress overload. This pattern is often repeated as the person moves quickly from one job, relationship, or church setting to another. The consequence: loss of intimacy, refusing to let anyone become emotionally close.
2. Desensitizing: Desensitizing occurs when someone *slowly* smothers emotions that are connected to people or a lifestyle that is believed to be creating the stress overload. The consequence: loss of a tender, caring heart, and an unwillingness to offer sympathy or kindness.
3. Distancing: Distancing will always follow desensitizing. It becomes evident as someone slowly withdraws from people or a lifestyle that is believed to be creating the stress overload. This pattern is more likely to become repetitive within the *same* job, relationship, or church setting. The consequence: loss of vulnerability and the refusal to risk exposure to emotional hurt.
4. Deadness: Deadness occurs after repeated hurts as one builds a shell of self-protection from people or a lifestyle that is believed

to be creating the prolonged stress overload. The consequence: apathy and loss of passion and purpose.

There are many different ways that these four Ds of the world system are accomplished. Even after being born into God's family, believers may continue to use one or more of these "coping mechanisms" because they do not yet have an understanding of the work and power of the Holy Spirit. It is His Presence that makes it possible to live victoriously in a system that drives stress overload, emotional short circuits, and the "earthing faults" of failure in relationships.

Which of these "coping mechanisms" have you used?

____

____

____

What result did these "coping mechanisms" produce in your relationships or life experience?

____

____

____

The Holy Spirit desires to replace the devices of the world system with a likeness to Jesus in each believer. An awareness of how God designed people is necessary to cooperate with God's work. The four Ds of the Holy Spirit are:

1. Decontaminated: The cleansing blood of Jesus has set us free from the contamination of sin. Sin is not eliminated, but we are now dead to its power. Because we are decontaminated, we can choose intimacy in our human relationships as our intimacy with God grows deeper.

2. Daring: As we recognize the incredible power of God residing

in us, we can choose to risk the emotional pain that comes from involvement with imperfect people. We can choose a tender, caring heart, willing to offer sympathy or kindness.

3. Defended: Because the Holy Spirit lives in a profoundly personal relationship with us, we can risk lowering our own defensiveness toward others. Close relationships cannot exist without vulnerability, but as we mature in our relationship with God, we trust Him to be our Defender and give us wisdom to know when and how to develop relationships.

4. Diligent: Passion and enthusiasm are antidotes for deadness. Knowing Jesus as a close and personal Friend brings deeper understanding of the incredible privilege we have to live in daily partnership with Him. We grow more determined to work through the difficult things instead of running away or building walls of self-protection.

Describe a specific relationship or circumstance in which you will exchange old, flawed, coping mechanisms for the Holy Spirit's plan:

Which of the Holy Spirit's Ds do you plan to use in this relationship or circumstance?

Describe how you will apply the Holy Spirit's plan of action to your particular situation:

____

____

Describe the changes you think this will make in you:

____

____

Describe the changes you think this will make in your circumstances:

____

____

God's Grace: It Really is Amazing!

At the very beginning of His ministry, Jesus made some radical statements that excited His followers and offended the religious leaders. "You are the light of the world... the salt of the earth." He was telling His disciples, men and women like we are, that because of His righteousness and the power of the Holy Spirit in us, we can dispel the darkness of the world. There is no reason for God's people to fear darkness, death, or sin.

Paul stood firmly against legalism as he traveled, planting new churches, instructing and admonishing those that were already established and growing. Paul understood that the intimidation of legalism puts God's people back under the hopelessness of trying to perfectly keep a Law that cannot be perfectly kept.

> Then after an interval of fourteen years I went up again to Jerusalem with Barnabas, taking Titus along also. And it was because of a revelation that I went up; and I submitted to them the Gospel which I preach among the Gentiles, but I did so in private to those who were of reputation, for fear that I might be running, or had run in vain. But not even Titus who was with me, though he was a Greek, was compelled to be circumcised. But it was because of the false brethren who had sneaked in to spy out our liberty, which we have in Christ Jesus, in order to bring

> us into bondage. But we did not yield in subjection to them for even an hour, so that the truth of the Gospel might remain with you. But from those who were of high reputation (what they were makes no difference to me; God shows no partiality) well, those who were of reputation contributed nothing to me.
>
> Galatians 2:1-7 (NASU)

Paul refused to submit to their legalistic demands because he knew that to give in would be to return to the slavery of the Law.

Finding the Biblical Balance

Truly understanding grace prevents both license and legalism, but because most of us have learned that we have to obey the "rules" or maintain certain "standards" to ensure that we live a Godly life, it feels at first as if we're "throwing the baby out with the bathwater." It may seem that we're saying that sin or failure doesn't matter.

Obviously sin matters! Sin cost Jesus His life, so it cannot ever be considered insignificant. However, the emphasis in Scripture is not on *sin* but on *righteous living*. As long as we are focused on self and "how not to sin," sin will inevitably increase. Colossians explains clearly that a legalistic, self-focus, never produces righteousness.

> Let no one defraud you by acting as an umpire and declaring you unworthy and disqualifying you for the prize, not holding fast to the Head , from Whom the entire body grows with a growth that is from God. If then you have died with Christ to material ways of looking at things and have escaped from the world's crude and elemental notions and teachings of externalism, why do you live as if you still belong to the world? Why do you submit to rules and regulations?—such as: Do not handle (this), Do not taste (that), Do not even touch (them), Referring to things all of which perish with being used. To do this is to follow human precepts and doctrines. Such (practices) have indeed the outward appearance (that popularly passes) for wisdom, promoting self-imposed rigor of devotion, and delight in self-humiliation and severity of discipline of the body, but they are of no value in checking the indulgence of the flesh (the lower nature). (Instead, they do not honor God but serve only to indulge the flesh.)
>
> Colossians 2:18-23

In fact, according to Romans 7:8, rules actually arouse sin!

> If it had not been for the Law, I should not have recognized sin or have known its meaning. For instance, I would not have known about covetousness and would have had no consciousness of sin or sense of guilt if the Law had not repeatedly said, "You shall not covet and have an evil desire for one thing and another."

Grace is a word that is used a lot, but understood very little. "Unmerited favor" is a favorite definition, but what does it really mean? How does "grace" apply in a practical way?

There is no specific definition of *grace* in Scripture. The Hebrew term *chen* means "to bend or stoop" and came to mean "condescending favor." It carries the idea of a superior being kind to an inferior when there was no obligation on the part of the one who is superior.[27] If we have not understood God's great love toward humankind, we will interpret this as meaning that "God offers grace, but He's rather annoyed about having to do it."

Grace covers a wide range of meanings, but all through Scripture the common tone is that of pleasantness. A dancer is described as graceful; good manners and courtesy communicate graciousness. Jesus never used the word *grace*, but His entire life modeled what grace is. We see grace in His response to the woman caught in adultery when He said with tenderness, "Neither do I condemn you. Go and sin no more." When He told the story of the rebellious sons and the loving, generous father in Luke 15:11-32, grace radiates from each word spoken by the father. In His observation about Martha's habit of worry and fretting, there is no tone of condemnation but a gentle reminder that she was responsible for her own misery, not Mary.

Living from the grace that Jesus has given is our only defense against legalism. Just as legalism shows up on our faces as tight lips, tense jaws, and condemning frowns, grace becomes apparent in a face that says "welcome" and "yes" to others more often than "leave me alone" or "what part of *no* do you not understand?" Living from grace develops greater appreciation of all that God has already given. Grace makes it possible for us to mature so that we spend less time fretting over other people's choices and behavior and the negative effect it may have on “me.” Grace increases joy while reducing prejudice, criticism, and judgmentalism.

God's "Equipment" for Living Life under Pressure

When we are born into God's family, we are connected to God and “grounded” by the presence of the Holy Spirit when He takes up residence in our bodies. From the moment He moves in, we have available to us all the protection we need from the overload of stress, anxiety and depression. But unless we learn how to utilize that protection, we will continue to try to live out of the four worldly Ds: disengagement, distancing, desensitizing, and deadness, instead of Holy Spirit's Ds: decontaminated, daring, defended, and diligent.

Experienced travelers carry at least one indispensable item overseas in addition to their passports and digestive medications. It is a small device that fits in the hand, and at first glance, doesn't seem all that special. However, when used properly, it has the power to take something potentially destructive and transform it into something thoroughly useful. *Transform* is a good word because that is exactly what it does when plugged into a wall socket of the high voltage European electrical systems. The handy transformer enables American and Canadian visitors to use their low-voltage shavers, radios, hair dryers, and curling irons without melting their appliances into a puddle of useless plastic.

But even more importantly, we have a Transformer for the heat and pressure of everyday life! This Transformer takes all the negatives and positives that constantly bombard our lives and runs them through His power in a way that makes the pressure usable so that we can gain from our pain, and grow from our struggle.

When Jesus was leaving His disciples on earth, He promised them a Helper, the Transformer Who makes it possible to live in a world that doesn't match the lifestyle “voltage” of a believer. Jesus's promise is that the Holy Spirit will:

1. Regenerate: John 3:3, 5-6
2. Indwell: Romans 8:11
3. Anoint: 1 John 2:20, 27
4. Baptize: Acts 2:17-41

5. Guide: John 16:13
6. Empower: Micah 3:8
7. Sanctify: Romans 15:16; 2 Thessalonians 2:13
8. Comfort: John 14:16-26
9. Give joy: Romans 14:17
10. Give discernment: 1 Corinthians 2:6-10; 1 John 4:1-6
11. Give gifts: 1 Corinthians 12:3-11; John 16:13
12. Assure us that we are God's children: Romans 8:16
13. Intercede for us: Romans 8:26

Because of the Transformer who lives in each believer, the pressure and busyness Satan uses to kill, steal, and destroy instead become tools that build strength and integrity in us in the middle of life's difficulties. As the Holy Spirit continues His work in "all things," God's goal for us to look more and more like His Son, is realized (Romans 8:28-29). It is often in the pressure cooker of stress and turmoil that God's best work is done. In those times we have to make specific choices to trust God and give up the things we have depended on for security or approval.

The Transformer gives us the ability to discern between good and bad, and between better and best as we unload stress wherever possible. In those areas where we cannot eliminate stress, we are given strength to respond from the Spirit rather than out of our flesh.

Jesus assured us: Peace I leave with you, My peace I give to you; not as the world gives, do I give to you. Let not your heart be troubled, nor let it be fearful...these things have I spoken to you that in Me you may have peace. In the world you have tribulation, but take courage; I have overcome the world (John 14:27; 16:33).

Who in the World Is the Holy Spirit?

God we know about. We hear a lot about "God," although in our world "god" comes in many forms. As believers, we are clearly instructed to know and worship the living God of the Bible; the God of Abraham, Isaac, and Jacob.

We know about Jesus, and as we are drawn into relationship with our heavenly Father, through salvation, we come to know Jesus as our Savior, Lord, Friend and Elder Brother.

But the Holy Spirit? Who is He? Webster tells us that *spirit* is (a) a life giving force within a person which endows the body with life, energy, and power; (b) a supernatural being that enters into and energizes a person.

We learned in chapter three, that each person is a spirit being with a soul, living in a physical body. It is our human spirit that endows us with life and energy. When we accept the life of Jesus (salvation); the Holy Spirit, Who is the energy and power of God, comes as a supernatural Being, to enter into our bodies and give us that energy and power. First Corinthians 6:17, 19: "The person who is united to the Lord becomes one spirit with Him. Do you not know that your body is the temple (the very sanctuary) of the Holy Spirit Who lives within you?"

From the moment of the new birth, we are conjoined with Holy Spirit so that:

- We continually have access to the very mind of God. (1 Corinthians 2:16)
- We are guided into all truth. (John 16:13-15)
- We are strengthened with His supernatural power from the inside. (Ephesians 3:16)
- We are filled up with the love of God. (Romans 5:5)
- We have power and boldness to speak the truth in love. (Ephesians 4:15)

Holy Spirit is neither a "force" nor a disembodied cloud of mist. He is a Person who comes to live in our "house" of skin, blood, and bones as an intimate roommate. He is our Partner, Friend, Advisor, and Lover.

Conjoined with the Holy Spirit

The Discovery Channel has produced a documentary entitled "Joined at Birth" that might be more accurately entitled "Joined at Conception." It features twin girls born in 1990 in Minnesota. The unique conjoining of Abigail and Brittney Hensel is extremely rare and has resulted in live births only four times in recorded history. The two sisters share one body with two heads, and today they describe themselves as "perfectly normal" young women who love to swim, play baseball, and other sports.

Obviously it takes deliberate cooperation to brush their teeth and hair, and decide which twin will have "control" of the car when they drive. The girls were each required to obtain individual driver licenses.

To look at them, they appear to be one person with two heads. However, they are two individual young women who happen to share parts of one body. Watching these lively girls whirl through life gives us a picture of the believer's relationship with the indwelling Holy Spirit. We are conjoined with Him, sharing the dwelling place of our body. It is this intimate "one-spirit" relationship that makes it possible to live victoriously in an antagonistic world.

When we think and act differently than the Holy Spirit desires, it is because we have "two heads" in some areas of our spiritual growth and our daily practice. There has to be deliberate cooperation on the part of the believer in order to become more and more one mind with Him. It is an awesome thought that everything "I" do is actually "we" performing every action! It is because of this truth that Paul says so emphatically:

> Do you not know that your bodies are members of Christ? Shall I then take away the members of Christ and make them members of a prostitute? May it never be! Flee immorality. Every other sin that a man commits is outside the body, but the immoral man sins against his own body. Or do you not know that your body is a temple of the Holy Spirit who is in you, Whom you have from God, and that you are not your own? For you have been bought with a price: therefore glorify God in your body.
>
> 1 Corinthians 6:19-20 (NASU)

A Mind in Agreement with God

The Bible describes two "mind-sets." One is a way of thinking that is in agreement with God's design for human living and is always indicative of grace. The other is a way of thinking that is in disagreement with God. This second mind-set is called "flesh" and always produces legalism and rebellion.

Mind of the Sprit	References
Trusting God	Proverbs 3:5-6
Praise and Gratitude	Ephesians 5:20
Giving up personal rights.	Ephesians 5:21
Hearing and understanding God's thoughts and wisdom.	1 Corinthians 2:10-13
Resting	Matthew 11:28-30
Bearing fruit	John 15
Living under grace and receiving life.	Galatians 2:19-20 Romans 5:17
Saying "no" to sin and self	Romans 6:12-13

Mind of the Flesh	References
Trusting self	Jeremiah 17:5
Never satisfied	Ephesians 4:19
Demanding my own way	James 4:3
Pursuing demonic, earthly "wisdom"	James 3:14-16
Struggle	Romans 1:28-32
Living a futile, empty life.	Romans 1:21-22
Legalism—living under the law and death	1 Corinthians 15:56
Saying "yes" to sin and self	Romans 8:6-7

Being indwelt and directed by the Holy Spirit is not a one-time occasion that makes everything suddenly perfect. Rather, it is a moment-by-moment, day-to-day relationship in which we are continually changed to think, talk, choose, and behave more like Jesus. The Holy Spirit pours His power into us by His presence; our part is to recognize His presence and choose to live from Him rather than from our emotions and circumstances.

When our lives are changed by the Transformer, overload is eased, the lights come back on, and we become what Jesus called us to be: bright lights in a dark world.

Christianity: The Light That Dispels Darkness

Darkness is simply the absence of light. If we are being what God has made us to be, we will stand out, and not only will our conduct look totally different than what is going on around us, we will change our surroundings as inevitably as light changes darkness.

God made the lights, the "luminaries," to light up the darkness of space, and because of the intense blackness of outer space, the stars are conspicuous; they stand out. These solar lights don't shine because they think someone might be watching or because they think someone expects them to be "on" at a certain time. They shine simply because it is their nature to shine. It's what they were created to do, and they shine whether anyone watches them shine or not.

Jesus said in John 9:5 that while He was in the world He was the light of the world. He said to His disciples, including us, that we are the light of the world (Matthew 5:14). When Jesus ascended and was no longer physically in this world, we who follow Him became the light of the world because we are now His physical, visible Body. In Ephesians 5:8, Paul tells us that we were formerly darkness, but now *we are light in the Lord.* As such, we are to live as children of Light, learning daily what is pleasing to the Lord.

From the moment of salvation, we become Jesus's ambassadors, and we represent Him and His kingdom in the foreign land of the kingdom of the world. As His Body, we are to do what He does, and what it is now our nature to do, shine in the darkness that surrounds us. Because the Spirit of Christ lives in each believer, it is our nature to be conspicuous in a world that is filled with the hopelessness and frantic anxiety that comes from being in the dark. Philippians 2:12-15 explains very practically how the "shining" is done through attitudes and behavior:

> What I'm getting at, friends, is that you should simply keep on doing what you've done from the beginning. When I was living among you, you lived in responsive obedience. Now that I'm separated from you, keep it up. Better yet, redouble your efforts. Be energetic in your life of salvation, reverent and sensitive before God. That energy is God's energy, an energy deep within you, God Himself willing and working at what will give Him the most pleasure. Do everything readily and cheerfully—no bickering, no second-guessing allowed! Go out into the world uncorrupted, a breath of fresh air in this squalid and polluted society. Provide people with a glimpse of good living and of the living God. Carry the light-giving Message into the night... (from *The Message: The Bible in Contemporary Language*)

The admonition in Philippians 2:12 to "keep on doing what you've done from the beginning" is not telling us that we have to earn our salvation. Rather, Paul is telling us to take this Gospel of truth that lives in each of us in the Person of the Holy Spirit, and bring it to its fullness at home, at school, and at work. We are to cultivate the seed of salvation that has been planted in us and bring it to harvest. That harvest is obedience to the love of God, which shows the world around us that Jesus is the Son of God.

Philippians 2:13 explains that the energy and the desire to accomplish this is God's power in us. God Himself is working out what gives Him great pleasure: bringing each of us to our fullest potential. The source of energy and power is God, but the choice to cooperate with that work is the privilege and responsibility of each believer.

List two areas of darkness (hint: confusion, hopelessness, depression) in your thinking:

____

____

Describe two practical ways that you can bring light (clarity of thought and hopefulness) into those areas:

____

____

The Counter-Culture Church

A *subculture* is a group within a society that has the same goals, interests, and behaviors. For example, a public school in a rural town would be a subculture of the American educational system. Even though it is a separate entity and is physically separated from the larger group, it has the same goals for training students and uses generally the same materials and teaching techniques. A *counter culture* is a group with a lifestyle that stands in opposition to the prevailing culture and by its influence, brings change to that culture .

The city of Philippi was a military outpost in Macedonia and is an example of a counter culture. The position of the city on the main road from Rome to Asia, the Via Egnatia, made it strategically important. The Roman citizens who lived there had all of the rights and privileges of Rome itself, including citizenship. They introduced Roman shops with Roman merchandise, Roman tax structure, and Roman laws into the settlement of Philippi so that it became a small reproduction of the city of Rome. Rome gained access to this city and changed it completely, not by violent overthrow, but by the gradual infiltration of Roman culture.

The Church is a counter-culture of light, and just as Philippi became a Roman reproduction in a Greek culture, so the Church is to reproduce heaven's light in a culture of darkness. Paul says in Philippians 3:20 that "our citizenship is in heaven" and we are to show our heavenly citizenship by our behavior; living a lifestyle that is conspicuously different in our situation in order to "heavenize" our surroundings.

We have an enemy who operates through the realm of darkness. That darkness is a poison more toxic than anything we can be exposed to physically. Because God "has delivered us and drawn us to Himself out of the control and the dominion of darkness, and has transferred us into the kingdom of the Son of His love," (Colossians 1:13) we are now able to recognize that our world is being poisoned by the enemy.

When there has been exposure to poison, neutralization of the toxin is necessary to avoid death. Jesus is the "antidote" for sin poisoning, and our behavior causes others to see the effectiveness of the antidote and desire it for themselves. To accomplish that, in partnership with Holy Spirit, we:

1. Choose to act like heavenly people.
   Write out Ephesians 5:3:

   ____

   ____

   ____

   Describe one specific change you can make, empowered by the Holy Spirit, to act like a "citizen of heaven."

   ____

   ____

   ____

2. Choose to view time from a heavenly perspective.
   Write out Ephesians 5:16:

   ____

   ____

   ____

   Write out Romans 13:11-14:

   ____

   ____

   ____

Describe one specific change you are willing to make in the use of your time in order to gain a "heavenly perspective" of time.

3. Choose to live by heavenly laws.
Write out Hebrews 10:15-16:

Describe a specific change in behavior you are willing to make in order to make the "moral integrity" of the Holy Spirit visible to others.

4. Choose to use the sort of words that express a heavenly language.
Write out Ephesians 5:4:

Describe a specific change you are willing to make in the way you talk (words, tone of voice, etc.) so that others—especially your family—will become familiar with "heavenly language."

5. Choose to have heavenly attitudes and thoughts.
   Write out Colossians 3:1-2:

   ____

   ____

   ____

   Name one specific thought and one specific attitude you are willing to replace:

   Thought:

   ____

   Attitude:

   ____

   What specific thought and attitude will you replace it with?

   Thought:

   ____

   Attitude:

   ____

Sanctification Is an Impartation, Not an Imitation

The word *sanctification* is used twenty-eight times in the New Testament, always in the context of separation or setting apart. Sanctification of the believer is the process of God's grace by which the believer is separated from sin and becomes dedicated to God's righteousness. Sanctification is accomplished by:

- The Word of God (John 17:17)
- The Holy Spirit (1 Thessalonians 5:23)

Sanctification results in purification from the guilt and power of sin.

This concept of being set apart for relationship and service to God is found throughout the Bible. The land of Canaan, the city of Jerusalem, the tabernacle, the temple, the Sabbath, the feasts, the prophets, the priests, and the garments of the priests were spoken of as "holy" or "set apart" in the Old Testament. In 1 Peter 3:15, we are told to "sanctify Christ as Lord in your hearts, always being ready to make a defense to everyone who asks you to give an account for the hope that is in you, yet with gentleness and reverence." God is sanctified (set apart from all others) by His perfectly righteous judgments upon sin (Ezekiel 38:16). Jesus also was "sanctified and sent into the world" (John 10:36).

There is sanctification for us in the atonement, based on the sacrificial death of Christ. In his letters to the churches, Paul noted that God has chosen and reconciled us to Himself in Christ for the purpose of sanctification (Ephesians 1:4; 5:25-27; Titus 2:14).

Sanctification is a work of God. We are sanctified by:

- God the Father (Jude 1:1)
- God the Son (Hebrews 2:11)
- God the Holy Spirit (2 Thessalonians 2:13; 1 Peter 1:2)

Paul describes practical holiness in Colossians 3:3-14

> Your old life is dead. Your new life, which is your real life — even though invisible to spectators — is with Christ in God. He is your life… and that means killing off everything connected with that way of death: sexual promiscuity, impurity, lust, doing whatever you feel like whenever you feel like it, and grabbing whatever attracts your fancy. That's a life shaped by things and feelings instead of by God… it wasn't long ago that you were doing all that stuff and not knowing any better. But you know better now, so make sure it's all gone for good: bad temper, irritability, meanness, profanity, dirty talk. Don't lie to one another. You're done with that old life. It's like a filthy set of ill-fitting clothes you've stripped off and put in the fire. Now you're dressed in a new wardrobe. Every item of your new way of life is custom-made by the Creator, with His label on it. All the old fashions are now obsolete… so, chosen by God for this

> new life of love, dress in the wardrobe God picked out for you: compassion, kindness, humility, quiet strength, discipline. Be even-tempered, content with second place, quick to forgive an offense. Forgive as quickly and completely as the Master forgave you. And regardless of what else you put on, wear love. It's your basic, all-purpose garment. Never be without it. (From *The Message: The Bible in Contemporary Language*)

Holiness is not just a suggestion; it is God's command, (1 Thessalonians 4:7) and it is the ultimate conclusion of God's work in each person. Paul prayed for believers, "Now may the God of peace Himself sanctify you completely" (1 Thessalonians 5:23). The process of sanctification is referred to as both an immediate event and a process in Hebrews 10:14, "because by one sacrifice He *has made perfect* forever those who *are being sanctified* and made holy."

Sanctification is also the believer's work as we make the decision to "grow up" and become mature. There are numerous commands in the Bible that indicate the believer's responsibility in the process of sanctification. We are commanded:

- To "be holy" (Leviticus 11:44; 1 Peter 1:15-16)
- To "be perfect" (Matthew 5:48)
- To "present your members as slaves of righteousness for holiness" (Romans 6:19)

These commands imply choices and determination on our part. We must choose to believe in Jesus, since we are "sanctified by faith in Him" (Acts 26:18). Through the Holy Spirit we must also choose to "put to death the evil deeds of the body" (Romans 8:13). Paul itemized the many "works of the flesh" from which we must choose to separate ourselves (Galatians 5:19-21). Finally, we are to live our daily lives in the power of the Spirit, exercising our wills so that our life experience displays the fruit of the Spirit (Galatians 5:22-24). Writing to the church of the Thessalonians, the apostle Paul made a strong plea for purity:

> This is the will of God, your sanctification: that you should abstain from sexual immorality; that each of you should know

> how to possess his own vessel in sanctification and honor, not in passion of lust, like the Gentiles who do not know God.
>
> 1 Thessalonians 4:3-5

The problem with our part of the process of sanctification is that it often seems so impossible in light of how we feel or what we are currently experiencing in our Christian walk. But when we entered into a new relationship with God, we instantly received our "new identity" (2 Corinthians 5:17).

Living out of this new identity results in a new life experience, but unlike the immediate transformation in our spirit, a new lifestyle does not happen instantly or automatically. Many Christians struggle with their life experience still looking too much like their old way of life, even after salvation. The message we often receive from the Christian community is "since you are a Christian, you shouldn't feel or think or act that way." This leaves the disgruntled Christian believing that everyone else lives in victory; he alone is left to struggle with wrong thinking and behavior. He believes that since God has already done His part, the rest is completely up to him and he is failing miserably.

Defining the words *justified* and *sanctified* provides a better understanding of what is our part and what is God's part in this process. *Justification* deals with our relationship with God. When we are "born again" we come into a condition that the Bible refers to as being justified: released from the guilt of sin and accepted as righteous. Romans 3:24 says that we "are justified freely by His grace through the redemption that came by Christ Jesus." Our justification is complete and given without condition. We can do nothing but accept the gift. Justification not only means that we are now "just as if we had never sinned," it means that we are now accepted by God *just as if we had always obeyed*!

Sanctification deals with our character, conduct, and growth after we have been justified. There are two aspects to sanctification. When we receive salvation, God sanctifies us and sets us apart, but we are then commanded to *sanctify ourselves* and set ourselves apart unto the Lord (1 Thessalonians 4:3). This second aspect of sanctification has to do with personal human relationships and the influence we have on people.

When doctrine goes no further than the teaching of justification, then "babies in the Lord" remain childish and self-centered. Just as we desire for our children to grow up, our heavenly Father intends for us to mature spiritually.

Hebrews 5:11-14 says that maturity is achieved through the deliberate practice of rejecting wrong and choosing right:

> Concerning this we have much to say which is hard to explain, since you have become dull in your [spiritual] hearing and sluggish … in achieving spiritual insight. For even though by this time you ought to be teaching others, you actually need someone to teach you over again the very first principles of God's Word. You have come to need milk, not solid food. Everyone who continues to feed on milk is obviously inexperienced and unskilled in the doctrine of righteousness … he is a mere infant, not able to talk yet! But solid food is for full-grown men, for those whose senses and mental faculties *are trained by practice to discriminate and distinguish between what is morally good and what is evil.*

Living the sanctified life is only possible when we understand what the death and resurrection of Jesus accomplished for us. He did not come to change our old life or "help us" live our old life more successfully. Jesus came to destroy and bury our old life. In exchange, He resurrected us with His own life. Paul shouts triumphantly in Galatians 2:20:

> I have been crucified with Christ; and it is no longer I who live, but Christ lives in me; and the life which I now live in the flesh I live by faith in the Son of God, who loved me, and delivered Himself up for me.
>
> (NASU)

Sanctification is an impartation, not an imitation. The secret to growing in holiness does not lie in *imitating* Jesus. If we try to imitate Him, the result is a fake life. Rather, we are to let Jesus live His own genuine life through our soul and body. As we know Jesus better and make our choices out of what we hear Him say and see Him do, the real life of Jesus becomes visible in our behavior. The wonder of sanctification is that all the wisdom and power of Jesus is at our disposal. As His perfection flows through our thinking, choices, and behavior, our lives increase in sanity and holiness. Sanctification is not some "thing" that Jesus Christ puts into us; it is *Himself* in us.

So how does knowing that Christ lives in us make a difference as we live "life in the real world"? In her book *Hope Has Its Reasons*, Rebecca Pippert describes the new life this way: "One of the most important things to remember when we come to know God is that everything is the same, yet nothing is the same. We still walk the same ground, breathe the same air, drink the same water, buy the same groceries, and get buried in the same earth. But like someone falling in love, our senses are so heightened that the sky really seems bluer, the grass greener, and every second charged with the grandeur of God."[28]

The Holy Spirit does not take away the God-designed personality we were given at conception. Being indwelt by the Holy Spirit does not remove our *humanity*; it removes the *sin* that poisoned our beautiful human design. Second Corinthians 4:7 explains that we have the treasure of God's life in the "earthen vessels" of our bodies.

Being indwelt by the Holy Spirit does not make us immune to the assault of temptation, but because of His life in us, temptation no longer involves the *necessity to sin*. Temptation does not become sin until we say yes to it. Sanctification makes saying no to temptation *possible*, not necessarily *easy*.

The indwelling presence of the Holy Spirit does not automatically produce maturity. Maturity requires time, discipline and watchfulness, and, according to Scripture, sanctified maturity is to be our goal:

> As a result, we are no longer to be children, tossed here and there by waves, and carried about by every wind of doctrine, by the trickery of men, by craftiness in deceitful scheming; but speaking the truth in love, we are to *grow up in all aspects* into Him, who is the Head, even Christ.
>
> Ephesians 4:14-15 (NASU)

> But the path of the righteous is like the light of dawn that shines *brighter and brighter until the full day*.
>
> Proverbs 4:18 (NASU)

> Like newborn babes, long for the pure milk of the word, that

by it you may *grow in respect to salvation*, if you have tasted the kindness of the Lord.

1 Peter 2:2-3 (NASU)

The indwelling presence of the Holy Spirit enables us to:

- Choose to live a life of faith in a world that depends almost totally on the five senses. Second Corinthians 4:17-18 sounds like such a paradox to our American way of thinking. Rearranging our understanding of what is lasting and what is temporary will make revolutionary changes in our choices.

  Write out 2 Corinthians 4:17-18

  ____

  ____

  ____

- Choose to live well-disciplined lives in a world system that describes respectful obedience to authority as restrictive. We have learned to believe the lie that perfect freedom means never having to say "no," never having any restrictions on what we can do or say, or where we can go.

  So, since we're out from under the old tyranny, does that mean we can live any old way we want… or anything that comes to mind? Hardly. You know well enough from your own experience that there are some acts of so-called freedom that destroy freedom. Offer yourselves to sin, for instance, and it's your last free act. But offer yourselves to the ways of God and the freedom never quits. All your lives you've let sin tell you what to do. But thank God you've started listening to a new Master… (Romans 6:15-17 from *The Message*: *The Bible in Contemporary Language*)

  Write out 1 Corinthians 6:12:

  ____

____

____

Write out Romans 6:22-23:

____

____

____

This change in thinking makes radical changes in our choices concerning use of time, friendships, work, and leisure.

- We choose to live humbly in a world filled with pride and prideful teaching. When we realize we have nothing that we have not received as a gift, we can choose to enter into relationships with a heart of humility and kindness rather than with self-centered demands. We are called to say *no* to self and egotism. This makes a complete change in our interaction with others at home and at work.

  > Do nothing from selfishness or empty conceit, but with humility of mind let each of you regard one another as more important than himself; do not merely look out for your own personal interests, but also for the interests of others. Have this attitude in yourselves which was also in Christ Jesus.
  >
  > Philippians 2:3-5 (NASU)

- We choose to live gratefully in a world that says what we have is never enough, and is always less than we deserve. The focus of the world is on positions, power, and possessions, all of which become stale over time. When we focus on God, we think more about what He has done by saving us than on what He "should" be giving us. *Self-indulgence* is a key word in our twenty-first century American culture. The call to self-denial sounds strange, even impossible, at first. However, this change in mind-set makes a radical difference in why we go to work every day, how we do our jobs, and how we manage the resources God has given us.

> For we have brought nothing into the world, so we cannot take anything out of it either. And if we have food and covering, with these we shall be content. But those who want to get rich fall into temptation and a snare and many foolish and harmful desires which plunge men into ruin and destruction. For the love of money is a root of all sorts of evil, and some by longing for it have wandered away from the faith, and pierced themselves with many a pang.
>
> 1 Timothy 6:7-10 (NASU)

- We choose to live quietly in a world that tries to outdo itself in noise and activity. Our culture is filled with people so frightened of honestly facing their thoughts that nearly every moment is spent finding distractions from quietness. Psalm 46:10 tells us to "Cease striving and know that I am God; I will be exalted among the nations, I will be exalted in the earth." The implication is if we are never still, we will not learn to know God. And until we understand what He is really like, our own failures will be too terrifying to face. As we come to know Him better in times of quietness, fear of failure will decrease and we will live more in the freedom of "doing all things" in His strength.

- We choose to live without idols in a world that is immersed in idolatry. An idol is anything or any person other than God that we depend on to get our needs for security, worth, and acceptance met. American believers would not consider setting up an altar in a corner and praying to a little statue twice a day. But without thinking, we choose to give the best of our time and energy to the earthly things that make us feel the most valuable and appreciated.

Many of those things are good, and perhaps we are doing work that God wants us to do, but the motivation for doing them has been twisted by the world around us. Good works come as the *result* of God's approval and love; they are not the *cause* of His approval and love. Understanding this keeps us from depending on works as a condition for keeping salvation, even after we have accepted it as a free gift.

We learn early to be suspicious of a "good deal." We're taught "if it sounds too good to be true, it probably is," and "there is no such thing as a free lunch," or "there are always strings attached." The "buy and sell" nature of our culture is so ingrained in us that we naturally think we have to deal with God the same way.

We may bargain with God:

- "You do this for me, God, and I'll do this for You."
- "God, if you just get me out of this, I promise ... "

At its core, a bargaining mind-set is legalistic and rooted in idolatry. God does not operate according to this principle. Instead, we have the privilege of approaching Him in trust, believing by faith that His promises and love for us are unchangeable (Matthew 6:33). Receiving God's complete acceptance frees us from the bondage of depending on ourselves and what we can do for God in order to get Him to provide for us.

Until we are aware that our needs are met in Christ, we will be driven by our own sense of emptiness to manipulate those around us into meeting our needs. As we recognize that we are fulfilled by the presence of God, we will be freed from a self-centered preoccupation with our own needs. Only then will our possessions, relationships, and jobs be safe for us to enjoy. Only then will we be able to offer ministry to those around us.

We have choices to make in each moment of life, and it is the power of the Holy Spirit in us that enables us to choose a disciplined way of life. Our choices are made out of who we now are, rather than out of how we feel or how our circumstances happen to look.

Spiritual disciplines are often seen as a form of legalism, but properly applied, these disciplines make a vast difference in the quality of the Christian life. The Scriptural concept of discipline is training that serves the Christian like a training program prepares an athlete. We need to learn the practical methods of spiritual discipline that get us "in shape" to live the Christian life with strength and enthusiasm.

Spiritual disciplines are not a program for inflicting punishment. They help us focus our spiritual energy on accomplishing creative things. A jogger may first begin to run under doctor's orders but then looks forward to his daily run because it makes him feel better physically. In the same way, spiritual disciplines help us to enjoy our Christian walk.[29] We live with confidence because we can choose to cooperate with God's sanctifying work in our everyday lives.

The sanctification of our mind, will, and emotions by the indwelling Holy Spirit should not be compared to a graduation exercise that occurs once and then becomes a distant memory. It is a *process* of deeper intimacy with God, empowered by the Holy Spirit and activated by our will. This process, which takes us into a lifestyle of growth, maturity and victory, continues for the rest of our lives.

Questions for Personal Reflection

1. Are there any areas of your life where you feel unaccepted by God?

 ___

 ___

 ___

2. Is there something you have done for which you think God could not forgive you?

 ___

 ___

 ___

3. What behavior do you adopt to try to gain more acceptance from God?

 ___

 ___

 ___

4. What family standards were you expected to maintain as you were growing up?

____

____

____

5. What church standards were you expected to maintain as you were growing up?

____

____

____

6. What standards do you use to judge the acceptability or worthiness of others?
(Hint: what annoys you? Do you have a "pet peeve"? What do criticize in others?)

____

____

____

As you identify your standards, sit quietly with the Lord and give them to Him. Make a choice to accept yourself and others in the same way Jesus has accepted you.

Write out Romans 15:7

____

____

____

Chapter 8: Getting Our Brains Washed with God's Detergent

Renewing the Mind

What Are You Thinking?

Do you really know what you think? Most of us would quickly answer "Well, of course I know, but sometimes I just put my mind out of gear, and I don't think at all."

The fact is we really don't pay much attention to our minds outside of a classroom. With a few exceptions, little effort is given to keeping our minds from becoming clogged by the "trash" that surrounds us and is being absorbed into our thinking. Expensive filters keep swimming pools and fish tanks clean by trapping the debris that is in the water. Vacuum cleaners and air purifiers help us breathe easier in our homes as contaminates are pulled from the air by specially designed filters. But these filters are only effective when they are properly installed and used the way they are designed.

God has given us His Word as a filter that traps the "thought trash" that surrounds us. Unfortunately, as ignorance of God's Word grows, the minds of believers are left largely unprotected. The Bible shows us how the spiritual "filtering system" of knowing and applying God's Word works:

> For the Lord gives skillful and Godly Wisdom; from His mouth come knowledge and understanding.
>
> Proverbs 2:6

> How shall a young man cleanse his way? By taking heed and keeping watch [on himself] according to Your word [conforming his life to it].
>
> Psalm 119:9

> The reverent and worshipful fear of the Lord is the beginning and the principal and choice part of knowledge [its starting point and its essence]; but fools despise skillful and Godly Wisdom, instruction, and discipline.
>
> Proverbs 1:7

Write out Ephesians 5:26-27:

____

____

____

____

Write out 1 Peter 1:22-23:

____

____

____

____

Neglecting to use God's specially designed filter often happens because we believe it's too much trouble to exercise our mental capabilities. We are bombarded with the idea that by age forty we can expect our ability to think and remember to deteriorate so that we can no longer learn. If we believe our minds are going to quit working just a few years after our education is completed anyway, it's just a hopeless waste of time and energy take thoughts captive and renew the mind.

It is a terribly sad commentary on our culture that far more time, research, and effort is given to convincing us that we can be like a thirty-year-old sexually at age sixty than keeping our minds active and alert after age forty. Billions of dollars are spent annually to keep our air clean and our world "green," but the litter and pollution from a world system under the control of Satan floods the minds of Christians with little awareness or resistance.

The truth from our owner's manual is that *the mind is central to our quality of life*. We cannot have a pessimistic, hopeless, selfish mind-set and enjoy an optimistic, enthusiastic, righteous lifestyle. Scripture also teaches that we cannot continue in pessimism and hopeless thinking if we really know and trust God. Complaining and negativism simply announces to the world around us that we really don't believe what God says about His desire and ability to take care of us.

The Bible emphasizes repeatedly that it is essential to pay close attention to our thoughts because we become what we think (Proverbs 23:7). God commands us to:

- Choose to meditate (think) on things that please God. (Psalms 19:14)
- Take thoughts captive. (2 Corinthians 10:5)
- Renew the mind with its attitudes. (Romans 12:1-2)
- Set the mind on eternal things. (Colossians 3:1-2)
- Choose the mind of the Spirit instead of the mind of the flesh. (Romans 8:5)
- Prepare our minds for action. (1 Peter 1:13)
- Be sober in our minds. (1 Peter 5:8)

Burning the "CD" of the Mind

We develop thought patterns from birth that are deeply ingrained into our minds, like sounds burned onto a CD. As we learned in chapter five, emotions are like warning lights on a vehicle's dashboard that help us recognize which thought pattern is playing in the mind. If it is a pattern rooted in rage, bitterness, or resentment, those thoughts need to be taken captive (2 Corinthians 10:4-5) and replaced with God's way of thinking, which will ultimately produce emotional peace (Romans 12:2-3).

We often blame our circumstances for the misery, fear, and anger that pull us down into discouragement. But attitudes actually control our response to circumstances. An attitude is a state of mind that produces a reaction in the emotions and body, resulting in particular choices and behavior. Much more than our actual situation, it is what we *think* about the situation that determines whether we are:

- victorious or defeated
- joyful or gloomy
- hopeful or hopeless

Right Actions Follow Right Thinking; Wrong Actions Follow Wrong Thinking

If someone who can accurately type seventy words per minute sits down at a computer keyboard and quickly fills the screen with every vulgar, disrespectful four-letter word she has ever heard and then clicks print, the words "For God so loved the world" (John 3:16) are not going to print onto the page. What has been typed in will print out.

The same thing is true of our lives: if we constantly meditate on all the hurts we have experienced, how unfair life is, or how hopeless the economic situation is, we are cultivating wrong thoughts. For example:

- *Fear*: anxiety and worry are reinforced by listening to and meditating on a secular perspective of current events and the future.
- *Lust*: a strong desire to satisfy our own selfish cravings is reinforced by absorbing our culture's definition of "need" through commercials, excessive window shopping, or by looking with envy over our neighbor's fence at their house, spouse, cars, or other possessions.
- *Hopelessness*: despair is reinforced by listening repeatedly to the cultural commentary on the state of the world or to what the latest psychological "guru" has to say about relationships.
- *Rage*: bitterness and bad temper is reinforced by keeping a list of every hurtful thing that has ever happened in our lives.

If we nurture these kinds of thoughts by dwelling on them, fear, lust, hopelessness, and rage are exactly what will "print out" in our behavior.

> (Jesus said): You have heard that it was said, "You shall not commit adultery. But I say to you that everyone who so much as looks at a woman with evil desire for her has already committed adultery with her in his heart."
>
> Matthew 5:27-28

Jesus fully understood that a thought is the beginning of an action. If the mind dwells on angry thoughts, murder in some form is inevitable; perhaps the murder of someone's character through slander or death in relationships.

If we allow our minds to dwell on lustful thoughts, we will manipulate circumstances to get the relationships or things we lust for. Thoughts always precede choices and actions. Our behavior today is simply an announcement of a thought we entertained yesterday.

Getting Our Brains Washed

"Renewing the mind" is a phrase we're familiar with if we have been in church for any length of time, but when it comes to applying it in a practical way, there's a lot of confusion. To renew the mind simply means:

> I choose to stop thinking the way I've learned to think from TV, music, movies, books, and friends that don't agree with the Word of God, and I choose to think progressively the way God teaches me to think through His Word.

This change in our thinking is a *process* that happens "little by little"; not all at once through "ten easy steps." In Exodus 23:28-33 God tells Moses what He is going to do for the people when they come into the land of promise. Remember, these are the people who eventually died in the wilderness because they refused to believe what God was saying to them. God said to Moses:

> And I will send hornets before you which shall drive out the Hivite, Canaanite, and Hittite from before you. I will not drive them out from before you in one year, lest the land become desolate (for lack of attention) and the wild beasts multiply against you. Little by little I will drive them out from before you, until you have increased and are numerous enough to take possession of the land. I will set your borders from the Red Sea to the Sea of the Philistines, and from the wilderness to the river (Euphrates); for I will deliver the inhabitants of the land into your hand and *you shall drive them out before you*. You shall make no covenant with them or with their gods. They shall not dwell

> in your land, lest they make you sin against Me; for if you serve their gods, it will surely be a snare to you.

Using our sanctified imagination, we can change this scripture to describe driving out wrong thinking:

> And I will send My truth before you that shall drive out the lust, the hopelessness, depression, bitterness, and unforgiveness. I will not remove it all from you in one year, because the beasts of pride in your own strength and accomplishments would multiply against you. So little by little, My truth will drive the thoughts out, until your confidence in My truth has increased enough to take possession of My promised land of truth. I will deliver those old thoughts into your hand, and *you shall drive them out.* You must refuse to enter into covenant with them by agreeing with them. Those old thoughts shall not dwell in your mind; if they do, they will cause you to sin against Me and they will keep you in bondage. (my paraphrase)

There are five things that are emphasized in this passage:

- If God changed our thinking for us all at one time, we would be overwhelmed by all the truth that He gives us.
- He will give us time to grow into this new land of truth.
- God will deliver the enemy of untruth into our hands, but we have to do our part and fight the old thoughts.
- We must refuse to take part in the pagan culture around us.
- We must destroy the "enemy" thoughts, or they will cause us to sin and keep us in bondage.

A Goal without a Plan Is Just Wishful Thinking

The process of renewing the mind could be compared to a family taking a vacation road trip. First, the family discusses their options concerning the destination. "Should we go to the West Coast to see the ocean or to the Midwest to see Mount Rushmore?" The destination is crucial; no other part of the planning can be done if the family doesn't know where they want to spend their vacation time. After some discussion, it is decided that since two of the children have studied about Mount Rushmore it would mean a lot for them to be able to actually see it.

First, Dad pulls out the maps and chooses the best route. Financial preparation is the next item on the list, followed by reservations at appropriate hotels and tourist attractions. On the appointed day, the family settles into the car, ready to begin their vacation.

The family soon discovers that there are many things along the way that may interrupt the original plan. Stops to accommodate different family members have to be made more often than anticipated, but by driving a bit faster, the family's arrival at the first night's hotel is only an hour later than originally planned.

The second day's schedule flowed smoothly until they encountered a detour for highway repairs. The alternate route took them twenty miles out of the way, and as they bumped over a gravel road, a sharp rock punctured a front tire. The day ended with everyone tired and irritable. The night at the hotel was too short, and they began the next day with far less enthusiasm for seeing Mount Rushmore. In fact, one of the children who had insisted that "life would hardly be worth living" if she didn't get to see it was now suggesting that they should just go back home! Another chimed in declaring that he was tired of the car and ready to be back in his own room where he was comfortable and he didn't think those big faces on the side of a cliff were going to be worth all this misery.

Mom and Dad looked at each other in desperation. What to do? Suddenly Mom remembered the video tucked away in the luggage that documented the process of carving the faces in the rock, the tools which were used, and how the measurements were taken from the blueprint onto the side of the mountain. Without consulting the children, they decided to cancel one of the stops planned for the next day so they could sleep later and swim longer before resuming the drive.

The next afternoon, after everyone got settled in the car, rested and happy, Mom plugged the DVD player in, and all three children became engrossed in the account of the obstacles that had to be overcome as the faces were carved into the side of Mount Rushmore. The discomfort of being away from home and riding in a car for hours was superseded by the renewed anticipation of seeing this great national monument.

You may be thinking, "*What does this family vacation have to do with renewing the mind?*"

- The family trip is the journey we take away from our old, familiar thought patterns into unknown territory.
- First we choose a destination. For example, we may decide that we want to think differently about our spouse. That's the destination or the goal.
- The map is instruction from the Word of God.
- The detour and road hazards are things like boredom, discomfort, disappointment, hopelessness, frustration, and sometimes just plain laziness and apathy.
- Because we live in a culture that insists life "should be" easy, pain free, trouble free, and stress free, we may whine to God because it's uncomfortable or difficult to change our thinking. We may think longingly about our old "room" of thought that we were familiar with; we may look ahead at our chosen destination and think it isn't worth the trouble and effort.
- The Holy Spirit is the "video" that will continue to show us why it is worth the effort. He offers opportunities to rest and be refreshed through our relationship with Jesus. He continually gives wisdom so that we know how to deal with the detours and road hazards.

But just as the destination on a road trip cannot be achieved without organization and effort, neither will the goals we set for changing our thinking be reached without careful planning.

Perhaps one of the reasons believers stay in bondage to lies even after receiving salvation is we believe that just knowing about the truth will somehow negate *The Lie*. But it is not enough to only *believe* the truth. We must recognize *The Lie* for what it is and eliminate it if we are going to enjoy increasing freedom from bondage.

What Are We Being Renewed from … To?

There are eight basic mind-sets that keep us in turmoil and bondage and six mind-sets that set us free to enjoy the abundant life our Father longs for us to have and enjoy.

1. The Sluggish Mind
   People with a sluggish mind-set will often say:

   - "I watch TV so I can just turn my mind off."
   - "I just want to sit down and veg."
   - "I'm too tired to think about anything."

   Mental sluggishness develops mostly through neglect. People who have a sluggish mind wish for things to be different but do nothing to make the changes needed; often expecting others to carry out the necessary work. As they sit trying not to think about anything, they sigh, complain and moan:

   - "Well, I just wish things would be different."
   - "I just wish he wouldn't act that way."
   - "I just wish I wouldn't get depressed … "

   "Empty" space is a place. If we are not deliberately filling our minds with what God tells us to put in there, that space will be filled by anything Satan can manage to slip in while we aren't paying attention. It is impossible to put our minds in neutral. We dream because even when we sleep our minds are working. Our minds are designed to always be thinking; therefore, they will always be thinking about something. *It is up to us to choose what we are going to think about.*

   Webster defines sluggish in this way: 1. Habitually idle and lazy; slothful; dull; inactive: 2. Slow; having little motion. Synonyms: inert; idle; indolent; dronish; drowsy.

   Jesus addressed the problem of a sluggish mind. He equated it with foolishness and being slow to believe Him.

> And (Jesus) said to them, O foolish ones (sluggish in mind, dull of perception) and slow of heart to believe (adhere to and trust in and rely on) everything that the prophets have spoken!
>
> Luke 24:25

A sluggish mind is a mind that continues to think but is not being disciplined and transformed in obedience to Jesus. It is being controlled by Satan and his world system through neglect. Unfortunately, the person who has a sluggish mind is generally unaware of that control.

There is no quick fix for a sluggish mind. The long-term solution is choosing to pay attention; being deliberately aware of what is entering our minds through our eyes and ears, and noticing carefully what our mind is doing with that information.

Identify two areas in your thinking that have become "sluggish." (For example, what you think about the importance of knowing God's Word or how it applies to everyday life.)

____

____

How do you plan to energize these two areas of thinking?

____

____

2. The Drifting Mind:
   A sluggish mind becomes a mind that rambles without purpose, drifting aimlessly, and following whatever tangent comes along. A drifting mind is undisciplined. Western cultures reject the idea of discipline and self-control and seek to find pharmacological "solutions" for the emotional and physical symptoms that result from this lack of discipline. The resulting loss of self-control is labeled "conduct disorders."

   Out-of-control emotions in children are the result of too much video and audio stimulation; too much stress combined with diets high in starches and sugar; not enough quiet, parental restraint, and an almost complete absence of stillness. This lack of discipline on the part of both parents and children receives the "bipolar" and "ADD or ADHD" labels.

The National Association of School Psychologists states, "The term ADD/ADHD has come to act like a set of blinders so that the many other potential sources of inattention are oftentimes bypassed and not even considered."

The very first group of severely ADD people ever studied were people who suffered from encephalitis, or a swelling of the brain. Birth defects and brain injury from toxic chemicals such as lead often cause ADD. However, over the last several decades the ADD diagnostic criteria have been greatly broadened to include many people with no brain defects at all. Experts in the fields of temperament and creativity have objected that perfectly healthy people are being classified as disordered. As time passes, we find it more likely that many so-called ADD people are simply not ADD in the original, classic sense. Yet currently, 8 million school-aged children in the United States are regularly given highly addictive, class 2 drugs to combat a "disorder" that is diagnosed by a list of vague, subjective observations.

The consistent, loving discipline of children takes time and energy, and in our "pressure-cooker" world where both parents usually work, that time and energy is not available. But if we stop to evaluate what stress does to adults, we will understand the enormity of the impact this pressure and anxiety-soaked world has on children.

- Children who are not taught by consistent repetition how to answer appropriately, sit still for periods of time, and take part in family activities (such as household chores) on a daily basis will grow up lacking the discipline needed to study and hold a job.
- Children who are not getting enough quietness, rest, and downtime spin out of control in behavior.
- Children who are exposed to a lot of noise and activity (fighting in the home, loud TV and video, constant noise

> through their iPods) will respond with agitation and loudness. We call it "bouncing off the walls" and attempt to fix it by increasing stimulation through chemicals and entertainment, rather than by decreasing stimulation and teaching them to be more comfortable with quietness.

An undisciplined child with an undisciplined mind will grow up to be an undisciplined adult who will raise more undisciplined children. If we think the way the world thinks about ADD or ADHD in both children and adults, we'll reach for a temporary solution: a pill bottle. To break this deadly cycle, we must think the way God tells us to think about childish, undisciplined behavior.

Undisciplined childishness is not new. Paul commented about this problem in 1 Corinthians 13:11:

> When I was a child, I talked like a child, I thought like a child, I reasoned like a child; now that I have become a man, I am done with childish ways and have put them aside.

Identify two areas of childishness in your thinking. (Hint: childishness is usually characterized by a focus on yourself.)

____

____

How do you plan to mature in these two areas of thinking? Be specific.

____

____

____

____

3. The Bewildered Mind
   A mind that drifts with no consistent direction is persistently bewildered: puzzled, confused, and unstable as described in James 1:5-8:

> If any of you is deficient in wisdom, let him ask of the giving God (who gives) to everyone liberally and ungrudgingly, without reproaching or faultfinding, and it will be given him. Only it must be in faith that he asks with no wavering (no hesitating, no doubting). For the one who wavers (hesitates, doubts) is like the billowing surge out at sea that is blown hither and thither and tossed by the wind. For truly, let not such a person imagine that he will receive anything [he asks for] from the Lord, (For being as he is) a man of two minds (hesitating, dubious, irresolute), (he is) unstable and unreliable and uncertain about everything (he thinks, feels, decides).

When believers try to reason everything out using information from an unbelieving world system, we become as confused and bewildered as our unsaved culture, surrounded by a "whatever" mind-set. A bewildered mind finds it difficult and frightening to make a commitment to anything or to make a decision for which we will be held accountable. "Whatever!" is a common response of a bewildered mind.

This attempt to figure things out and make choices out of our own wisdom is a remnant of believing *The Lie* that Satan told the first human couple; that if they just had enough knowledge, they could figure things out and, just like God, be able to fix everything.

Rational thought is not a bad thing; after all, God did not say that we would be transformed by the *removal* of our minds, but the *renewal* of our minds. He gave us the ability to think and tells us to ask Him for wisdom in our thinking. The problem comes when we try to reason through every aspect of a situation and manipulate it to our best advantage. When we are determined to get what we want, how we want it, when we want it, the Bible describes that as acting from our "flesh."

Bewilderment is prevalent because the compass of our world (worldly, demonic wisdom) is constantly spinning off in a different direction and we can't find our footing. The diagnosis of the anxiety produced by this spiritual need for God's moral compass is "bipolar" or "Generalized Anxiety Disorder (GAD)." But this anxiety is not a mental disease to be cured with drugs. It is simply the accumulated result of not training and renewing the mind according to God's direction. The permanent solution is to place the bewildered mind under the authority of God's unchanging Word.

Identify two areas of confusion in your thinking:

____

____

How do you plan to bring clarity into these two areas of thinking?

____

____

____

____

4. The Doubting Mind

Bewilderment is like being surrounded by a dense fog, and the longer it lingers, the more uncertainty, anxiety, and doubt increases. *Vine's Expository Dictionary* defines doubt as: "to stand in two ways—implying uncertainty which way to take . . . being anxious through distraction . . . wavering between hope and fear."

Some doubt and uncertainty is simply a normal part of "little" faith growing up into a greater faith. When a child takes her first steps, there is a great deal of uncertainty, and she is hesitant about letting go of dad's hand. And it is certain that when she finally does let go, she will fall and bump her head. But if she never takes the risk of falling, she will never get beyond those first uncertain steps.

If we don't stretch our minds into uncomfortable, sometimes threatening new areas of knowledge about God, our minds remain immature and uncertain. We continue to be childish and filled with vagueness about who God is and about who we are.

Identify two areas of doubtful thinking:

____

____

How do you plan to change from doubt to greater certainty in these two areas of thinking?

____

____

____

____

5. The Skeptical Mind
   Uncertainty that is not eliminated through study and growing faith becomes skepticism. Doubt and skepticism are related, but they are not the same thing.

   - Doubt is immaturity.
   - Skepticism is *accepting immaturity as normal*, refusing to grow up and live life as a spiritual adult.

Mark 16:9-14 is the account of Jesus's resurrection, His conversation with Mary Magdalene, and her announcement to the other disciples that she had seen Him.

> Now Jesus, having risen (from death) early on the first day of the week, appeared first to Mary Magdalene, from whom He had driven out seven demons. She went and reported it to those who had been with Him, as they grieved and wept. And when they heard that He was alive and that she had seen Him, *they did not believe it*. After this, He appeared in a different form to two of them as they were walking (along the way) into the country. And they returned (to Jerusalem) and told the others, *but they did not believe them either*. Afterward He appeared to the Eleven (apostles themselves) as they reclined at table; and He reproved and reproached them for their unbelief (their lack of faith) and their hardness of heart, *because they had refused to believe* those who had seen him and looked at him attentively after he had risen [from death].

This was not a case of doubt and uncertainty wondering, "Could it really have been Him?" Jesus reproved them because they were deliberately choosing not to believe an eyewitness account simply because they weren't the witnesses. Grumbling, rebellion, and cynicism are the fruit of spiritual skepticism or unbelief.

Paul said this to his Jewish listeners, and it still applies today:

> Paul interrupted: "I have just one more thing to say to you. The Holy Spirit sure knew what He was talking about when He addressed our ancestors through Isaiah the prophet: Go to this people and tell them this: 'You're going to listen with your ears, but you won't hear a word; you're going to stare with your eyes, but you won't see a thing. These people are blockheads! They stick their fingers in their ears so they won't have to listen; They screw their eyes shut so they won't have to look, so they won't have to deal with Me face-to-face and let Me heal them.'"
>
> Acts 28:25-27 (The Message)

Identify two areas of spiritual skepticism:

____

____

How do you plan to replace skepticism with confidence?

____

____

____

____

6. The Apprehensive Mind
   Skepticism produces a mind-set characterized by apprehension and dread. This is also often treated as a medical condition in our culture, referred to as "mental illness." But the Bible tells us clearly that anxiety and apprehension are emotional responses rooted in skepticism.

> Anxiety in the heart of man causes depression, but a good word makes it glad.
>
> Proverbs 12:25, (NKJV)

Jesus was equally clear about the solution:

> Peace I leave with you; My own peace I now give and bequeath to you. Not as the world gives do I give to you. Do not let your hearts be troubled, neither let them be afraid. Stop allowing yourselves to be agitated and disturbed; and do not permit yourselves to be fearful and intimidated and cowardly and unsettled.
>
> John 14:27

Anxiety produces a lifestyle of self-pity, complaining, and hopelessness. Choosing to exchange dread for trust in the goodness of God produces peace.

Identify two areas of apprehension and dread in your thinking:

____

____

What new thoughts do you need to plant and cultivate to "choke out" apprehension?

____

____

____

____

7. The Condemning, Suspicious Mind
   Apprehension creates a self-centered mind-set that is suspicious of the motives and actions of others, believing that "if other people would just do what they are supposed to do, my life would be easier." A person who thinks like this always has a list of what others "should have done." They see life through

a judgmental, perspective that constantly blames others for any inconvenience or discomfort they may experience.

This person's focus is predominately on self; on other people and circumstances next, with an occasional glance toward God. They believe they need to figure out exactly what other people are thinking and planning in order to make their own future more secure. Assumptions and mind reading are a common characteristic of the condemning, suspicious mind-set:

- "I know exactly what they're thinking when they look at me like that."
- "I know what she *really* meant when she said . . . "
- "If I was him I would never say that."
- "I know why they do what they do. Their motives are all wrong."

We are not God and we cannot accurately know what someone else is thinking, but once again, *The Lie* that Satan brought into Eden goes into action. We believe, "If I just have enough knowledge, I can be just like God (knowing all things, including what other people think), and I won't need Him or anyone else." A condemning, suspicious mind is another unsuccessful attempt to live out of *The Lie.*

Identify two areas of suspicion and condemnation in your thinking:

____

____

What specific thoughts do you need to plant and cultivate to move from suspicion and condemnation to acceptance and encouragement of others?

____

____

____

8. The Critical, Unforgiving Mind
When we exercise a suspicious, judgmental attitude, criticism and unforgiveness grows. This produces bitterness and physical tension that will eventually become visible in illnesses such as cancer, arthritis, and irritable bowel syndrome, just to name a few. It manifests in relationships through divorce, church splits, and families who refuse to speak or interact, sometimes for years.

Once again, the physical and emotional symptoms produced by the unforgiving mind are called "mental illness." Drug companies feverishly produce and promote their latest "silver bullet" for anxiety, depression, and agitation.

But Jesus says, "Come to Me, all you who labor and are heavy-laden and overburdened, and *I will cause you to rest.* I will ease and relieve and refresh your souls (mind, will, emotions). Take My yoke upon you and learn of Me, for I am gentle, meek and humble ... in heart, and *you will find rest, relief... refreshment... blessed quiet for your souls* (mind, will, emotions). (Matthew 11:28-29, emphasis added)

What Kind of Mind Should We Have?

1. Believers have the mind of Christ through the presence of the Holy Spirit:

> For who has known or understood the mind, the counsels and purposes of the Lord so as to guide and instruct Him and give Him knowledge? But we have the mind of Christ (the Messiah) and do hold the thoughts (feelings and purposes) of His heart.
> 1 Corinthians 2:16

This ability to absorb the truth of God's Word and grow in our understanding of Him is a gift that comes with salvation. It doesn't mean that we can know everything that God knows; after all, He is infinite, and we are finite. However, it does mean that we are able to continually absorb more insight and understanding in the same way that a child who has learned that 1 + 1 = 2 can move on to more complicated formulas.

Write out Proverbs 1:7

____

____

____

Write out Proverbs 9:10

____

____

____

2. Believers have been given a calm, well-balanced mind.

> For God did not give us a spirit of timidity (of cowardice, of craven and cringing and fawning fear), but (He has given us a spirit) of power, love and a calm, well-balanced mind, with discipline and self-control.
>
> 2 Timothy 1:7

A sound mind is one that is disciplined to think in agreement with the Father. We find an example of this in the story of the prodigal son.

> But when he came to his senses, he said, "How many of my father's hired men have more than enough bread, but I am dying here with hunger!"
>
> Luke 15:17

Coming to his senses didn't mean the young man had lost his mind. It means that he was living in the flesh, in complete inconsistency from what his father wanted for him. When he began to gain his father's perspective of what he was doing, and what his inheritance really was, it is described as coming to his senses.

Write out Romans 12:3

____

____

3. Believers must choose to develop a renewed mind.
   Because we have been given the mind of Christ as a gift, and because He has given us a calm, well-balanced mind, we can now choose to develop a renewed mind and think in agreement with God.

Write out Romans 12:1-2

____

____

____

____

4. Believers must choose to develop a prepared, organized mind
   A renewed mind, thinking in agreement with God, becomes an organized mind that is prepared to face life.

   Obviously, because we are each different and have different personalities, we are not going to think, study, and learn in the same way. But we can continue to study and learn within the way we have been gifted and designed. Peter and Paul did not excuse us from preparing our minds for action simply because it's hard for us to sit still or because we have difficulty concentrating. They simply instructed us to do it.

Write out 1 Peter 1:13

____

____

Write out Philippians 4:13

____

____

5. An organized, well-disciplined mind becomes a single mind. Jesus had to focus His attention on His purpose: the salvation of the human race. We have to focus on our purpose: to receive the love of God and learn to love Him in return. Jesus could not have achieved His purpose if He had not been single minded in His walk through life. He did not allow inconvenience, discomfort, or conflict in relationships to distract Him from his goal.

Write out Isaiah 50:7

____

____

Write out Luke 9:51

____

____

6. A single mind is a mind that is focused on heavenly things. Most of us have heard the statement credited to Oliver Wendell Holmes, "Some people are so heavenly minded they are of no earthly good." It's a claim sometimes used to collectively describe Christian people, accusing us of being useless for life on the earth. Taking a closer look at the body of Christ these days, we are more likely not heavenly minded enough to make a real difference here on earth! Our faith actually increases and we grow stronger in our Christian walk as we focus our attention on eternal principles and activities.

   C.S. Lewis said, "If you read history, you will find that the Christians who did most for the present world were just those who thought most of the next. The Apostles themselves, who set on foot the conversion of the Roman Empire, the great men who built up the Middle Ages, the English Evangelicals who abolished the slave trade, all left their mark on Earth, *precisely because their minds were occupied with Heaven*" (*The Joyful Christian*, p.138).

Write out Colossians 3:1-2

____

____

____

____

Extreme Makeover

A young couple decided to buy a fairly new house that had been repossessed. They knew that the family who built it had been pretty careless about keeping things clean. In fact, the musty, stale odor that washed over them when they opened the door made it very evident that the house had not been cleaned for many months.

But the price was right, and this young couple knew they could clean the house up. Their research showed that it was well built and the foundation was stable and strong. As they walked through the house, they imagined how it would look cleaned and remodeled.

But what if they just moved into the house, expecting that their knowledge of what the house could be would automatically eliminate the smell, the trash, and the dirty walls? Would that make the smell go away? No, they have to roll up their sleeves and do the unpleasant and hard work of hauling the trash out, scrubbing and repainting the walls, and pulling up the old, soiled carpet.

Remodeling Is Hard, Dirty Work

In the same way, just knowing that we have been given a new spirit—a new foundation for living life—will not automatically eliminate *The Lie* from our minds. Freedom from *The Lie* is not a supernatural "zap" that God does while we allow our minds to continue thinking the same old thoughts. Carrying out the trash of old thoughts, stripping off the torn "wallpaper" of self with its evil practices, tearing up the soiled "carpet" of lies and half truths is hard, dirty work, but it is essential if we want our life experience to match what the Holy Spirit has already accomplished on the inside.

An important feature of new or remodeled homes is an alarm system that warns of intruders. The Holy Spirit is our alarm. He promises that when He moves in He will let us know when intruders are coming. He tells us specifically what to watch for:

> The Holy Spirit distinctly and expressly declares that in latter times some will turn away from the faith, giving attention to deluding and seducing spirits and doctrines that demons teach, through the hypocrisy and pretensions of liars whose consciences are seared.
>
> 1 Timothy 4:1-2

> But refuse and avoid irreverent legends (profane and impure and godless fictions, mere grandmothers' tales) and silly myths, and express your disapproval of them. Train yourself toward godliness, piety, keeping yourself spiritually fit.
>
> 1 Timothy 4:7

Unholy thoughts are those that disagree with the Word of God. They are like intruders, and as long as they are living with us, we can't enjoy the privacy of our "house" because they are always interrupting and telling us what to feel, say or do. It's hard to invite guests—thoughts that we really enjoy—when the intruders are whining and complaining.

But our mind is our "house," and since Holy Spirit is now permanently living with each believer, we can take charge and decide who comes in. We can say no when the intruding thoughts come up on the porch, and we can stop feeding the ones who sneaked in.

We start by making a guest list and an intruder list. This takes practice because some of the intruders have been a part of our lives so long they feel like guests! But the more we practice, the easier it is to recognize and choose between the two.

If we go by our feelings during this process, we will throw up our hands and say:

- "God could change this if He wanted to."
- "Why doesn't God answer my prayers?"
- "It's too hard!"
- "It's no use."
- "I shouldn't have to suffer this pain!"
- "I deserve better than this."
- "It's not fair!"

It is necessary to remind ourselves that our *emotions do not have a brain and cannot think*. They can only react to what is going on around us. During the times of intensive remodeling, we must renew our minds to agree with God's perspective of both the process and the results. Because God's intentions toward us are only good, His work in us is good even when it becomes uncomfortable and often painful.

Just as the young couple had a lot of hard work to do before they could enjoy their home, we must cooperate with the hard work that the Master Carpenter is doing in us so that we can enjoy the newness of life.

List five thoughts that you recognize as intruders:

____

____

____

____

____

List five thoughts that you want to invite as guests, whose company you will enjoy:

____

____

____

____

____

Exchanging Negative for Positive

We need to be able to identify the patterns that produce negative results in our lives. This chart is a listing of "root thoughts" followed by the "leaves, branches, and fruit" thoughts that are produced by each one:

"Root" Thought	Branches	Leaves	Fruit
Apathy	Self-pity	Jealousy	Resentment
Baffled	Confusion	Procrastination	Failure
Critical	Scorn	Pride	Contempt
Doubting	Fearful	Isolation	Depression
Envy	Resentment	Self-pity	Depression
Fretful	Discontentment	Boredom	Procrastination
Greedy	Stingy	Envy	Workaholism
Harsh	Critical	Rage	Abuse
Inadequate	Shy	Anxiety	Depression
Jealous	Clinging	Pouting	Manipulation
Know-it-all	Boastful	Critical	Scorn
Lukewarm	Lethargic	Boredom	Resentment
Mean	Abusive	Vulgar speech	Violence
Narcissistic	Self-centered	Insecurity	Clinging
Obnoxious	Bully	Manipulation	Harassment
Passive	Detachment	Loneliness	Depression
Quandary	Perplexity	Doubtful	Procrastination
Resentful	Irritation	Annoyance	Abuse
Self-Pity	Discontentment	Whining	Complaining
Toxic	Scheming	Bitterness	Hostility
Used	Victim	Self-pity	Isolation
Violent	Manipulation	Power struggle	Abuse
Weak	Shy	Self-pity	Victim
X-rated	Self-centeredness	Abusive	Pornography
Yearning	Envy	Discontentment	Irritation
Zany (silly, foolish)	Thoughtlessness	Selfishness	Loud

Each of these words describes a pattern that, if left to run unchecked through the mind, will produce chaos and darkness.

The process of changing the direction of our thought life can be defined by the acrostic:

R-E-N-E-W-A-L:

- Recognize: Recognize the emotion that is being stirred up by the thoughts. For example, if you are experiencing a great deal of anger, you can be sure that discontented, bitter, resentful, self-pitying thoughts are playing a dominant role in your mind.
- Express: Express your thoughts and emotions to the Lord.
- Notice: Notice what kind of behaviors these thoughts and emotions have produced, including speech habits.
- Evaluate: Evaluate and determine which part of your life experience agrees with God's Word, and which things need to be replaced.
- Wrong: Refuse wrong thoughts. Choose thoughts and attitudes that come from God's Word.
- Absorb: Absorb new thought patterns that agree with God's Word. These will need to be "planted" and "cultivated" in order for your life experience to change.
- Listen: Listen carefully as the Holy Spirit gives you instruction, wisdom, and assurance of His love for you.

As we work through this RENEWAL process, we replace each negative thought pattern with these:

"Root" Thought	Branches	Leaves	Fruit
Appreciative	Grateful	Contentment	Joy
Blessed	Benevolent	Generosity	Generous harvest
Calm	Quietness	Understanding	Peace
Devoted	Loyalty	Faithfulness	Commitment
Enthusiastic	Excitement	Anticipation	Enjoyment
Forgiving	Merciful	Sympathetic	Kindheartedness
Grateful	Contentment	Fulfilled	Satisfaction
Honest	Authentic	TRUE	Faithfulness
Imaginative	Resourceful	Inspired	Creativity
Joyful	Grateful	Glad	Contentment
Kind	Sympathy	Gentleness	Compassion
Loyal	Trustworthiness	Reliability	Stability
Merciful	Kindness	Gracious	Generosity
Neighborly	Hospitable	Generous	Friends
Obedient	Respectful	Polite	Gracious
Patient	Longsuffering	Endurance	Serenity
Quiet	Peaceful	Stillness	Tranquility
Reasonable	Realistic	Understanding	Wisdom
Sympathetic	Compassionate	Sensitive	Benevolence
Tender	Affectionate	Caring	Kindness
Understanding	Supportive	Thoughtful	Considerate
Vibrant	Energetic	Lively	Cheerfulness
Wise	Insight	Cautious	Understanding
X-uberant	Enthusiastic	Cheerful	Energetic
Youthful	Childlike	Enthusiastic	Uncomplicated
Zestful	Dynamic	Fervent	Passionate

Choose four thought patterns from the "negative" list that you struggle with fairly often:

____

____

____

____

Choose the four thought patterns from the "positive" list that will replace these old patterns:

____

____

____

____

Describe four specific ways you plan to replace the old with the new:

1. ______________________________

____

2. ______________________________

____

3. ______________________________

____

4. ______________________________

____

Squeezed and Shaped

To make cookies into certain shapes, a specially shaped cutter is pressed into the dough. As the dough squeezes into the cookie cutter, it is pressed into the shape of the cutter, and the remaining dough is trimmed away. The result is a baking sheet filled with identically shaped cookies.

Paul had that in mind when he wrote to the believers in Corinth about the need to think differently than the culture that surrounded them. He told them that if they adopted their culture's way of thinking they would be "squeezed into" the same mold and their behavior would look exactly like their culture.

To the Christians in Rome, he wrote:

> For those who are according to the flesh set their minds on the things of the flesh, but those who are according to the spirit set their minds on the things of the spirit. For the mind set on the flesh is death, but the mind set on the spirit is life and peace, because the mind set on the flesh is hostile toward God for it does not subject itself to the law of God, for it is not even able to do so.
>
> Romans 8:5-7

Write out Romans 8:29

____

____

____

What is God's plan for "those who love Him and are called according to His purpose"?

____

____

What You Think Is What You Get

The words that we speak both in the mind to ourselves and out loud to others determine what our life experience will be.

- Words are thoughts that produce emotions.
- Emotions drive our choices.
- Choices become behavior.
- Repeated behavior becomes habit.
- Habits become character traits.
- Character traits determine our life experience.

Thoughts lie at the very root of our life experience. It is critically important that we be aware of our thoughts and get rid of the ones that sabotage the abundant life God has given us through His Son.

The process of renewing the mind can be difficult, especially at the beginning. As we learned in chapter five, emotions follow our thought patterns. We have to choose by faith to think differently than we feel. For example, let's suppose it has been part of Charlie's normal routine to get out of bed in the morning grouchy and irritable. If he wants to change, he'll have to choose to speak cheerfully to his wife at breakfast, even when his emotions feel like snapping at her. The more consistently Charlie chooses a cheerful response, the more quickly his emotions will change to agree with his new way of thinking and acting.

God's Word + Holy Spirit + My Will = Renewed Mind

Jesus said that if we really love Him, we will choose to do what He tells us to do (John 14:21). We need to have determination, but a renewed mind and different behavior are goals that cannot be reached apart from salvation and the indwelling power of the Holy Spirit.

Following a set of rules or principles equipped only with our own determination always results in legalism and eventual burnout. A relationship with the living God produces life. Dependence on the power of the Holy Spirit sets us free from bondage to the law, other people's standards, and our old way of thinking.

Colossians 3 lists some specific actions we can choose in order to make our relationship with Jesus and our new way of thinking visible through our behavior. The word *you* is inserted in each place that we are instructed to make a choice. Since you have been raised to new life with Christ, you and Holy Spirit together can make these choices:

Bible Study: Colossians 3

Finish the statements from each verse:
Verse 1: Choosing to know God: *You* keep seeking…

____

Verse 2: Choosing a new focus: *You* set your mind...

____

Verse 3: Recognizing our new eternal position: *You* are hidden…

____

Verse 4: Believing the promise that we will always live with Him, now and forever: When Christ is revealed *you*…

____

Verse 5: Viewing our earthly life from an eternal perspective: *You* consider or reckon yourself dead to…

____

Verse 8: Recognizing the works of the flesh: *You* put aside…

____

____

____

____

____

Verse 9: Recognizing the motivation behind our new choices: *You* do not…because…

____

____

Verse 10: Recognizing our new identity: *You* have put on…

Verses 12-13: Recognizing our new life, choices, and behavior in the Spirit: Since *you* are chosen of God, now *you* put on…

Verse 14: Choosing our new attitude: *You* put on…

Verses 15-16: Recognizing our new authority: *You* let…

Verse 17: Recognizing and acting from our new motivation: Whatever *you* do….

Verses 18-22: Growing up in family and business relationships: *You who are wives choose:*

___

You who are husbands choose:

___

You who are children choose:

___

You who are fathers choose:

___

You as employees choose:

___

Verse 23: Recognizing and acting from our new motivation: Whatever *you* do...

___

___

Verse 24: Recognizing the rewards of new choices and behavior: *You* will receive...

___

Verse 25: Recognizing the connection between choices and consequences: The one who does wrong...

___

> For I through the Law (under the operation of the curse of the Law) have (in Christ's death for me) myself died to the Law and all the Law's demands upon me, so that I may (henceforth) live to and for God.

I have been crucified with Christ (in Him I have shared His crucifixion); it is no longer I who live, but Christ (the Messiah) lives in me; and the life I now live in the body I live by faith in (by adherence to and reliance on and complete trust in) the Son of God, who loved me and gave Himself up for me.

Galatians 2:19-20

Endnotes

Chapter 1

1 Gary R. Collins: *Can You Trust Psychology* (Downers Grove, IL; Intervarsity Press, 1988) p. 127

2 The American College Dictionary (Syracuse, NY; Random House 1947-1967) p. 1229

3 'Psychology: A Study of Science', 1983 article

4 The American Heritage® Dictionary of the English Language, Fourth Edition Copyright © 2006 by Houghton Mifflin Company. Published by Houghton Mifflin Company. All rights reserved.

5 Gary R. Collins *Can You Trust Psychology?* Downers Grove, IL: InterVarsity Press, 1988

6 http://www.christiantherapist.com/online/news/WhatIsChristianPsychology.htm *What is Christian Psychology?*

Chapter 2

7 Kosfeld M et al. 2005. Oxytocin increases trust in humans. Nature 435:673-676. PDF PMID 15931222

8 Zak, P.J. Stanton, A.A., Ahmadi, A. 2007. Oxytocin increases generosity in humans. PLoS ONE 2(11): e1128. [1]

9 Anderson, G; Moore, E; Heworth, J; Bergman, N. Early skin-to-skin contact for mothers and their healthy newborn infants (Cochrane Review). 2003. In *The Cochrane Library, 3*. Oxford: John Wiley.

Chapter 3

10 Walter Kaiser; *"Hard Sayings of the OT"*; Downers Grove; intervarsity Press, 1988. pp 23-26

11 Joseph E. Coleson, Professor of OT; Nazarene Theological Seminary; *"Ezer*

Cenegdo:A Power Like Him, Facing Him As Equal"

12 Biblesoft's New Exhaustive Strong's Numbers and Concordance with Expanded Greek-Hebrew Dictionary Copyright © 1994, 2003 Biblesoft, Inc and International Bible Translators, Inc

13 S.G. Green: *A Handbook to Old Testament Hebrew* pp 74, 154

14 1 Timothy 2:14-15; 2 Corinthians 11:2-3

15 Job 31:33; Hosea 6:7

16 Romans 5:14, 15, 16, 19; 1 Corinthians 15:22, 45, 47

17 *Who Switched Off My Brain?* Dr. Caroline Leaf : Printed in USA by Switch On Your Brain, PO Box 4227 Rivonia 2128, South Africa

18 *Who Switched Off My Brain?* Dr. Caroline Leaf : Printed in USA by Switch On Your Brain, PO Box 4227 Rivonia 2128, South Africa

19 *Will Medicine Stop The Pain?* Elyse Fitzpatrick and Laura Hendrickson, M.D.: Moody Publishers, Chicago, ILL, 2006; p. 56-57

20 *Who Switched Off My Brain?* Dr. Caroline Leaf : Printed in USA by Switch On Your Brain, PO Box 4227 Rivonia 2128, South Africa

21 *Holoubek, JE; Holoubek AB (1996). "Blood, sweat and fear. "A classification of hematidrosis".". Journal of Medicine* **27** *(3-4): 115-33.*

Chapter 6

22 from Bible Knowledge Commentary/Old Testament Copyright © 1983, 2000 Cook Communications Ministries; Bible Knowledge Commentary/New Testament Copyright © 1983, 2000 Cook Communications Ministries. All rights reserved.)

23 Krister Stendahl *Paul Among the Jews and Other Essays* (Philadelphia, PA Fortress Press 1976)

24 Macmillan, John A. *The Authority of the Believer* (Camphill PA Christian Publications 1980)

25 Kraft, Charles H. *Christianity with Power* (Ann Arbor MI Servant Publications 1989)

Chapter 7

26 Dr. Dixie Yoder: *The Church Snatchers: The Ultimate Identity Theft*

27 Norman H Smith, "Grace" in *A Theological Word Book of the Bible,* MacMillan Paperbacks ed., Alan Richardson (New York, NY; Macmillan Co., 1962) p. 100

28 Rebecca Manley Pippert *Hope Has Its Reasons* (CA Harper and Row 1989)

29 Luke Keefer, Jr. *Everything Necessary* pp. 92, 102 (IN: Evangel Press 1984)

Author Bio

Dr. Dixie Yoder is an ordained minister with nearly thirty years of experience in Biblical personal guidance ministry. She is a Bible scholar who loves the Word of God and its day-to-day application to life and brings considerable practical wisdom into the individual, parental, and marital guidance she offers along with the knowledge she has gained in her years of study. She is founder and executive director of *Infinite Grace Ministries, Inc.*, a nonprofit ministry whose mission is to help hurting people find emotional wholeness through knowing God more intimately. Dr. Dixie currently has offices in Oklahoma City and Weatherford, Oklahoma, for one-on-one personal guidance and offers seminars and conferences on a variety of life issues.

Dr. Dixie has ministered to many across the United States and in other countries. In 1995, she was involved in ministry for victims of the Murrah Building bombing in Oklahoma City. Dr. Dixie worked with pastors and evangelists from twenty-five countries in Amsterdam at the Amsterdam 2000 conference sponsored by the Billy Graham Evangelistic Association. In October 2001, she spent two weeks at Ground Zero in New York City, offering spiritual guidance to policemen and victims of the attack on the World Trade Center. She also worked in the Family Assistance Center and answered phones in the Billy Graham Crisis Phone Center in Lower Manhattan. She spent time in New Orleans as a police chaplain following hurricane Katrina in 2005.

Dr. Dixie is the author of *Church Snatchers: The Ultimate Identity Theft*. This important book is a study of why so many believers have a life experience that is very similar to that of their unsaved neighbors, revealing the cultural influences that have seeped into the thinking of American Christians—so silently that many are unaware of how deeply their way of thinking and choosing have been compromised. She has authored numerous booklets.

Dr. Dixie says, "I am absolutely passionate about the difference that really *knowing God* will make in the life of a believer. I have always loved the Word of God and have read and studied it regularly since grade school. Even during the times of my life that I wasn't sure God was entirely trustworthy, I somehow knew that the answers to life's problems are in the Bible and in knowing God."

In 2006, Dr. Dixie became septic following a root-canal procedure and lay near death for several days. Seventeen days of medical treatment in critical care included a week in a coma, her breathing assisted by a ventilator. While in the coma, Dr. Dixie had a personal encounter with the Lord in what she refers to as a "near *life* experience." "I have taught for years that God loves us absolutely and that absolute love calls for absolute obedience. Since that encounter with the Lord, I am even more convinced that true freedom and the quality of life we search for so desperately is found in God's perfect love, combined with our single-minded obedience to the One who loves us perfectly."

Dr. Dixie is active in Bethany Church in Thomas, Oklahoma. She served six years on the board of directors for the Wesleyan Holiness Women Clergy Conference, an international biannual conference for women in leadership. She enjoys ministry in music with her sister, dad, and youngest son and grandchildren. Dixie and her husband have been married forty years and are blessed with two wonderful sons, two beautiful daughters-in-law, and four *amazing* grandchildren.